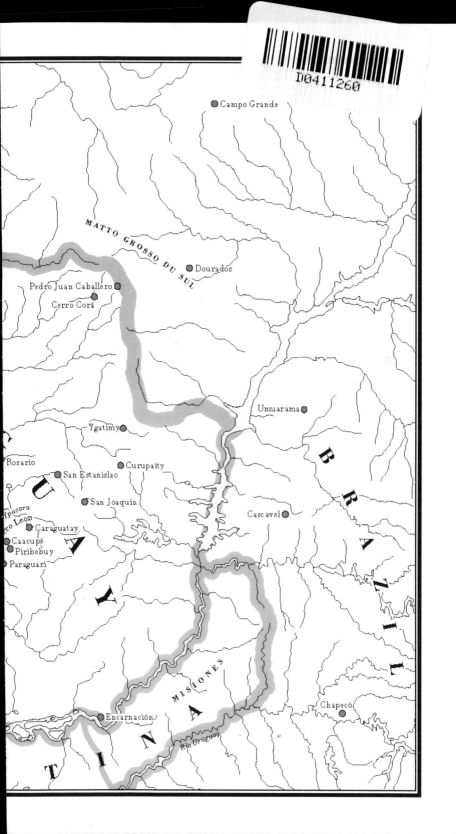

The Empress of
South America

The Empress of South America

Nigel Cawthorne

WILLIAM HEINEMANN : LONDON

First published in the United Kingdom in 2003 by William Heinemann

1 3 5 7 9 10 8 6 4 2

William Heinemann
The Random House Group Limited
20 Vauxhall Bridge Road, London, SW1V 2SA

Random House Australia (Pty) Limited
20 Alfred Street, Milsons Point, Sydney
New South Wales 2061, Australia

Random House New Zealand Limited
18 Poland Road, Glenfield
Auckland 10, New Zealand

Random House (Pty) Limited
Endulini, 5a Jubilee Road, Parktown 2193, South Africa

The Random House Group Limited Reg. No. 954009

www.randomhouse.co.uk

A CIP catalogue record for this book is available from the British Library

Papers used by Random House are natural, recyclable products made from wood
grown in sustainable forests. The manufacturing processes conform to the
environmental regulations of the country of origin

ISBN 0 434 00898 2

Typeset by SX Composing DTP, Rayleigh, Essex
Printed and bound in Great Britain by
Clays Ltd, St Ives Plc

CONTENTS

PICTURE CREDITS

1. South American Pictures
2. British Library
3. From Manlio Cancogni and Iván Boris, *El Napoléon del Plata*, Noguer, 1972
4. Collection Edgar L. Ynsfrán, reproduced in A. Nagy and F. Pérez Maricevich, *El Mariscal de la Epopeya*
5. From Diego Abad de Santillán, *Historia Argentina*
6. Collection José Antonio Vázquez. Museo del Barro
7. From Jorge Rubiani, *La Guerra de la Triple Alianza*
8. From Jorge Rubiani, *La Guerra de la Triple Alianza*
9. From *Album Gráfico de la República del Paraguay* edition Arsenio López Decoud
10. From *Album Gráfico de la República del Paraguay* edition Arsenio López Decoud
11. From J.E. O'Leary, *El Paraguay en la Unificación Argentina*, Asunción, 1924
12. Collection M&MC, reproduced in Miguel A. Cuarterolo, *Soldados de la Memoria*
13. From Miguel A. Cuarterolo, *Soldados de la Memoria*
14. From Jorge Rubiani, *La Guerra de la Triple Alianza*
15. From Jorge Rubiani, *La Guerra de la Triple Alianza*
16. From *Album Gráfico de la República del Paraguay* edition Arsenio López Decoud
17. From *Album Gráfico de la República del Paraguay* edition Arsenio López Decoud
18. From Jorge Rubiani, *La Guerra de la Triple Alianza*
19. British Library
20. From Jorge Rubiani, *La Guerra de la Triple Alianza*
21. From Jorge Rubiani, *La Guerra de la Triple Alianza*
22. From Miguel Al Cuarterolo, *Soldados de la Memoria*
23. From Miguel Al Cuarterolo, *Soldados de la Memoria*
24. From CABICHU'I, edition Museo del Barro
25. Photo by W. Bate, 1866, from the album *La Guerra del '70. Una visión fotográfica*
26. Library of Congress, Washington

❧ 1 ❧

A NATIONAL HEROINE

One night in May 1961, a Paraguayan of Lebanese descent named Teófilo Chammas scaled the walls of Père Lachaise cemetery in Paris. The gates were locked but the high walls were not topped with barbed wire as they are today. Nor was the cemetery patrolled at night. And then, as now, young lovers climbed into the graveyard to lose themselves in the darkness there.

Chammas, however, had something altogether more shady in mind. Once inside Père Lachaise made his way down the Avenue Carette, past the tomb of Oscar Wilde, to Division 92 of the cemetery. There he began searching for plot number 6/42 – 18/90. The nearest landmark was the reclining brass figure of journalist Victor Noir whose lips and crotch have been burnished by the countless caresses of female mourners lavished on his effigy since he was shot by Prince Pierre Bonaparte in 1870, hastening the end of the Second Empire. Six rows behind Noir and eighteen from the Avenue Carette, Chammas found what he was looking for.

At the foot of the ornamental sarcophagus at plot 6/42 – 18/90 was the label '*C.A.P.*' – Concession à Perpétuité – '*No 542 année 1886*'. An inscription on the lid of the sarcophagus noted that the tomb belonged to the *Famille Martin*. The grave, according to another inscription, housed one Estelle Martin, who had died on 18 February 1900. But it was not Estelle Martin that Chammas was interested in. There were other curious clues on the sarcophagus. On one side there was the puzzling legend *Paz y Justicia* – 'peace and justice' in Spanish. Beneath it was the figure of a dancing lion holding, on a stick, a Phrygian cap – once worn by freed Roman slaves, but better known as the French Revolutionary's 'red cap of liberty'. This figure was borrowed from the great seal of Paraguay. The other side of the sarcophagus bore the five-pointed star and olive branch of the Paraguayan flag. At the end of the sarcophagus nearest Victor Noir there was an escutcheon bearing three stylised shamrocks. Above it appeared a wolf; below, the motto read: *Lupus me fugit inermen* – 'The wolf flees from me though I am unarmed'.

Although the meaning of these inscriptions would have been lost on the casual visitor, they would have told Chammas that he was in the right place. To those familiar with the troubled past of South America, their significance would have been explained by a small marble plaque on the other end of the sarcophagus, which said in Spanish:

Monument erected
by
Enrique, Federico and Carlos Solano López.
To the illustrious memory
of their always beloved and unforgettable mother
Doña Elisa Alicia Lynch-López.
Died 25 July 1886.

Reading this, students of Latin American history would instantly recall the bloodiest war in the history of the Americas, a war which left more dead that the United States' bitter Civil War and all but destroyed a wealthy nation, through the weakness of a man and the ambition of a woman. It was this woman, Elisa Alicia Lynch-López – better known as Eliza Lynch – that Chammas had come for.

A freelance import-exporter and general entrepreneur, Chammas was new to the grave-robbing business, but he had cultivated useful contacts among the staff at Père Lachaise. Money had changed hands and the tomb had already been opened. There were five coffins in the grave. The first two occupants were Estelle Martin and Eliza Lynch. They had been buried there in May 1900. Estelle Martin had died in February of that year and had been interred briefly elsewhere, while Eliza had languished in a tiny grave in Division 53 of Père Lachaise since 27 July 1886. As these two had been buried first, the other coffins were stacked up on top of them, making exhumation difficult. Manhandling a coffin out of a grave is a strenuous and time-consuming business at the best of times and coffins that had lain in the damp soil of Père Lachaise for any length of time would have been in a fragile state. So by the time Chammas reached those of Estelle and Eliza, it must have been nearing dawn.

According to Chammas, when he finally opened what he took to be Eliza's coffin, the corpse's long, black hair turned instantly to luminous gold. This may have just been hyperbole, but perhaps, at very moment he opened the coffin, the first rays of the spring sun burst over the horizon, bathing the corpse in golden spring sunlight. He certainly would not have been able to linger over the scene. Daylight would bring the workmen who tended the graves and officials who ran the cemetery. Soon after, Père Lachaise would be open to visitors. Chammas was certainly not eager to be caught. He hurriedly packed up Eliza's remains and made his escape.

At around this time the Paraguayan Ambassador to Paris, Dr Hipólito Sánchez Quell, was making official representations to the French government, formally requesting the return of the remains of Eliza Lynch. Although Eliza was an Irish woman, British by birth, French by marriage and Parisian by inclination, Paraguayan dictator General Alfredo Stroessner believed that her body belonged in Paraguay. The appropriate paperwork was lodged with the French authorities and, while the bureaucracy went slowly about its business, Dr Quell paid a visit to Eliza's grave with his ten-year-old daughter. It would have come as a shock to him when he discovered that Madame Lynch's remains had already been disinterred and had been hurried out of the country. But Dr Quell had no doubt who was responsible – a fellow countryman who he denounced as the chief *contrabandista*.

While Dr Quell had been seeking the removal of the remains through the proper channels, Chammas smuggled the corpse back to South America in a coffin packed with Lebanese hashish. It was intercepted by customs at Buenos Aires. From Argentina, the remains either travelled on to Paraguay in a gunboat after some diplomatic arrangement had been stitched together, or Chammas, a drug smuggler who had turned grave-robber to ingratiate himself to the dictator Stroessner, paid off the Argentine customs officials, chartered a seaplane and took Eliza's reamins back to Paraguay in a suitcase.

At least that is one version of the story. Bizarre, certainly. But it would have been a fitting postscript to the life of a truly remarkable woman. There are, of course, more prosaic accounts of her return to Paraguay.

The French authorities insist that Eliza Lynch was legally exhumed. The records clerk at Père Lachaise even says that the Paraguayan Ambassador was there when she was disinterred, though the cemetery records are closed to the general public. However, under French law, it is necessary to have the consent of the next of kin of all the people buried in a grave before it can be disturbed. The Prefecture of Police had the consent of Jorge Manuel and Elisa A. Solano López, Eliza Lynch's grandchildren, to remove her body. But it would have been difficult, if not impossible, to track down the families of the four other people buried there.

The Paraguayan authorities also maintain that the exhumation was done legally. But strangely, Dr Quell, who was both a prolific writer and passionate devotee of Madame Lynch, makes no reference to her exhumation in the extensive volumes he wrote about his endeavours in Paris, even though the return of Eliza's remains would surely have been his greatest diplomatic triumph.

The historian at Père Lachaise, Christian Charlet, says that this is easily explained. The request for the return of the remains of Eliza Lynch was handled covertly through the French embassy in Asunción, the capital of Paraguay. The Paraguayan Embassy in Paris was informed later and only discovered that the body was already gone when the ambassador visited Père Lachaise on 23 May.

'In view of the use made of Elisa Lynch-López's remains when they were returned to Paraguay, it is not impossible that the political power of the time (General-President Alfredo Stroessner) preferred to secure their return via a discreet approach, purely family,' says M. Charlet, 'rather than make an official political inter-vention that would be likely to provoke a negative reaction from the French Government.'

But the French Government were not that squeamish. President Charles de Gaulle visited Paraguay in 1964, just three years after the remains had been returned. He does not seem to have been bothered by any 'use' the remains were put to. And certainly it would not have been possible for the French President to have visited Paraguay if there was any outstanding dispute between the two countries – over a little grave robbing, say. So perhaps the whole thing was swept under the carpet. After all, it is not very difficult to make the appropriate adjustments to records that are not open to the public.

At the time, the Paraguayans maintained that Madame Lynch's remains were returned on a warship. But landlocked Paraguay did not have any ocean-going warships – and does not to this day. Its naval activity is limited to the three navigable rivers – the Paraguay, the Paraná and the Pilcomayo – that mark four-fifths of the borders of modern Paraguay. Nevertheless, the remains did arrive at the dockside in Asunción on 25 July 1961, the seventy-fifth anniversary of Eliza Lynch's death. General Stroessner, in a uniform befitting the president of a banana republic that grows no bananas, was waiting on the quay. He had proclaimed the day a 'Day of National Homage' and the entire government turned out, along with a guard of honour and a huge crowd. As the Paraguayan Army Band struck up Paraguay's operatic national anthem, the remains were brought ashore in a large bronze urn. This urn was identical to one said to contain the remains of another great hero of Paraguayan history, Eliza's lover and partner in crime, Mariscal Francisco Solano López – one-time dictator, former army chief and war hero, who was also variously described as the world's worst tyrant since Nero and the biggest mass murderer since Genghis Khan. Between the two of them they were responsible for the slaughter of practically the entire male population of Paraguay while, behind Francisco's back, Eliza bled the country dry.

However, according to General Stroessner's grandiloquent speech at the quayside, the beautiful Eliza was a national heroine and a national martyr, though she had died far from Paraguay and in much greater comfort than most of her victims. The huge funeral cortège then made its way up the hill to the Panteón de los Héroes – a replica of Napoleon's tomb in Les Invalides – which her consort Francisco had had built to house his own remains. Stroessner's intention was that the two lovers were to be re-united there. He had hoped that the two unlikely national heroes would lie side by side in the Panteón de los Héroes in perpetuity. But, at the last minute, the Catholic Church had raised an objection. Eliza and Francisco had never been married. Throughout her time in Paraguay, Eliza was married to a Frenchman and her liaison with López had been adulterous. The Panteón de los Héroes stood on sanctified ground and, according to the Church, it would be an affront to God for the two of them to lie there together – even though it was unlikely that they would break the seventh commandment again, given the fact that they were dead.

The Church's scruples did not hugely concern Alfredo Stroessner, the strongman who had ruled Paraguay unopposed since he seized power in a coup in 1954 – he would continue to do so until 1989, making him the longest-standing ruler of any South American country in the twentieth century. However, just six years before, he had seen his old friend Juan Perón ousted from Argentina after the Church turned against him. Perón had had the temerity to petition the Pope to have his late wife, the one-time prostitute Eva Perón (née Duarte) – Evita – canonised. And Eliza Lynch's reputation was no more savoury. Privately Stroessner would accede to the demands of Mother Church. But publicly he was not going to be robbed of his moment of glory. As Pallbearer in Chief, Stroessner led Eliza's funeral procession into the Panteón de los Héroes. In a scene rich in symbolism, Eliza's urn was solemnly marched in through the front door of Francisco's mausoleum, then – after the briefest reunion with the supposed remains of her lover – it was whisked out of the back door again.

From there, the remains were spirited down the Avenida Mariscal Francisco Solano López to the Ministry of National Defence. On the second floor, a small 'Museo Madame Lynch' had been prepared in what was essentially a broom cupboard, next to the gentlemen's lavatory. It contained a rusty sword said to have belonged to Francisco López, a book of homage containing some 87,000 signatures and a portrait of the national heroine, showing Eliza's dazzling beauty at its imperious height. There the remains were left to gather dust for the next nine years.

❧ 2 ❧

THE RIVER AND THE SEA

Paraguay is a relatively small South American country, around the size of California. Trapped between the regional giants of Brazil, Argentina and Bolivia, it lies at the centre of the long tapering point of the chilli pepper that is South America. Once the richest and most powerful nation in the region, it was destroyed by the War of the Triple Alliance in the 1860s when it fought, simultaneously, Brazil, Argentina and Uruguay. The war was largely the result of the ambitions of Eliza Lynch and the failings of Francisco López. Three-quarters of the population of Paraguay died. The country was looted, bankrupted and dismembered. Yet since the 1960s the authors of Paraguay's destruction have been honoured as national heroes. But then, Paraguayan history has always read like the blackest of black comedies.

Paraguay was discovered by accident by Sebastian Cabot in 1526. The family was dogged by such mishaps. Sebastian's father John Cabot had suffered a similar misfortune when, in 1497, he had stumbled upon North America, planted the Tudor flag in it and claimed it for England, possibly naming it for his patron, the High Sheriff of Bristol Richard Ameryk. The following year,

John Cabot was lost on an expedition to find a north-west passage around the barren and unwanted continent that blocked Europe's westerly trade routes to the Orient. However, there is evidence that suggests he sailed down North America's eastern seaboard and into the Caribbean where he was captured – and perhaps murdered – by the Spanish to protect their discoveries there. This would make it all the more ironic that in 1526 his son Sebastian was sailing for the Spanish, searching for a south-west passage when, in April that year, he entered a broad channel which he thought might lead to the Pacific. He soon discovered that this was the mouth of the Río de la Plata – the River of Silver or River Plate. Cabot gave it this name after the Indians on its banks gave him some silver trinkets and told him that there were vast quantities of the stuff further upstream.

Abandoning his commission to find a trade route to the Moluccas – the Spice Islands – Cabot headed on up the Paraná River, thinking that it would lead him to the silver mines of Peru. This was another mistake, but the prospect of finding a water-borne route to loot the wealth of the Incas excited him so much that he named the whole area Río de la Plata.

Cabot established the first Spanish settlement in the region at San Espiritu. But this was lost the moment his back was turned when the enterprising underlings whom he had left behind to hold the fort headed off in search of El Dorado, the fabled city of gold, never to be seen again. Meanwhile, Cabot continued upstream into the Paraguay River which branches off northwards about 700 miles from the sea where the Paraná swings sharply to the east, now forming the southern border of Paraguay. It is said that the name Paraguay means, in the language of the area's peaceful Guaraní Indians, 'the river that gives birth to the sea' – even though the Guaraní seem to have been pretty content with their jungle existence and it is unlikely that they ever ventured as far as the ocean. Others say that Paraguay means the 'river that runs from the sea' as the river was thought to have its source in Lake Xarayes. But Xarayes is no sea. It is a fetid swamp that only floods in summer. Other proposed derivations include the 'the river of the crown' – the fetid Xarayes swamp being the crown; 'the sea-water hole'; 'the river of many colours' for the colourful flowers and birds along its banks; 'the river of feathers', again for its birds; and 'the water of the Penelope bird', though that particular species is not seen south of Ecuador. However, the most likely explanation is that the river was named for the warlike Payaguá or Canoe Indians, renowned for the artificially distended breasts of their womenfolk, or, more particularly, their one-time chief Paragua.

About 125 miles further up the river from Tres Boccas – the 'Three Mouths' where the Paraguay flows into the Paraná – Cabot ran into the Payaguás at the narrows of Angostura. The Indians stood no chance against the Spaniards' matchlocks and cannon. Cabot lost just two men in the encounter. Even so, he decided that reinforcements were called for. He returned to Spain, where he was arrested for failing in his mission to find a south-west passage and banished to Africa. After two years, he was pardoned and back to England where, undeterred, he began looking for a north-east passage to the Indies.

Despite Cabot's downfall, the River of Silver took a fierce grip on the Spanish imagination. In 1534, four years after Cabot's return, another expedition set out under a wealthy member of the royal household, Don Pedro de Mendoza. Hernando Cortés had needed just 500 men to butcher the ferocious Aztecs in Mexico and make off with their gold. With less than 200 men, Francisco Pizarro had slaughtered the highly organised Incas of Peru and looted their empire. So Mendoza took 2,650 heavily armed men on fourteen ships to face the primitive and defenceless Indians of the Río de la Plata.

Things began to go wrong even before they reached South America. During the Atlantic crossing Mendoza grew jealous of his popular and experienced military commander Don Juan de Osorio and had him arrested. At a hearing in Rio de Janeiro, a misunderstanding resulted in Osorio being stabbed to death by Mendoza's Chief of Police Juan de Ayolas.

Next Mendoza founded Buenos Aires – universally recognised as the worst port in the world in the days of sail. Ships had to lie as much as nine miles off shore. It cost as much to lighter a cargo ashore as it did to freight it from Liverpool or New York. The rocky bottom meant that, with a slight change of wind, ships would drag their anchors, beaching themselves high up the river and leaving them fit only for firewood. Things were no better on the landward side. Inland from Buenos Aires there is a level and treeless plain, given to dust storms in the dry season. And in the rainy season, mud made it impassable.

Even from Mendoza's limited perspective, the settlement at Buenos Aires was impractical. There were few provisions at hand to feed his men. The local Querandi Indians provided some game, but the amount was far from adequate. In an effort to wring more out of them,

Mendoza decided to attack them with his cavalry. But the Indians simply lured the mounted troops into a bog and killed half of them, including Mendoza's brother Don Diego. The Querandis then stormed Buenos Aires with bolas – the traditional South American three-balled throwing weapon. Burning faggots tied to the tails of the bolas set fire to the fort and several ships.

The Spaniards clung on, but the foraging parties Mendoza sent out were picked off by the Querandi, leaving the Spaniards close to starvation. Fortunately the Timbus Indians who had supplied Cabot were still friendly, Mendoza headed off up the Paraná and established a fort at Corpus Christi, near the site of Cabot's abandoned San Espiritu.

By this time there were only 600 men left out of the 2,650 Mendoza had started out with the previous year. Half of them then set off up river with Juan de Ayolas in search of Peru. They did not return. After a year, Mendoza sent more men out to look for them, including another kinsman Don Gonzalo. When they did not return either, Mendoza gave up and headed back to Spain. The strain had all been too much for him. He lost his reason and died a raving madman on the way.

However not all Ayolas's men were lost. Domingo Martínez de Irala and a force of 100 men had established Fort Olimpo on the Paraguay River, some 240 miles above the site of the present capital Asunción. There he made peace with the Payaguás and sent regular search parties for Ayolas, who had continued up the river. Don Gonzalo de Mendoza reached Irala there, but as there was no news of Ayolas, he decided to head back to Corpus Christi. On the way, he spotted a tall bluff at a dog-leg in the river where the Paraguay met its principal tributary, the Pilcomayo. At the bottom of the bluff was a deep-water harbour. From the top you could see for miles across country. This would be the perfect place for a trading post on the road to Peru – at least it would have been if you could reach Peru this way. So, with the help of the mild-mannered Guaraní Indians, Mendoza began work on a fort there on 15 August 1537. This was the feast of the Assumption of the Virgin, so he named the outpost La Asunción. Older than any town in the United States, the capital of Paraguay was founded 70 years before the first English settlers reached Jamestown and 83 years before the Pilgrim Fathers landed at Plymouth Rock.

When the small party of men who were still holding Buenos Aires heard the news from Asunción, they decided to swap imminent starvation and hostile Indians for the fertile soil and fine climate upstream. But when they reached the upper reaches of the river, they were greeted by scenes of devastation. A plague of locusts had swept through the area, stripping the crops, poisoning the wells with their corpses and filling the air with pestilence as they decayed.

Meanwhile the bloodthirsty Ruiz de Galan had taken over command in Asunción. When Domingo Martinez de Irala came downriver from Fort Olimpo to challenge Galan's authority, Galan had him arrested and sent back. While Irala was away, the Payaguás had had time to change their minds about Europeans invading their ancestral lands and ambushed him. They met with a terrible defeat. Irala killed twelve of their strongest men single-handed, it was said.

At the same time, Galan set off down the river to Corpus Christi where he massacred the Timbus Indians who had provisioned both Cabot and Mendoza. Other Indians struck back. In the middle of the ensuing battle, on 3 February 1538 – St Blaise's Day – St Blaise himself appeared on the battlefield with a fiery sword in his hand. This blinded the Indians, making them all the easier to slaughter, and bloody St Blaise became, appropriately, the patron saint of Paraguay. Mind you, Galan could be just as brutal without heavenly assistance. When he found a Spanish woman who had gone to live with the Indians to save herself from starvation, he left her tied to a tree to be devoured by wild animals.

When a new ship-load of colonists arrived on the coast, Galan decided that it would be best to abandon Buenos Aires and group everyone together at Asunción – the only place the Spaniards had not yet succeeded in alienating the Indians. They arrived to find Irala firmly in control. With Don Pedro de Mendoza gone and Juan de Ayolas now almost certainly dead, an election was conducted to select an interim governor. Irala won. He decided that as they depended on the Indians for food, it would be a good idea to abandon Mendoza's and Galan's policy of killing them. Instead the Spanish men should shack up with the bare-breasted, brown-skinned and compliant Guaraní women and learn the local tongue. When the Guaraní menfolk objected and rebelled, the ringleaders were rounded up and executed, and the Indians were forced to hand over their remaining wives, sisters and daughters. A Spanish chronicler later claimed that the Indians were happy to give up their womenfolk. They felt no jealousy and were cold when it came to sex, performing the act without preamble or any demonstration of affection, he said. With no wives or priests to suggest otherwise, most of the Spaniards kept 30 to 50 Guaraní concubines. Irala himself had 70. However, he seems to have been an enlightened man. To promote racial harmony, he insisted that the Spaniards' children speak Guaraní and learn Indian ways.

Irala's policy of racial mixing resulted in the rapid growth of the colonial population of Paraguay. Other towns were founded, bringing the settlers into conflict with more belligerent tribes. However, these hostile Indians had customs that practically guaranteed their extinction. Each woman was only allowed one child. The young women were beaten regularly around the belly to keep them nubile and childless as long as possible. Their first-born were slaughtered automatically. Only when a woman was reaching the end of her child-bearing years was she allowed to keep an infant. The rest were killed. When these tribes were defeated by the Spaniards and their mestizo offspring, the men were slaughtered and the women taken as concubines and allowed to keep as many babies as they could bear, turning the whole of Río de la Plata into a burgeoning Spanish colony – albeit one that spoke Guaraní and followed Guaraní customs. It was later noted that Paraguayan ladies could deport themselves as elegantly as any European at a ball of an evening and be seen the next day walking barefoot, wearing only a chemise and smoking cigars like an Indian. Irala's race-mixing policy also meant that the Guaranís were saved from regular bonded slavery. A far worse fate awaited them.

Río de la Plata was a peaceful and prosperous colony

under the elected governor Irala, but his governorship was only ever meant to be temporary, until a new governor was appointed by the King. His choice was Álvar Núñez de Vera Cabeza de Vaca – *cabeza de vaca* means 'cow's head'. He had a colourful past. In 1528, he had been sent as treasurer on an expedition to conquer Florida. Shipwrecked in Tampa Bay, he found himself alone and naked in what is now Galveston, Texas. Apparently, the local Indians, a smooth-skinned race, were impressed by his two beards – the one on his face and the one down below. They took him for a god and made him their chief. In 1536, Cabeza de Vaca, was rescued by a party of *conquistadors* from Mexico and told them of the fabulous riches of the Seven Golden Cities of Cíbola that he had heard lay to the north. 'Cow's Head' returned to Spain where he published an account of his time in 'New Spain' – the Spanish possessions in North America. Expeditions were duly despatched to look for the Seven Golden Cities. They were never found. As in South America the search for El Dorado was still on, Cabeza de Vaca was plainly the man to send to Asunción.

After a terrible sea crossing, Cabeza de Vaca's fleet of four small ships made land on the Brazilian coast at Santos, the port of modern-day São Paulo. Rather than continue the gruelling journey by ship, Cabeza de Vaca and his men struck out to cross 700 miles of virgin forest on foot. Cabeza de Vaca's time with the Indians in North America stood him in good stead. He lost just one man on the trip, who accidentally drowned crossing a river. After four months and nine days in the jungle, Cabeza de Vaca's party arrived at the Paraguay River in better health than when they had left the coast. But the moment

Cabeza de Vaca set foot in Asunción, Irala arrested him and sent him back to Spain, where he was tried for failing in his mission and, like Cabot, banished to Africa.

In 1580, a new colony was established at Buenos Aires. Despite its shortcomings as a port, it quickly over-shadowed its older rival 1,000 miles up river. By then it had been definitely established that Asunción was not on the road to Peru, but rather on the road to nowhere. But although the riverine route through Paraguay yielded no Inca silver, it did produce the New World's first saint. In 1589, Francisco Solano stumbled into Asunción. A native of Spain, he had arrived in Peru in 1582. From there he had scaled the Andes and crossed the Gran Chaco, the wasteland to the west of the Paraguay river that makes up more than half Paraguay's land mass. On the way, according to Francisco Solano's own account, he had out-baptised John the Baptist, immersing over 200,000 converts and explaining the mysteries of the Trinity, transubstantiation, the transfiguration of Christ and the papal succession to his new congregation. However, subsequent expeditions found no Christians in the area. In fact, there were very few people at all. Those there spoke languages with vocabularies of less than a thousand words, by and large related to the natural world around them – not the sort of languages that could be used to explain the finer points of theology. Nevertheless, Francisco Solano was beatified in 1675 and canonised in 1726.

Paraguay was formally separated from Río de la Plata and the Buenos Aires colony in 1620 by Hernando Arias de Saavedra. From then on, Paraguay's only outlet to the sea was through other countries' territory, making war with its neighbours, some say, inevitable. As a young man Saavedra had travelled in Patagonia. His battles with the Indians there taught him that there were simply too many to exterminate. Instead, they would have to be converted so, in 1608, he sent for the Jesuits. Ignoring the mestizo heritage of Paraguay, the Jesuits tried to enforce strict racial segregation. They corralled the Indians in their missions and introduced the Guaraní to the love of God with the brand and lash – no means were too extreme to do the Lord's work. The Indians, who had so far been saved from the rigours of commercial slavery, became slaves of the Society of Jesus. The Indian schools established by the Franciscans were closed and the only thing the Indians were taught from then on was the catechism. However, Paraguay has one proud boast of its time under the Jesuits – it was the world's first country run entirely without money, beating Pol Pot's Kampuchea by over three-and-a-half centuries.

This state of affairs was not to last. When Don Luis de Cespedes Jaray was appointed governor, his Portuguese wife saw the docile Indians at the Jesuit missions as cheap labour for her plantations in Brazil and persuaded her husband to let the slavers in. But once they had cleared out the Jesuit missions in eastern Paraguay, they began raiding the nearby Spanish towns for slaves. As a result the entire province of Guayrá east of the Paraná River was lost to Brazil.

The Jesuits made another enemy in the Bishop of Paraguay, Bernardino de Cardenas, an irascible Franciscan much given to excommunication. In 1644, he excommunicated the governor, Gregorio de Hinistrosa, who then had to beg for absolution at the bishop's feet.

The regional parliament, or Audience, in Charcas and the Spanish Viceroy in Lima heard about this and felt the bishop had overstepped his authority. They ordered Hinistrosa to arrest the bishop – which he did amid a blizzard of anathemas. Cardenas was expelled from f Asunción to the sound of church bells and general rejoicing. He retired to Corrientes, 200 miles downstream in what is now Argentina, where he spent five years scheming. When Hinistrosa died in 1648, Cardenas succeeded him as governor. Figuring the Jesuits were against him, when he returned to Asunción, he loaded them on to boats without sails or anchors and cast them adrift. Many drowned. The Viceroy banished Cardenas once more in 1649, though he was later pardoned by the Pope. Meanwhile, the Jesuits returned.

In 1717, Don Diego de los Reyes Balmaceda was appointed Governor, but serious charges were laid against him at the Audience in Charcas. A five-year investigation followed. In the meantime, Don José de Antiquera y Castro, who had been named as Balmaceda's successor, got tired of waiting. He marched into Asunción to arrest Balmaceda, only to find he was away in Corrientes at the time. The Viceroy repudiated Antiquera and ordered him to withdraw. Antiquera ignored his orders and sent men to Corrientes to seize Balmaceda. The military governor of Río de la Plata, Don Baltasar Garcia de Ros, was then sent to bring Antiquera to heel but when Antiquera defied him Ros withdrew for reinforcements.

Thinking that Ros had been successful, the governor of Buenos Aires, Bruno Mauricio de Zavala, sent him a letter, asking for troops to defend Montevideo, which was under attack by the Portuguese. But the letter fell into the hands of Antiquera. Hoping to ingratiate himself with Zavala, Antiquera sent 600 men and, suspecting that the Jesuits sided with Balmaceda, expelled them from Asunción once more. Zavala had little attention to spare from the Portuguese in Montevideo and sent Ros back Paraguay with just 200 Spanish troops to crush Antiquera. Zavala also gave Ros permission to conscript Indians from the Jesuit missions. Although they were not a warlike people, the Guaraní had been taught by the Jesuits to obey orders without question. Later, when battle hardened, they would prove to have the makings of great troops. But this first time out under Ros, they were met by 3,000 men and soundly defeated. Some 1,800 Indians were killed.

The Viceroy then ordered Zavala to go in person to Paraguay and arrest Antiquera. Realising the whole force of the Spanish government in South America was ranged against him, Antiquera fled to Charcas and threw himself on the mercy of the Audience. They forwarded him to the Audience of Peru, where he was tried. But the trial dragged on for years and, during that time, public opinion swung in Antiquera's favour. When he was eventually found guilty of high treason and sentenced to death by beheading, crowds turned out to protest the injustice of the sentence. As Antiquera was paraded through the streets on the way to the scaffold, an angry mob jostled the Viceroy. He panicked and ordered his troops to open fire on the prisoner. Antiquera and two friars on horseback beside him were killed. Even though Antiquera was now dead, the Viceroy ordered that the sentence be carried out to the letter. So Antiquera's dead body was placed on the scaffold with its head on the block and the corpse was duly decapitated.

While Antiquera was on trial in Lima, the Jesuits had returned to Asunción. But when the people heard of Antiquera's execution, they blamed the Jesuits and expelled them from the city yet again. This time, the Jesuits were prepared to resist. In the countryside, they had built up a slave army of 7,000 Guaraní, who had now been blooded in battle. Civil war broke out. The Jesuits backed the winning side, then imposed their merciless authority on the country as a whole. However, the international power of the Jesuits was already on the wane. In 1759, they were expelled from Portugal. France and Spain soon followed suit. In 1767, the order came to expel them from Paraguay and free the Indians. But it was feared that the Jesuits, with their huge army, might overrun the Spanish garrison. The fear was unfounded. For even though the Jesuits had seemingly reduced their Indian converts to a state of total obeisance, they feared that the Guaraní might rebel if they were forced to fight to maintain their own enslavement; the Jesuits left the country without resistance. The Guaraní, having been coerced by a single authority under the Jesuits, now found themselves trying to obey the orders of both the local priests and civil administrators. When these conflicted, the Indians were flogged and bastinadoed. The Jesuits had also kept them ignorant of money, so the Guaraní would supply any goods requested, without thought of payment or exchange. Inevitably they were ruthlessly exploited by a series of corrupt Spanish governors and their favourites, who dominated the export of tobacco, hides, tallow and *yerba maté* – the local narcotic, also known as Paraguayan or Brazilian tea.

Maté is the dried and powdered leaf of the *Ilex paraguayiensis*, a shrub of the holly family though in size and foliage it resembles an orange tree. The powder is mixed with water in a cow's horn or gourd and the infusion is sucked through a *bombilla*, a silver straw with a bulbous end full of fine holes – though poorer people used the hollowed leg bone of a chicken with a piece of cotton wrapped around the stump. To this day, when Paraguayans have nothing else to do, they sit around sucking *maté*. But in the nineteenth century, its use outside Paraguay was widespread and its export was the origin of the country's wealth.

Back in Europe in 1808 the Emperor Napoleon forced Charles IV of Spain and his son Ferdinand VII to abdicate and placed his own brother Joseph Bonaparte on the Spanish throne. This act of nepotism undermined the authority of the Spanish viceroys in the Americas, who ruled in the name of the king. Meanwhile, the Peninsular War – Spain's War of Independence – tied up Spanish troops at home. In 1810 – the same year Simón Bolívar began his campaign to liberate Venezuela – the newly established viceroyalty in Buenos Aires was overthrown by a junta who, though seeking independence, claimed to rule in the name of the deposed Ferdinand. They invited Paraguay to join their revolution. But the Paraguayans saw no reason to favour Ferdinand over Joseph. They had suffered plenty under Spanish kings, not at all under French ones, and were currently enjoying the liberal governorship of the enlightened Don Bernardo Velasco.

To persuade them to join the cause, the Buenos Aires

junta sent an envoy, perversely selecting the worst possible candidate, José Espinola, who had been the ruthless lieutenant of the previous corrupt governor Lazaro Ribera Espinosa and was consequently the most hated man in Paraguay. Before Espinola arrived in Asunción, few Paraguayans cared one way or the other about who was king nearly 6,000 miles away in Madrid, but after Espinola arrived they turned emphatically against Ferdinand. General Manuel Belgrano, the Argentine hero who had thwarted Britain's attempted invasion of Río de la Plata in 1806, then decided that he could convince the Paraguayans of their need for liberation, arriving with an army on the borders of Paraguay on 4 December 1810. He issued a proclamation in Ferdinand's name, offering to free all those 'enslaved' by the colonial yoke in Paraguay. To the Paraguayans, this seemed disingenuous. If they were slaves now under Joseph, they had been slaves before under Ferdinand. It further muddied the waters that Velasco had been appointed governor, not by Joseph Bonaparte, but by Charles IV, Ferdinand's father – so, technically, Velasco and Belgrano were on the same side.

Belgrano then sent a letter asking Velasco to submit to the authority of the junta and to send a deputy to the Congress that was being held in Buenos Aires. The messenger was taken in chains to Asunción. Belgrano saw this as a hostile act and proclaimed that anyone caught with arms or who fired on his troops would be shot. This stiffened the resolve of the Paraguayans. The man claiming to be their liberator was threatening to execute anyone who tried to defend their homeland. To make it clear that he was there only to free them from colonial rule, Belgrano singled out a Paraguayan soldier of Spanish blood from among his prisoners and had him shot. This raised Paraguayan national fervour to fever pitch. The Paraguayans called Belgrano a butcher for shooting an unarmed prisoner of war – hardly the result he had intended. On the other side, however, the council in Asunción showed an extraordinary political naïvety in accepting an offer of help from General Sousa, the commander of the Portuguese Army that was suppressing the breakaway Brazilian province of Banda Oriental, now Uruguay. Velasco had to seize their letter of acceptance from the Portuguese Embassy – otherwise Sousa would have ridden to the defence of Paraguay, annexed the country for the Portuguese Empire and Paraguay would now be part of Brazil.

Supremely confident in the justice of his cause, Belgrano crossed the Paraná into Paraguay with just 400 men and two artillery pieces, leaving behind a company of cavalry he felt were unnecessary. He had come to liberate the country from colonial rule and still believed that he would be greeted as a hero. In the face of Belgrano's advancing army, Velasco's men fell back. Civilians also fled from their self-styled liberator. Finding no one to liberate, Belgrano simply burnt everything he came across *en route*, making himself a victim of a self-inflicted scorched-earth policy. The more the Paraguayans fell back, the more confident Belgrano became – and the more his supply lines were stretched across the scorched landscape he himself had turned into a desert.

At the same time, the six-week rolling retreat concentrated the Paraguayan forces. By the time Belgrano caught up with them he found himself facing a force outnumbering his own by seven to one and in a strongly fortified position. Along the way he had also lost his baggage train. Nevertheless he decided to go on the offensive. But at the same moment he staged a surprise attack on the Paraguayan camp, the Paraguayans staged a surprise attack on his. The Paraguayans were raw troops and, at their camp, the defenders fled. The Argentinians chased them as far as the village of Paraguari where, thinking they had won the war, they began to get drunk.

At Belgrano's camp, in the face of the Paraguayan onslaught, battle-hardened Argentine soldiers stood firm but were soon out of ammunition. Believing themselves to be cut off, they had fired on a cavalry escort bringing them fresh cartridges. The drunken pillagers of Paraguari were soon rounded up, while the rest of Belgrano's forces fled. But the Paraguayans were far too disorganised to pursue them. This gave Belgrano a chance to rally his men. After all he had come to help Paraguay throw off the shackles of Spanish rule, even if he did so in the name of the royal family that had imposed them. He regrouped, but was attacked by a superior force. As losses mounted, his men clearly expected him to surrender. But when a flag of truce appeared and the Paraguayans demanded that either he capitulate or every man would have his throat cut, Belgrano refused to lay down the arms of the king. He persuaded his men that their only chance lay in a swift attack. This sent the enemy reeling. He then sent out his own flag of truce. It was during this cease-fire that Belgrano spelt out for the first time that he was not there to conquer Paraguay in the name of Ferdinand, but rather to free the country from colonial rule and invite them to join the Argentine Confederation. To show his good faith he distributed gold to the widows of the Paraguayan men killed in the fighting.

Belgrano's talk of independence quickly convinced the Paraguayans. But he did his job too well. They decided that they wanted independence, not just from Spain, but from Buenos Aires too. So in a bloodless coup in May 1811, the military deposed the governor in Asunción and Paraguay became an independent republic before Argentina did. In the process they rid themselves of Don Bernardo Velasco, the first truly enlightened man to govern Paraguay, only to replace him with someone very much worse.

❧ 3 ❧

El Supremo

The history of Paraguay may seem like a terrible and bloody farce up to this point, but things would only get worse after independence. After the Paraguayans had deposed Governor Don Bernardo Velasco, they faced the problem of how to replace him. Velasco's secretary Dr Pedro Somellera – an old friend of General Belgrano from Buenos Aires who had been working for independence behind the governor's back all along – suggested forming a three-man junta. Two of its members would be the popular military leaders Don Juan Pedro Cavallero and Colonel Fulgencio Yegros. Unfortunately, these two men, it was said, knew as little about government as the horses they rode. Worse, they were Spaniards, not native Paraguayans.

The only native Paraguayan in the country obviously qualified to sit on the junta was Dr José Gaspar Rodríguez Francia. His rule was to set the tone for that of Francisco Solano López. Born in Asunción in 1758, Francia was the son of a Brazilian army officer who had come to Paraguay to grow tobacco. Like Eliza Lynch and Francisco Solano López, Dr Francia was a francophile. He changed his name from the Portuguese França or

Franza to Francia – the Spanish for France – and claimed French descent. He had spent a couple of years at school during the time the Jesuits had been expelled and, as his parents were relatively wealthy, he was sent to study theology at the University of Cordoba, across the river in what is now Argentina. Back in Paraguay he became a provincial *tinterillos* – essentially a lawyer without any legal qualifications, a glorified form-filler. A man of simple tastes, he had little use for money and no time for his family. When his father lay dying and feared that he would not be admitted into heaven unless he was reconciled with his son, Francia sent a message telling him to go directly to hell. He hated his neighbours and seems to have had no friends. However, thanks to the Jesuits, Francia was the only native Paraguayan with any form of education. He could do mathematics to elementary school level and had a handful of books on his shelves at home. This was an impressive library in a country where the reading of the vast majority of people was limited to the prayer book. He was also the owner of an old theodolite, whose telescope he used to study the stars – leading superstitious Paraguayans to conclude that he was communing with the demons of the night, a myth he encouraged.

Although Francia took no part in the revolution – and was probably opposed to it – at Dr Somellera's suggestion, he was selected to sit on the junta. As the other two members knew nothing of government and the law, it was left to Francia to write a constitution. It ran to just four lines. When it was ratified by a hastily convened Congress, Paraguay became the first independent republic in South America, at a time when Buenos Aires was still searching for a spare European royal to take over as head of state.

Francia rapidly tired of sharing power with the two gold-braided generals who were his companions on the junta. So he withdrew, leaving the government paralysed. Back in the countryside he stirred up discontent among the landowners – already troubled by the fact that Buenos Aires was at war with Spain and the river, essentially the only way for goods to get in and out of Paraguay, was closed. He also ingratiated himself with the Guaraní by treating the wealthy and those of Spanish blood with ostentatious contempt. Soon he was seen as the coming man.

The 21-year-old Scottish merchant John Robertson was in Paraguay at the time, consorting with the amorous 84-year-old widow, Doña Juana Ysquibel. On 27 May 1814, Doña Juana's saint's day, he attended a party at her *quinta*, her country house at Ytaphá, 25 miles from Asunción. Doña Juana performed a lively *sarandig*, or heel dance, with a seven-foot giant named Bedoya. But at the end of the evening as lovers headed off into the darkness of an orange grove, a sense of foreboding hung in the air.

'Ah, Mr Robertson,' said Don Velasco. 'I am afraid that this is the last scene of festivity we shall ever see in Paraguay.'

He was right.

'Both the light and the music of the revels must have reached Dr Francia's cottage,' wrote Robertson. 'At this very time he was planning those schemes which . . . at once hushed hilarity and extinguished the light of liberty.'

Francia seized his moment when the junta in Buenos

Aires once again sent a diplomat to Asunción to invite Paraguay to join the Argentine confederation. Francia put out the word that the Argentines were attempting by diplomacy what they had failed to do by force. Although in Francia's absence the junta had been expanded to five, they were still all Spaniards and the people did not trust them to put the interests of Paraguay first. Rejecting the junta, there was no choice but to recall Francia. His price was that he be allowed to rule alone. He became first consul, then the Perpetual Dictator of Paraguay, known informally as 'El Supremo' – a title that Francisco Solano López would also adopt. Francia's coup was not entirely unopposed. The troops under Yegros rebelled. Cavallero intervened to restore order. Both were jailed. Cavallero strangled himself in prison some years later in 1821; Yegros was executed.

Dr Somellera, a fellow graduate of the University of Cordoba, was arrested even though it had been he who had originally proposed Francia for the junta. He was jailed along with his brother Benigno and the former governor Velasco. In theory, Somellera was held incommunicado, but his cell door was often left open, enabling him to be informed about a planned counter-revolution to restore Velasco to the governorship. On the morning of 29 September 1814, soldiers took to the streets. But this was no counter-revolution; it was a trap. Those who rallied to the cause were shot down, their bodies hung from a gallows while the soldiers who had seemingly led the counter-revolution paraded under the gibbet, shouting patriotic slogans. With this simple ruse Francia disposed of the opposition. Somellera, knowing Francia well, had avoided falling into the trap and was allowed to leave the country. Velasco died in prison.

Francia immediately instituted a reign of terror, jailing anyone who criticised him on trumped up charges. It was said that the blacksmiths in Asunción could not forge shackles fast enough. Anyone who had previously held political office in the country was arrested and their property seized, and the houses where Francia fancied that plots were being hatched were burnt down.

Francia took over the running of the courts personally. Confessions and the indictment of co-conspirators were obtained by torture behind closed doors in the so-called Chamber of Truth. He created a police force and set up a spy system so effective that it was said he even knew the thoughts of the dying. Brother informed against brother; son against father; servant against master; husband against wife. Prisoners often had no idea what they had been imprisoned for. No one dared ask. Some were simply arrested and held until a ransom was paid, though they were rarely released even then. Few emerged from Francia's prisons. Prisoners were left there, ill-fed, unwashed, unkempt, with no medical attention until they died. Their relatives knew they were still alive only because they were permitted to send them food.

Francia also acted as chief executioner, issuing the bullets to his firing squads. But he was stingy with the bullets, usually handing over only two or three at a time. His men were not very good shots and, if they failed to kill the prisoner, the victim would be cruelly bayoneted to death. These executions always took place early in the morning. The *banquillo* – the stool where the condemned man sat – was set up under an orange tree outside Francia's window. He watched to make sure the deed was done and insisted that the body remained outside his window in the heat all day to make sure the victim was dead before the family were allowed to take it away.

A merchant named Mendez was arrested merely for having a party. When he was exiled to a penal colony, no one dared take over his business, act as his agent or buy his property in case they suffered the same fate. After that, a general gloom settled over the country.

In the eyes of Paraguayans, Francia was more powerful than God. A reader of Voltaire and Rousseau, he ignored their espousal of the rights of man but adopted their anticlericalism. He made himself head of the Church in Paraguay, seized all church property, closed the monasteries, banned church services and had his own likeness carved above every church door.

'If the Holy Father should come to Paraguay,' he said, 'I would do him no other honour than to make him my personal chaplain.'

Francia was also a follower of Benjamin Franklin, who he declared to be the 'first democrat of the world'. Within forty years, he said, every Latin American country would be ruled over by a man like Franklin, bringing to them a liberty that they had not been prepared for by Spanish rule. But in his 28 years in power, Dr Francia did little to promote this end. Worse, within 40 years, Paraguay would be ruled over by Francisco Solano López.

Like López, Francia was terrified of assassination. Even though the cigars he smoked were made by his sister, every one was carefully unrolled to see if it contained poison – his sister was not above suspicion because he had imprisoned her husband, along with his own brother and another brother-in-law, and had had one of his nephews executed. He checked on the ingredients of his meals and made his own *maté*. No one was permitted to come into his presence with even a cane in his hand nor approach him within six paces; their hands had to be kept well away from their sides. Francia himself was never without a loaded pistol and an unsheathed sabre within easy reach. To guard against insurrection, no man in the army was promoted above the rank of captain. Nor did he trust his own government ministers, who were made to stand in the hot sun while he harangued them, and they were regularly imprisoned.

No one was allowed out on the street when Francia rode out with his escort. All shutters had to be closed along his route and orange trees, shrubs and other potential places of concealment were uprooted. Anyone caught in the streets had to prostrate themselves or risk being cut down by sabre. When his horse shied at an old barrel outside a house, the owner was instantly arrested.

Francia himself held the only keys to his palace. Each night, he locked and barred the doors himself, and slept with a revolver under his pillow. The only person he confided in was the unwashed drunken mulatto who dressed his hair each morning. However, he had a servant boy imprisoned for hitting his dog, then thought better of it and had the boy shot.

The only person other than his hairdresser to whom Francia showed any respect – or even any mercy – was José Artigas, the 'father of Uruguayan independence', who spent his last years in exile in Paraguay. With the reputation of having cut more throats than any man alive, Artigas was granted a handsome pension of thirty dollars a month.

The whole apparatus of terror was run by Francia's

soldiers, who were conscripted for life. They were not paid, receiving only a daily ration of beef and an extravagant uniform designed by Dr Francia himself. And Francia never enforced the law against his own troops, so they were free to get drunk, steal and rape with impunity.

As a mark of respect, all adults were compelled to doff their hats to Francia's soldiers. Indians who could not afford a hat had to wear a brim. Silver spurs were very much in fashion in Paraguay at the time, even among those who could not afford a horse, and it was not uncommon to see Guaraní striding through the streets of Asunción naked except for a hat brim and spurs long after Francia was dead.

Francia banned education and sealed the borders of Paraguay, preventing his subjects escaping and precluding any trade with the outside world. Outsiders who stumbled into the country fared little better than the natives. The Scottish trader John Robertson and his brother William, who arrived in Asunción in 1812, were only released in 1816 when John promised to present the products of Paraguay at the bar of the House of Commons, though it remained unsure as to how he would get them past the Sergeant at Arms. Two Swiss naturalists, Johann Rengger and Marçel Longchamp, crossed the border on a field trip in 1819 and were only permitted to leave in 1825 when the British chargé d'affaires in Buenos Aires promised to provide arms in exchange for their release. Francia claimed he wanted to make Paraguay the first nation in South America, as Britain was the first in Europe. He was to be disappointed. The British did not supply the arms.

The world-famous French botanist Aimé Bonpland,

who had explored much of South America with the great German explorer Alexander von Humboldt, did not even have to enter Francia's hermit state to find himself in trouble. Noting the market for *yerba maté* in Buenos Aires and Rio, he set up a farm on the western side of the Paraná River, outside Paraguay. Around him he gathered a colony of Indians whom he instructed in the cultivation of *maté*. Arguing that growing Paraguayan tea outside the country was a threat to the Paraguayan economy, Francia sent 400 troops across the river. They slaughtered the Indians, razed the plantation and brought Bonpland, badly wounded with a sabre-cut to the head and wreathed in chains, back across the Paraná into Paraguay. Exiled to the remote settlement of Santa Maria, Bonpland made use of his skills as a doctor and built up a carpentry business and a smith's. Then after nine years, when he was relatively prosperous again, he was expelled from Paraguay with less than twelve hours' notice. He was forbidden to take anything with him and was dumped, alone, at night, with the minimum of ceremony, on the other side of the Paraná, where he started all over again.

Although Francia insisted on only a modest salary and living a modest lifestyle, he appropriated the assets of the aristocracy and acted as if the entire wealth of the country was effectively his own private property – not that he needed to spend any of it. All public works were accomplished with forced labour. The Guaraní, long cowed by the Jesuits, did what they were told without recompense. With the help of his theodolite, Francia executed a radical plan to straighten the streets of Asunción. But Francia had little flair for architecture and he left the city looking worse than when he started. His urban development plan involved the arbitrary demolition of large tracts of housing. When distraught property-owners asked where they were going to live, Dr Francia said he was only too happy to find accommodation for them in his prisons. Others were sent to a penal colony some 300 miles north of Asunción, which was subject to frequent floods, famines, malaria and Indian attacks. Few of its inmates lasted more than a year or two.

Apparently having been disappointed in love, Francia had little time for women. When the wife of a prisoner threw herself at Francia's feet and begged for her husband's release, Francia merely ordered that another set of iron fetters be placed on his legs – and a further set every time she approached him. Her husband died in chains, along with a friend who also had the temerity to intercede on the poor man's behalf.

Another woman who tried to rally opposition on the day of her husband's execution was thrown into jail loaded with chains. During her incarceration, the only words she uttered – and repeated hour after hour, day after day – were: 'Had I a thousand lives to lose, I would risk them all to destroy this monster.' The one life she had did not suffice. She was flogged to death, while Francia watched from his window in his dressing gown.

Some people used his harshness for their own ends. One woman, in a fit of jealousy, denounced her husband for speaking disrespectfully of Francia. The unfortunate man was sentenced to 100 lashes, though he was entirely innocent. Foolishly he said he would rather be shot. His wish was granted.

Francia turned to women for one thing only. He kept

an account book detailing his sexual prowess. Like their unfortunate mothers, his seven illegitimate children were left penniless. But when one of his daughters tried to support herself by becoming a prostitute and plied her trade outside the gates of his palace, he proclaimed prostitution to be a highly respected calling and ordered that working girls wear a golden comb in their hair as the badge of their calling. Consequently, they became known as the *peinetas de oro*. He did this not to honour his daughter, but to dishonour high-born Spanish ladies who traditionally wore their hair in that style. More than anything Francia hated the Spanish. To humiliate them further, he passed a law that permitted the white patrician classes to marry only African slaves or mulattos.

After 28 years in power, people began to believe that Francia was immortal. Then suddenly at the age of 79 he died on 20 September 1840. He caught a chill during a thunderstorm, which flooded his room, and took to his bed. When his doctor approached within six paces to examine him, Francia stabbed him with a sabre, then had a fit. The doctor called for help, but the sergeant of the guard refused to enter the room without direct orders from Dr Francia. The doctor explained that Francia was unconscious and unable to speak, but the sergeant said: 'Even so, if he comes round, he will punish me for disobedience.' The storm saved the Spanish officer Captain Pascual Urdapilleta and his two sons who, after surviving twelve years in jail, were scheduled to be shot next following day. The thunderstorm washed away the *banquillo* and next morning Francia was too weak to issue the necessary bullets. Untended, Francia died and Urdapilleta and his two sons were released, only to be horribly tortured and shot in the reign of terror begun by Eliza Lynch and her boyfriend, Francisco.

For several days after Francia's demise, none dared believe that he was really dead. People were afraid that it might be a trap. They feared they were being enticed into expressing relief or joy – only to bring down the wrath of the miraculously undead *El Supremo*. Indeed, Paraguayans feared even to mention his name decades after his death. He was known simply as '*El Difunto*' – the deceased.

Despite his contempt for religion, Dr Francia was laid out in state before the high altar of the cathedral in Asunción. Afraid that the dictator still might rise from the dead, a priest delivered a glowing eulogy which exhorted Paraguay to weep for the saviour of the country and described Francia as the 'guarantor of our national freedom'. Meanwhile, Francia's rule was praised by misguided Scottish radical Thomas Carlyle for its 'rigour'.

The night after the eulogy, Dr Francia's body disappeared from the cathedral, giving rise to the legend that the devil had claimed its own. Probably the old Spanish families of Paraguay had taken their revenge on the great man's cadaver, chucking it in the river for the alligators to eat.

Dr Francia's lasting legacy was the machinery of a ruthless authoritarian state, later to be exploited by Francisco Solano López. But first, horror was succeeded by farce. Like many dictators, Francia failed to groom a successor. Worse, he had systematically killed off anyone talented enough, educated enough or even fit enough to take over. The reins of power resided temporarily in the hands of Francia's secretary Polycarpo Patiño, who decided to set up a new junta. Its first act was to throw Patiño in jail where he hanged himself.

Without Patiño, no one seemed to have any idea how to ru˜˜˜government. Soon the junta was overwhelmed by petitions from the families of people Francia had thrown in jail, but could not make up its mind whether it had the authority to set them free. The junta was replaced in a military coup which was led, not by some beribboned generalissimo, but by two sergeants. They failed to inspire confidence and a Congress was called, playing into the hands of a greedy and ambitious man who had the foresight to turn up with a written constitution in his hands.

His name was Carlos Antonio López. Born in 1790, the son of a shoemaker in La Recoleta just outside Asunción, Carlos López was of mixed Guanari, Spanish and African blood. Despite his humble background, he studied theology and philosophy at the *Colegio* in Asunción. Then, like Francia, he began to practise law. When Francia came to power, López had the foresight to realise that other lawyers would be seen as a threat. He saved his skin by coming to the aid of the wealthy landowner Don Lázaro Rojas, who had married a widow and carelessly impregnated her daughter. In 1826, López married the heavily pregnant and vastly overweight Doña Juana Pablo Carillo – as he had African blood, this was legal under Francia's race laws. He then discreetly withdrew from the capital to run the remote ranch his father-in-law had so thoughtfully provided as part of a generous dowry. It was there that, alone at night, Carlos wrote his constitution. It was a straightforward document that put all executive power, along with control of the judiciary and the military, into the hands of the President. Along with power it also gave him patronage. The appointment and dismissal of every government official, along with the fixing of their salaries, was also the responsibility of the President. Admittedly the constitution limited his term to ten years, but the President had to be re-elected by a Congress which he alone had the power to call and whose members he hand picked. It had no legislative power either. The President's word was law. The congressmen simply turned up on the appointed day, one of them would propose that all the President's acts be ratified and the motion would be passed unanimously without question or debate. For a dictator, things do not get much better than that.

When Francia died, after a brief period of chaos under the junta, Congress held an election. Perhaps unsurprisingly, as Carlos López was the only person in Paraguay to come forward ready-equipped with a constitution, he was unanimously elected President – a result that was to be repeated in subsequent elections. In later life, López would coyly decline the nomination, only to be forced to accept it by the tears and entreaties of the people. He had learnt this trick from his old enemy the Argentinian tyrant Juan Manuel de Rosas. Rosas repeated it every year until 1852 when he was defeated by General Justo José de Urquiza, Governor of the Argentine province of Entre Rios, and forced to flee to England, where he died a gentleman farmer in Hampshire. However, Carlos López was not as adept as his model. On one occasion he declined the nomination without telling anyone his plan. Congress, thinking he wanted his son Francisco Solano

López to take over, voted unanimously for him instead, before Carlos declared the process void and had himself proclaimed President again.

Carlos López was 47 by the time he came to power. He was already too obese to sit on a horse and could be seen riding around Asunción in a coach, guzzling cakes and throwing banana skins out of the window. Although he had no military background, he took to wearing extravagant uniforms with enormous epaulettes and huge cocked hats which, according to Charles Washburn, the US Ambassador to Paraguay from 1861 to 1868, 'would have led one to suppose that some harmless, demented buffoon was playing king for the diversion of the rabble'. Carlos routinely surrounded himself with a large guard of good-looking young men, which made his squat figure look even more ludicrous by contrast. Sir Richard Burton, the great explorer and orientalist who was then British consul in Brazil, described him as 'hideous, burly and thickset . . . With chops flapping over his cravat, his face wears, like the late George IV, a porcine appearance'.

López always received guests sitting down. Visitors were impressed by his informal manner but it was actually to conceal the fact that one of his legs was shorter than the other. He also spoilt the effect by insisting on wearing a hat when receiving foreign ambassadors. The British Ambassador claimed it showed disrespect for the Queen of England. López pointed out that the Queen wore a crown on similar occasions. However, he was forced to back down when the ambassadors all refused to remove their own hats during official interviews.

Compared with *El Supremo*, 'Citizen López', as he styled himself, was a breath of fresh air. He re-opened the elementary schools – though they were still run along Jesuit lines, discouraging young minds from questioning authority. Even so, by his death, literacy in Paraguay was still only a quarter of what it had been in Governor Velasco's time.

Carlos started the country's first newspaper, *Paraguayo Independiente*, as a mouth-piece for his own home-spun philosophy. He was also the first head of state in the western hemisphere to ban slavery, declaring presumptuously: 'All men are equal before God and me.' Nevertheless, so as not to have to compensate slave owners, he freed the slaves only gradually. After the anti-slavery law was introduced in 1842, those who were already slaves remained slaves, while children born to slaves were freed when girls reached 24 and males when they reached 25. Then, after 1867, all children of slaves were to be free from birth.

Carlos opened the borders and soon the country grew rich on the export of *yerba maté*. Twenty-five pounds of *maté*, bought from pickers in Paraguay for one shilling, sold for between 24 and 32 shillings in Buenos Aires and Brazil. Paraguay's exports also included hides from the huge herds of cattle in the south-west of the country, tobacco, cigars, maize, tanner's bark, hard woods – and firewood for Buenos Aires which had none – oranges, starch, slate and *caña*, the local rum. In 1858, some 230 steamers and sailing vessels arrived at the port of Asunción and the Paraguayan steamer *Rio Blanco* made several trips to London and back. Despite the booming economy it was felt that the wealth of country had only just begun to be exploited. In Brazil to the east and Bolivia to the north, gold and precious stones had been discovered and it was thought that similar finds would be made in Paraguay's outlying cordilleras.

With this new-found wealth, Carlos invited foreigners, particularly Britons, into the country to trade and develop its infrastructure. However, López had never been out of Paraguay, knew next to nothing of the outside world and was diplomatically inept, and his open-door policy courted disaster. The United States almost went to war with Paraguay when López's troops fired on the USS *Waterwitch*, killing an American sailor. Relations with Great Britain soured when a Uruguayan resident of British parentage named James Canstatt was implicated in an assassination plot that Carlos had dreamt up to rid himself of some political enemies.

The French broke off diplomatic relations with Paraguay when emigrants from Bordeaux were beaten and tortured. And Brazil sent a squadron of warships when Paraguay withdrew navigation rights up the Paraná River, preventing the development of Brazil's wealthy western province of Matto Grosso. They were seen off only by the hurried construction of fortifications at Humaitá, downstream from Asunción. López was also unable to resist getting involved in the civil wars that raged in Uruguay and Argentina.

At home, while Citizen López may have been a liberal ruler when compared to Francia, he maintained Francia's system of spies and his tendency to imprison arbitrarily. And no one was allowed to upstage him. When a wealthy landowner imported a carriage from Europe, it was confiscated on the grounds that no one could have a better carriage than *El Presidente*. There were also summary executions. When a merchant was overcharged at the customs house, lost his temper and trampled on a government paper bearing a stamp with Carlos's picture on it, López had the man shot for stamping on his portrait. Nevertheless, by Paraguayan standards, his regime was relatively benign – though two Frenchmen were deported for practising mesmerism without permission.

'Probably in no country in the world has life and property been so secure as all over Paraguay during his reign,' wrote a visitor. 'Crime was almost unknown and, when committed, immediately detected and punished. The mass of people was perhaps the happiest in existence. They had hardly to do any work to gain a livelihood. Each family had its house or hut in its own ground. Each hut had an orange grove and a few cows. They planted, in a few days, enough tobacco, maize and mandioca [cassava] for their own consumption, and the crop hardly wanted looking at till it was ready to be gathered.'

The better off had a European lifestyle and many families were well off and comfortable. However, anybody was liable to have his property 'pressed into public service, without payment'. But this power was not frequently abused and Carlos only allowed his family to tyrannise the people to any great extent.

After Carlos re-established relations with Rome – while still refusing to hand over the tithes or account for the treasures Francia had stolen – he managed to persuade Pope Gregory XVI to appoint his brother Basilio Bishop of Asunción. As a result the secrets of the confessional were reported directly back to *El Presidente*. His grotesquely obese wife over-ate and styled herself *La Presidenta* and lorded it over her subjects, while his overweight and ugly daughters, Inocencia and Rafaela, were allowed to buy torn banknotes at a discount of sixpence in the dollar and sell them back to the exchequer at full value. They also lent money on the security of jewellery but kept anything they liked. His three sons were granted monopolies of the nation's exports and were exempted from paying customs duties. They occupied any state lands they chose and built themselves impressive ranches and homes using unpaid labour. They were also noted for their libertinism. The youngest, Benigno, was universally detested. He was elephantine, syphilitic and cheated at cards. No Paraguayan dared refuse to play him and none dared win. Nevertheless, he was his mother's favourite. She doted on him and prevailed on his father to grant him all sorts of special privileges. Carlos's second son Venancio was fat and beardless with a high falsetto voice. Nevertheless, Venancio was the 'terror of those families that, not belonging to the upper class, had yet some regard for decency and the reputation of their daughters,' according to Washburn. And then there was Francisco . . .

~§ 4 §~

FRANCISCO LÓPEZ

Of an unattractive family, the oldest son Francisco
Solano López was undoubtedly the most unappealing.
Although he was not the natural son of Carlos Antonio,
he shared many of his father's grosser characteristics. He
was short, fat, ugly, barrel-chested and bandy-legged
from learning to ride early in life. And like Carlos, he
showed a predilection for extravagant uniforms, cut tight
in a misguided attempt to disguise his corpulence.

'His eyes, when pleased, had a mild expression; but
when he was enraged the pupil seemed to dilate till it did
not appear to be that of a human being, but rather a wild
animal,' wrote Ambassador Washburn undiplomatically.
'He had, however, a gross animal look that was repulsive
when in repose. His forehead was narrow and his head
small, with the rear organs largely developed. His teeth
were very much decayed, and so many of the front ones
were gone as to render his articulation somewhat difficult
and indistinct.'

Washburn concluded that Francisco made no effort to
clean his teeth and said those that remained were unwhole-
some in appearance and as black as the cigar he kept permanently clenched between them. His heart was blacker.

Born on 24 July 1826, Francisco Solano López was spoilt, arrogant, boastful and greedy. Nevertheless, while Benigno was his mother's favourite, Carlos doted on Francisco. After all he owed the child everything. It was the birth of Francisco, as the illegitimate son of Don Lázaro Rojas, that had saved Carlos from almost certain death under Francia, who had disposed of every other potential rival. The child had brought him wealth and the opportunity to plan his own bid for power. From the moment he became president, Carlos indulged Francisco as a crown prince and groomed him as his successor. He had also named him after a saint.

At the age of ten, under the tutelage of the Jesuit priest Padre Fidel Maiz – Carlos and Doña Juana's confessor and generally acknowledged as Paraguay's leading scholar – Francisco read *El Catecismo de San Alberto*, a narrative of the savage suppression of the insurrection of Tupac Amaru II, the last descendant of the Inca emperors. After being forced to witness the execution of his wife and sons, Tupac was mutilated, drawn, quartered and beheaded. This was the young Francisco's favourite bedtime reading. Later, at the school of Juan Pedro Escalada, a scholar from Buenos Aires, Francisco learnt about Napoleon who became his lifelong hero. After all, Napoleon, like Francisco, was a short man. Francisco was bilingual in Guaraní and Spanish. At home with Eliza, he spoke fluent French and, under her tutelage, his English was passable. However, his teachers said that he was not a 'desirable' pupil and Washburn said that he knew no more of history than a New England school boy of fifteen. He had no knowledge of music, art, literature or the classics; his only ideas of government were gleaned from Dr Francia.

Francisco left school at fifteen and joined the army. Within three years, he had risen to the rank of brigadier general, the highest rank in the Paraguayan army. At nineteen he became a war hero. In 1845, his father unwisely embroiled Paraguay in the civil war in Argentina. Francisco rode into the Argentine province of Corrientes at the head of 5,000 men, rode around a bit, then rode back into Paraguay without a shot being fired. *El Semanario*, the Paraguayan government newspaper that succeeded *Paraguayo Independiente*, declared him 'the Hero of Corrientes' and the greatest warrior since Alexander the Great. His father made him Minister of War. To prevent jealousy within the family, Benigno was appointed Commander-in-Chief of the Asunción garrison and Venancio was promoted to Major. However, Venancio complained that he was not cut out for the rigours of army life, so he was appointed Grand Admiral of the Fleet instead. This clearly proved less taxing as landlocked Paraguay had no fleet at the time and Venancio retired to one of the *estancias* he had seized.

Like his brother Venancio, Francisco seems to have inflicted himself on any woman he fancied. As a youth, he would visit brothels and send the bill to the palace, saying his father would pay. But while Venancio liked lower-class women, Francisco had a weakness for young aristocratic virgins and terrorised the first families of Asunción. If their daughters refused him, their fathers would be jailed and the families' property confiscated on Carlos's authority. Francisco was, as the US Ambassador put it, a 'licensed ravisher'.

Nevertheless a young woman regarded by many as the most beautiful in Paraguay named Pancha Garmendia –

known as the 'jewel of Asunción' – resisted him; her father had already been jailed and executed by Dr Francia. She took refuge in a convent – not a good move as Francisco was only too prepared to 'martyr' some of the nuns. He arrested her brothers and had them tortured. Still she refused him, so he tried to take her by force. He broke into her room at night, but she defended herself like a tiger. So, according to Washburn, he had her put in chains, and is said to have had her flogged and raped daily by his soldiers for the remaining 23 years of her life.

The Hero of Corrientes then took a fancy to another aristocratic beauty named Carmencita Cordal. She refused him on the grounds that she was engaged to be married to Carlos Decoud, a son of one of the leading families of Paraguay. Decoud was arrested, along with his two brothers. On the eve of the wedding, his naked, mutilated corpse was dumped in the street in front of her house – some say it was flung into her living room. The shock drove Carmencita insane. She spent the rest of her life wreathed in black and was seen in the dead of night sobbing over her dead lover's grave.

The murder of Decoud was one step too far. Aristocratic families with beautiful daughters began queuing up to get passports. Normally, Carlos was perfectly willing to issue them, provided families fleeing the country left behind all their property. But there was such a stampede to leave Paraguay that Carlos thought it best that Francisco absent himself until the scandal blew over. So the Hero of Corrientes was sent to win his diplomatic spurs in Europe. Francisco was to be the first Paraguayan of any note to travel abroad.

Carlos gave him vast sums of money, ostensibly to buy

a navy which, plainly, landlocked Paraguay did not need, and he travelled with a huge retinue including his brother Benigno. First they went to Britain which, in the wake of the Great Exhibition, saw itself as the world's leading nation and was at the height of its imperial expansion. London saw itself at the capital of the world and had a population nearly twice that of the whole of Paraguay. Nothing Francisco had seen in La Plata could have prepared him for the bustle of a big Victorian city – gaslight, railways, the telegraph – it was thanks to Francisco that Carlos López brought in British engineers to modernise Paraguay. He ordered huge quantities of guns and ammunition and two war steamers from J. & A. Blyth of Limehouse – paid for with worthless scrips and IOUs. But not everyone was impressed. Queen Victoria refused to see him. She had no time for the bandy-legged son of a Latin American dictator.

So Francisco headed for France. There he bought uniforms both for himself and his army, modelled on those worn by his hero Napoleon and his Grande Armée. As Francisco idolised Napoleon, he was eager to meet his nephew, Napoleon III, who had recently seized the throne and declared France's Second Empire. With the promise of buying more arms in France, Francisco was invited to court at the Tuileries Palace. Wearing the dress uniform of a field marshal, a cape of the finest lace and patent leather boots with monstrous silver spurs, the bow-legged Francisco strutted through a long series of ante-rooms, with the doors flung open by liveried servants along the way, until he was ushered into the presence of Louis-Napoléon and the Empress Eugénie. Francisco presented Louis with a hundred boxes of

Paraguayan cigars, which Louis promised to show at the following year's Paris Exhibition. Then, reeking of cigar-smoke which the Empress Eugénie detested, Francisco bent to kiss the Empress's hand. According to one observer, she turned away and vomited over an ormolu desk.

With impressive sang-froid, Eugénie explained that she was *enceinte* and suffering from morning sickness – which wasn't true. Louis-Napoléon then kissed Francisco on both cheeks and presented the Hero of Corrientes with the *Légion d'Honneur*.

Strangely, in the light of this decoration, none of Louis-Napoléon's generals sought the advice of the greatest warrior since Alexander the Great, although France was involved in the Crimean War at the time. This was, perhaps, because no one seemed to know where Corrientes – or, indeed, Paraguay – was. Few of those in the court in the Tuileries had ever heard of Brazil or the Argentine. Some joked that the newspapers from New York were late and they had missed news of the discovery of Paraguay. This failed to amuse Francisco; after all Asunción had been founded 87 years before the first Dutch settlers had arrived in New Amsterdam.

As Francisco left the royal presence, Louis-Napoléon said: '*J'espère que vous vous amusez à Paris.*' Which Francisco certainly did. With his vast entourage, he went drinking, gambling and whoring. He sprayed money around like champagne. This would not go unnoticed – especially by a nineteen-year-old courtesan named Eliza Lynch, who always had an eye on the main chance.

ELIZA LYNCH

Eliza Lynch was born in County Cork on 3 June 1835, to an Anglican family. She styled herself variously Eliza and Elisa, though intimates called her Ella. However, as she was christened Elizabeth, it is best, for our purposes, to called her by the diminutive Eliza, which is the one she used most often herself. She would claim subsequently that her father's side of the family boasted two bishops and more than seventy magistrates, while her mother's included a vice-admiral in the Royal Navy who, with four of his brothers, fought under Nelson at the Battle of the Nile and Trafalgar. All her uncles were officers in the British armed forces, or so she claimed, and her cousins occupied high positions in the establishment in Ireland. No records have been discovered of anyone who matches these descriptions, though it is possible that one uncle was a lieutenant in the navy.

It was also said that the family tree of Eliza's mother, Adelaide Schnock, included Queen Victoria's personal confessor, three members of parliament during the reign of Queen Anne, the leader of the opposition in Cromwell's Protectorate Parliament, the executioner who removed the head of Charles I, a royalist general, the rightful claimant to the Duchy of Warwick, the favourite catamite of Richard the Lionheart, the first 'white man' to land in Ireland and the man who had written the *Domesday Book*. No evidence can be found to this effect.

Stories circulated that Eliza's father, John Lynch, was a British naval officer who died in glorious circumstances off the coast of China during the first Opium War in 1840. He was in fact a doctor and was alive when she married in 1850. On the putative death of her father, Eliza's mother was said to have married a man named Kinkley. As a result, Eliza was sent to live with her maternal uncle, the Archbishop of Dublin, and was enrolled at Trinity College at the age of nine. This is, at best, fanciful. However, there is no doubt that she was a clever and cultured woman. She mastered French, Spanish and Guaraní, the tongue-twisting Indian language of Paraguay and she was the cultural superior of even the most highly educated in Paraguay at the time – though, as the schools had been closed throughout Francia's reign and the country had been closed to the outside world, this is not saying much.

Eliza wrote little about her childhood, though she claimed her family was wealthy – which seems unlikely. Few people living in Ireland in the early nineteenth century could claim that distinction. But, with a father who was a doctor, her family would certainly have been relatively well off. Even so they would not have been unaffected by the Great Irish Potato Famine, which struck in 1845. Within four years 1.1 million Irish people would be dead, another 1.5 million were forced to emigrate and Eliza's presumably comfortable and secure childhood had been turned into a nightmare. Indeed it was the humble potato, which itself had its origins in South America, that set young Eliza off on her eventual quest to become Empress of that continent.

The summer of 1845 was warm and must have been idyllic for a child of ten. The Irish countryside was thick with brightly coloured potato flowers. Although Irish peasant farmers planted corn as a cash crop to pay the rent, potatoes were their staple diet and everyone was delighted by the prospect of a bumper crop. There was no reason to suspect that anything was amiss until the autumn, when the leaves of the potato plants began to curl at the edges and turn black. Still no one foresaw the catastrophic consequences. When the crop was lifted, the tubers seem unaffected. However, they soon turned black and into a squelchy, stinking mess. Vast areas of the country were affected. Within a year, Eliza would have seen men, women and children starving, naked and reduced to a state of total despair.

Cork was particularly badly hit. Local magistrate Nicholas Cummins wrote to Sir Charles Trevelyan at the Treasury in London: 'The alarming prospect cannot be exaggerated. In the whole city and port of Cork there is only four thousand tons of food stuff. Unless great amounts reach us from other quarters, the prospect is appalling. I assure you that unless something is immediately done the people must die . . .'

Relief committees were set up, but had to close after a few days as supplies ran out. Some 2,130 died in the city of Cork workhouse between December 1846 and April 1847 alone.

The horrific scenes Eliza would have witnessed were vividly portrayed by Nicholas Cummins in a letter to the

Duke of Wellington, which was published in *The Times* on Christmas Eve 1846. It described a trip to a country village.

'Being aware that I would have to witness scenes of frightful hunger, I provided myself with as much bread as five men could carry,' he wrote, 'and on reaching the spot, I was surprised to find the wretched hamlet apparently deserted. I entered some of the hovels to ascertain the cause, and the scenes that presented themselves were such as no tongue or pen can convey the slightest idea of. In the first, six famished and ghastly skeletons, to all appearances dead, were huddled in a corner on some filthy straw, their sole covering what seemed a ragged horsecloth, their wretched legs hanging about, naked above the knees. I approached with horror, and found by low moaning that they were still alive – they were in fever, four children, a woman, and what had once been a man. It was impossible to go through the detail. Suffice it to say, that in a few minutes, I was surrounded by at least two hundred such phantoms, such frightful spectres as no words can describe, suffering either from famine or from fever. Their demoniac yells are still ringing in my ears and their horrible images fixed on my brain.'

How many sights like this Eliza saw we cannot tell. But we do know that she saw such things again. Next time, though, they would be caused, not by the innocent potato blight, but by the blight of her own ambition.

Other scenes from her Irish childhood would be replayed in her later life, when public works were begun in an effort to bring relief: 'It was melancholy and degrading in the extreme to see the women and girls withdrawn from all that was decent and proper and labouring in mixed gangs on the public roads,' wrote one English observer. Twenty-two years later and over six thousand miles away, Eliza would organise similar work details.

She would also be familiar with the diseases that famine brought with it to Ireland in later life. The most common was oedema.

'Many of the people were prostrate under that horrid disease – the results of long continued famine and low living – in which first the limbs, and then the body, swell most frightfully, and finally burst,' one eyewitness wrote. 'Perhaps the poor children presented the most piteous and heart-rending spectacle. Many were too weak to stand, their little limbs attenuated, except where the frightful swellings had taken the place of previous emaciation. Every infantile expression entirely departed; and in some reason and intelligence had evidently flown.'

Scurvy struck, causing people's teeth to drop out and their legs to turn black with broken blood vessels. Few could afford to wash or change their clothes or bedding. Their filthy rags were infested with lice, which brought with it typhus. The victims of typhus vomit uncontrollably and become covered with sores and rashes. Their faces swell and turn black and their whole body gives off an unbearable stench. For fear of the disease, parents abandoned their children and children their parents. Corpses were left unburied. There were riots and, by 1848, Ireland was in open rebellion. But it is unlikely that Eliza saw any of the fighting, which climaxed with a farcical shoot-out at Widow McCormack's house in County Tipperary where, due to a misunderstanding, one rebel was killed and several others wounded. Already familiar with sights of horror and the stench of death by the time she was twelve, Eliza left Ireland in 1847. Her older sister, Corinne, was already living in Paris and the Lynch family fled there.

The Stroessner government was to maintain that Corinne's husband was a famous musician called Tamburini, of whom no record exists. Apparently, his friend Victor Hugo considered the youthful Eliza to have a superior mind, while Franz Liszt wept openly when she refused to become a concert pianist. There is no evidence that she knew either man, and the name of Tamburini does not appear on the concert bills of the time.

In fact, for the Lynch family, the move to Paris would have been more a case of out of the frying pan into the fire. At the time France was just coming to the end of the so-called 'July Monarchy'. Under the 'Citizen King' Louis-Philippe, the country had enjoyed sixteen years of prosperity. But in 1846, crop failures made food both expensive and scarce. Businesses went bankrupt and unemployment rose. Rioting broke out in 1848 and 40 demonstrators were shot down by the army in front of the house of Louis-Philippe's Chief Minister, François Guizot. The Citizen King abdicated in favour of his nine-year-old grandson and fled to England. Paris was in political turmoil. The Chamber of Deputies was invaded by a mob demanding a republic. The establishment of 'national workshops' to provide relief for the poor attracted the unemployed from all over France to Paris. To pay for this, a 45-centime surcharge was levied on every franc of property tax. There were violent demonstrations on the streets. Elections solved nothing, rather they provoked a four-day civil war on the streets of Paris, with the army using artillery against the barricades. Over 1,500 rebels were killed and 12,000 arrested. In September 1848, Louis-Napoléon, the nephew of Napoleon Bonaparte, returned from exile in England. Several scheming monarchists backed him, thinking that he could be shunted aside later and the Orleans monarchy restored. In December, under a new constitution that some thought the most democratic in Europe, Louis-Napoléon was elected the first – and only – President of the Second Republic.

If Eliza's father had thoughts of restoring the family's fortunes by speculating on the Paris Bourse, he was out of luck. The economic boom of the July Monarchy was over by the time he arrived there. The rioting would have meant that there would certainly have been call for his medical skills, though it would have been unlikely that many of his patients had any money to pay him. And as Corinne's musician husband was not a well-known virtuoso, the family seems to have fallen on hard times.

But for the strong and independent-minded Eliza there was a way out. On her fifteenth birthday, 3 June 1850, she married Xavier Quatrefages, who she later claimed 'occupied a high ranking position in France'. He was a 40-year-old French army vet. Their marriage was not allowed under French law – the age of consent was sixteen in France. So the fourteen-year-old Eliza took her middle-aged Catholic lover across the Channel to Kent. They were married under the rites and ceremonies of the Anglican Communion in Folkestone parish church, dedicated, perhaps inappropriately, to the Virgin Mary and St Eanswythe, the King of Kent's daughter who fled to France to become a nun rather than marry. Eliza seems to have been keen both to marry and lose her virginity. On her marriage certificate it merely mentions she was 'under age'.

Official biographies in Paraguay claim that Quatrefages was a college chum of Eliza's elder brother. He met her when he was on secret mission to Dublin for French military intelligence, wooed her on the banks of the Shannon and they were married by her uncle the Archbishop. The Shannon, of course, does not flow within 60 miles of Dublin.

Perhaps a modest dowry from Quatrefages helped the family finances. The marriage would certainly have freed Eliza from the penury that had overcome the rest of her family. It also removed her from further bloodshed in Paris. Her husband was posted to Algeria to care for the horses of a cavalry regiment – or, in some accounts, become a senior inspector of military hospitals – and Eliza went with him. France had seized Algeria from the Ottoman Empire in 1830. Full-scale war raged until 1847 with a third of the French army, more than 100,000 men, stationed there. But by the time Eliza reached Algeria, that number had been reduced to 70,000, although sporadic fighting continued until 1871. The Algiers of that time was a sophisticated city said to have all the gaiety of Paris, the charm of eastern life and the enchantment of the Arabian nights. The French had gone to a great deal of trouble to install an efficient sewerage system. However, the cavalry were garrisoned outside town in the village of Lower Mustapha. As fighting to control the Saharan oases was still raging, the cavalry would sometimes be posted to dusty towns in the interior of French West Africa, hardly the place for a vivacious young woman when the Second Empire was establishing itself back in Paris.

Under the 1848 constitution, the President of the Second Republic was only allowed a single four-year term. So on 2 December 1851, Louis-Napoléon staged a *coup d'état*. A year later he proclaimed the Second Empire, naming himself Napoleon III – Napoleon Bonaparte had been Napoleon I, while his only legitimate son, the Duke of Reichstadt and one-time King of Rome, counted as Napoleon II, though he never reigned. But if the empire of the first Napoleon had ended in tragedy for France, the Second Empire was a farce. Napoleon III's aide-de-camp Emile Fleury explained that it 'was not exactly a proper empire, but we did have a damn good time', while Théophile Gautier described Louis-Napoléon as looking like 'a ring-master who had been sacked for getting drunk'.

Nevertheless, stuck out in Algeria, Eliza was missing all the excitement. She left her husband after three years of marriage – 'for reasons of ill health,' she said. They had no children. It was later contended that the marriage was never consummated. What really happened, it seems, is that Quatrefages's commanding officer, a colonel, took a fancy to her and her husband had neither the rank nor the inclination to defend her from his advances.

She was saved by an aristocratic young Russian cavalry officer named Michael, who just happened to be cantering across the dunes in search of adventure at the time. He challenged Eliza's elderly seducer to a duel and killed him. The two young lovers took off for Paris, while Quatrefages consoled himself with the fact that, under French law and as a Catholic, his wife was no wife at all. He later remarried.

Michael set up home with Eliza in a grand mansion in the Ruc de Bac in the newly fashionable district of Saint Germain. While Eliza had been away, it seems, her father had died, her brothers had joined the Navy and her mother and sister had returned to England. But Eliza had her Michael. Her story might have had a happy ending right there, but in October 1853 the Crimean War broke out. Russia was now the enemy of both Britain and France, and Michael, who had after all already killed a French officer, returned to his country to fight. Eliza's husband had returned to France, but he was not willing to support her. The beautiful seventeen-year-old found herself alone in the Paris of the Second Empire, which, under Napoleon III, had become the brothel of Europe. She had herself and a mansion to support, so Eliza entered the only lucrative career open to her. There was nothing too disreputable in this. The Second Empire was the era of the *grandes horizontales*. Women of all classes earned wealth and influence on their backs. The Emperor himself set the style. The only thing that Napoleon III had inherited from his uncle, it was said, was his insatiable sexual appetite. He was said to have paid £10,000 for a single night with the notorious Plymouth-born prostitute Cora Pearl. Cora went on to become the mistress of Louis-Napoléon's cousin Prince Napoleon, known universally as '*Plon-Plon*' – an expression that has now entered the language for casual sex.

The *grandes cocottes* were the unofficial aristocracy of Paris and wealthy with it. The Contessa di Castigilione charged one million francs a night. This was at a time when a thirteen-year-old serving girl, earning four francs a month, was jailed for four years for stealing jam from her employer. The Princesse de Sagan was one of the many mistresses of the Prince of Wales. So was Cora Pearl who is said to have had herself served to him on a silver salver, naked except for a string of pearls and a sprig of parsley. She danced naked on a carpet of orchids and bathed in champagne before an audience of paying guests. Her toilet seat was made of swan's down and she presented plaster casts of her sumptuous breasts to regular clients. She was also famous for her Billingsgate. When a jealous lover blew his brains out in her salon, her only comment was: 'That f***ing pig has ruined my f***ing carpet!'

Demi-mondaines mixed in the highest levels of society. *La Belle Otero* claimed to have bedded most of the crowned heads of Europe, while Hortense Schneider was so well known for distributing her favours to European royalty she was known as *Le Passage des Princes*. The Duc de Grammont-Caderousse once took the Prince of Wales to visit Guilia Beneni, who proudly claimed to be the 'greatest whore in the world' and worked under the name of *La Barucci*. *Zucca Barucca* is Venetian for 'roast pumpkin'. Rudely *La Barucci* turned her back on the Prince, then pulled up her skirt to reveal her naked *derrière*. When the Duc told her off for this breach of protocol, she simply replied: 'Well, you told me to show him my best side.'

Though the rewards of being a sexual adventuress were considerable, the competition was stiff. But Eliza had advantages. She was tall and supple with a delicate figure admired for its beautiful and seductive curves. Her hair was reddy gold, her skin calcium white and her eyes 'a blue that seems borrowed from the very hues of heaven and had an expression of ineffable sweetness in whose depths the light of Cupid was enthroned,' as Argentine journalist Héctor Varela put it. Varela also enthused about her lips which 'were indescribably expressive of the voluptuous, moistened by ethereal dew that God must have provided to lull the fire within her' and her mouth which was 'like a cup of delight at the banquet table of ardent passion'. Her hands were 'small, with long fingers, the nails perfectly formed and delicately polished'. She was plainly a woman who was proud of her looks. According to Varela, she was a woman for whom taking care of her appearance was a religion.

There is no doubt that Eliza could have scaled the heights of her profession. Élisabeth-Céleste Vénard – *Mogador* – became the Comtesse de Chabrillan and Marie Duplessis became the Comtesse de Perrégaux, although she is best remembered as the model for the tragic heroine of Alexandre Dumas fils's *La Dame aux camélias*. Born in the Jewish ghetto of Moscow, Thérèse Lachman used her attractions to rise from being plain Madame Villoing, to the Marquise de Païva, then to Countess Henckel von Donnersmarck. Had she lived a few years longer, there is every possibility that she would have become a princess. While the notorious Lola Montez became Countess of Landsfeld and ruled Bavaria by her lover King Ludwig's side, until her intrigues toppled the throne.

But Eliza set her sights even higher. She cannot have failed to notice that another red-headed young woman of humble birth had made her mark on Paris at the time. Her name was Eugénie de Montijo. Her grandfather William Kirkpatrick was a Scot, who claimed descent from the third-century Irish hero Fingal. When Louis-Napoléon failed to find a Hapsburg or a Romanov princess or any appropriate relative of Queen Victoria to marry, he chose the lowly Eugénie as his Empress. Cousin *Plon-Plon* teased him, saying: 'One does not marry women like Mademoiselle Montijo, one merely makes love to them.' In fact they had both tried unsuccessfully to do just that. When the frustrated Louis-Napoléon had asked her to tell him the way to her heart – though he surely meant her *con* not her *coeur* – she replied: 'Through the chapel, sir'. In 1853, that chapel turned out to be Nôtre Dame cathedral.

The Empress Eugénie became Eliza's model. Both were accomplished horsewomen. Both lived to see their first-born sons die. Both flourished as the consorts and mentors of physically unattractive and unfaithful men. Both urged their men into disastrous wars that destroyed them and damaged their nations. And both died in exile – though, by that time, the roles had been reversed. Eugénie died in England in 1920, some 34 years after Eliza was interred in France.

Eliza was well connected, so when she started in her new profession she avoided the Bohemian haunts of the *demi-monde* frequented by Cora Pearl and Blanche d'Artigny, the model for Zola's *Nana*. A friend of Princess Mathilde, the Emperor's cousin and a leading society hostess, Eliza attended soirées at the Princess's palace and was seen at first nights at the Opera, the *Variétés* and the *Comédie Français*. Soon she boasted a posse of suitors who spoilt her. But as fast as the money came in, it went out again on clothes, the upkeep of her mansion, her servants' wages and expensive food and wines. What Eliza needed was one really wealthy man who could take care of all her needs.

During the Second Empire, rich men from all over the world flocked to Paris. Eliza had cards printed, introducing herself as *Madame Lynch, Language Teacher*. Her servants were despatched to hand these out at hotels, embassies and Paris's fashionable night-spots. Meanwhile, she had gaming tables installed in her salon, so that her gentlemen callers could amuse themselves – and lose money – while they waited.

≈§ 6 §≈

THE TRYST OF FATE

There are various versions of how Francisco and Eliza met. Paraguayan historians of the Stroessner era claimed that they were introduced at a ball in Algiers, when the Governor had invited the beautiful women of the area to meet the dashing young war hero visiting from Paraguay. Others maintain that they met at the Gare St Lazare as Francisco first set foot in Paris. Ambassador Washburn, who knew both Francisco and Eliza well, had a different story to tell. He maintained that Francisco was not Eliza's first Paraguayan paramour. One of Francisco's entourage named Brizuela had got there first and, when he boasted of the experience, Francisco was keen to meet 'the lady whose charms were so vaunted by his subordinate'.

Apparently, Eliza was also keen to meet Francisco. Once Brizuela told her of 'the princely munificence of his chief, she contrived to make his acquaintance' – just the man for Eliza, who was always on the look-out for a free-spending lecher. 'She belonged to that class of public women so numerous in Paris,' Washburn wrote, 'always on the watch for strangers with long pockets and vicious habits.' He speculated that her affections were transferred from Brizuela to Francisco for 'valuable money considerations'. Others simply say that Francisco actually bought Eliza from her husband. Of course, Francisco may have received one of her cards. Perhaps the snaggletoothed generalissimo liked the idea of brushing up his French with an attractive linguist. Whichever way it happened, we can safely assume that money changed hands.

Francisco was 'greatly infatuated with her appearance'. Eliza, plainly, overlooked his. Within an hour they were in her boudoir. This must have been something of a shock to him. He had made love to beautiful women before, but he had probably never encountered one who went to bed with him without putting up a fight. Afterwards, he told her of the earthly paradise that was Paraguay. One day soon, his father would die and he would become *El Presidente*. But for a man whose ambition had been encouraged from an early age, being President of a small Latin American republic was not enough. Now he had met Napoleon III and wanted an Empire of his own. And Eliza would reign with him. After one night of bliss, he promised to make her the Empress of South America. The following day she gave her landlord her notice to quit.

It was quite clear that, from the very beginning, Francisco Solano López and Eliza Lynch were soul mates. But what was the attraction between them? The author R. B. Cunninghame Graham, who knew them both, said: 'No doubt the handsome, strong woman, with her Parisian accomplishments, quite captivated the half-civilised young man, with his head full of schemes of conquests, who saw himself as the Napoleon of the River Plate. She on her side may have been attracted by a type she could never have encountered in Paris or Algeria. For the wife of a government official, not very highly placed, and probably not highly paid, to the dictatress of a country that she well may have thought larger and more important than it really was, the step was great, and one that was well worth adventuring.'

Like most Europeans, Eliza would have known nothing about Paraguay, but tales of the great wealth to be found in South America had been commonplace since the Spaniards first arrived in Mexico and Peru. By the middle of the nineteenth century, Brazil was known for its vast untapped potential and it had been ruled by an emperor since 1822 – though the current incumbent, Pedro II, was a rather more modest emperor than Francisco intended to be.

'If I were not an emperor,' Dom Pedro said, 'I would like to be a schoolteacher.'

Naturally, if Eliza was going travel to a faraway continent and become its Empress she would need do some shopping and Francisco was soon seen trotting up and down the Rue de Rivoli by the side of Eliza's carriage, which was loaded with dresses, hats, petticoats, lingerie, crinolines and diamonds. Eliza would certainly have known what to wear in her imperial role. Eugénie had come to the throne that very year and was already the leader of Parisian fashion.

Eliza and Francisco took time out to visit Napoleon's tomb in Les Invalides where, hand in hand, they paid their respects to the great man – though there is some doubt that the remains returned to France from St Helena in 1842 and housed there are really his.

Eliza and her lover then set off on a trip around

Europe. They visited Queen Isabella II of Spain, notorious for her numerous lovers, and Eliza, it is said, held a 'wickedly obscene' dinner party for the Pope.

At the time, an unmissable part of the grand tour was a visit to the battle front in the Crimea. War then was still a spectator sport. Pavilions were erected on the hilltops and well dressed men and women would sip champagne and sup caviar, while the slaughter took place below. It was also an opportunity to study the latest military technology and tactics. Eliza must have longed to catch sight of her handsome Russian cavalryman, while Francisco was eager to see Napoleon III pay the Russians back for the disastrous retreat from Moscow in 1812. Eliza constantly fuelled his ego, inflating his fantasy that he would one day be the Napoleon of the New World – although in fact, when he went to war, the Buenos Aires press was to dub him the American Attila. And there would be no spectators in their war. Anyone who came as a casual observer got sucked in.

Eliza and Francisco's ersatz honeymoon came to an end when news arrived that Carlos López was ill and Francisco should return to Paraguay. At 10.30 am on 11 November 1854, Francisco and Eliza sailed from Bordeaux on the new 500-ton steamer, the *Tacuari*, which Francisco had bought from J. & A. Blyth of Limehouse. Its British crew would have made Eliza feel at home. They had loaded hundreds of trunks full of expensive clothes, fine linen, expensive furniture, splendid carriages, the finest silver cutlery and china from Sèvres and Limoges, along with a complete spectrum of gaudy uniforms made for Francisco by the finest French tailors, 70 pairs of hand-crafted leather boots with Cuban heels trimmed with silver, and a Pleyel piano. Eliza Lynch is thought to have been the first person in Paraguay to own a piano.

News of Madame Lynch's imminent arrival was already ruffling feathers in Asunción. In Paris, Benigno had tried to talk Francisco out of taking his fancy woman home with him. When he failed, Benigno headed off home to warn the family. At first, Carlos was not particularly concerned. His wayward sons already had numerous mistresses and had fathered countless bastards. However, when Benigno told his darling mama about *la ramera irlandésa* – the Irish prostitute – *La Presidenta* prevailed upon Carlos to bar her from the country. Francisco refused to return home without her, so the two of them disembarked at Buenos Aires. This in itself would have been quite a palaver. The *Tacuari* would have had to moor eight or nine miles off shore, then Francisco and Eliza would have had to clamber down into a lighter. The slightest breeze gave the passengers a soaking and even the lighter could not take them all the way to shore. When it grounded passengers had to climb on to a blood-red bullock cart driven by a gaucho who screamed at his team of half-drowned rheumatic horses as they struggled to find a footing. The humiliation of travelling in a bullock cart was too much for some upper class ladies who preferred to hoist up their skirts and wade rather than be carried ashore on such a lowly conveyance. This caused much amusement to the *porteños* – as the inhabitants of Buenos Aires are known – who gathered on the jetty. Passengers then had to climb up filthy steps on to a wooden pier that had numerous holes in it, was slippery under foot and crowded with 'loungers and promenaders'. At the end of it were a number of kiosks selling newspapers, books, the lyrics to erotic songs and saucy photographs. A scrum of porters swore at each other as they tried to grab the passengers' bags and carry them to customs where the officials would insist on opening every case, though they seemed to consider rummaging through them beneath their dignity and were quite happy to be told by passengers that they were carrying nothing but clothes. The lighter cost $50, the cart $20 and four porters $140. The entire bill came to the equivalent of one shilling and thruppence.

The Customs House and Government House behind it were just about the only two-storey buildings in Buenos Aires. In 1854, it was a relatively small city with a population of less than 100,000, no sewage system and ill-ventilated streets which boasted anything but 'good airs'. It was laid out around nine or ten public squares and the grid of streets and the white plaster walls of the houses made it appear neat. But when it rained the unpaved streets turned into a quagmire, or cut them into ravines, leaving the paved sidewalks up to five feet above the thoroughfare. Knife fights were common and murder the national sport. There was little else to do but hang around the cafés, mess about in boats or go riding. With her fair skin, Eliza would have had to stay indoors away from the sun. She would have had a chance to catch up on her reading as Buenos Aires boasted a British library. It also had a Fenian Club, though Eliza would not have visited it. She was too proud of her Anglo-Irish roots to have any sympathy with Home Rule.

The hotel where they stayed would have been expensive and the accommodation 'abominably bad . . . inferior to third-rate inns in a second-rate European city,' according to Sir Richard Burton who travelled extensively in the area. Only one establishment, the Hotel Universal, offered bathing facilities. An old tin bath filled with muddy river water 'cost as much as a first-class *bain complet* in Nice'. This was not the sort of thing Eliza was used to at all.

Fortunately she did not have to stay in Buenos Aires long. Carlos, fearing he had not long to live, backed down. He wanted his favourite son back in town to take over the reins of power and gave him permission to bring Eliza to Asunción. So in January 1855, they began their way up river. The journey upstream was depressing. The Paraná was not a well behaved river like the Seine or the River Lee in County Cork. It regularly overflowed its banks – particularly at that time of the year – drowning the trees and turning the landscape into a swamp as far as the eye could see. For mile after mile there was no sign of human habitation or any living creature, though occasionally an alligator would be seen lying menacingly on a sand bank. No life could be seen in the thick brown water and small aquatic birds gave low cries of alarm as the boat approached. Otherwise there was silence except at night, when the quiet was broken by the scream of parrots raiding the abundant orange trees.

For Eliza, the journey would have been particularly distressing. It was midsummer and, for an Irishwoman, it would have been unbearably hot. As ladies then were jealous of their pallid complexions, she would not have risked sunburn. If she sat out on the deck, it would have had to be under a thick awning.

Occasionally, along the banks, small towns huddled

behind stockades for protection from marauding Indians. But beyond the hot, dreary, sandy and smelly city of Corrientes, there was not another town for 300 miles. The *Tacuari* entered the Paraguay by negotiating the turbulent streams of the Tres Boccas. A barefooted local pilot from the village of Paso de la Patria would have guided them through. He would have spoken to Francisco in nasal Guaraní as he dodged the craft from bank to bank to miss the strongest of the currents, snags and sand banks. Then Eliza would have seen for the first time the curious soil of Paraguay, which is bright-red as if thirsty for blood. It was also the colour of her hair. Next she would have seen the huge fort being constructed at Humaitá to guard the country's only entrance. Then, for a hundred miles, ugly stunted palm trees stood on both shores as far as the eye could see. Every so often a cluster of huts stood around a barn-like church or a military outpost. But there were few people as all trade was confined to the capital so that Carlos could collect his customs dues. However, to the east there were at least some signs of human activity. This was the fertile heartland of Paraguay. To the west was the mysterious Gran Chaco, an uncharted desert of scrub and swamp that stretches some 600 miles to the foothills of the Bolivian Andes. In Eliza's time it was inhabited by ferocious Indians mounted on horseback who were only too willing to plunge their long spears into those they called *Cristianos* regardless of nationality.

As the *Tacuari* steamed under the Lambaré, a hill that towered above the yellow Paraguay river like a sugar-loaf, Eliza would have caught her first glimpse of Asunción, which rose on a gentle slope from the river for about a mile. If she had thought Buenos Aires was small, Asunción was barely large enough to make a decent county town in the old country. At that time its population was under 20,000, less than a quarter of that of the city of Cork when she had left Ireland. And Eliza had just come from Paris, a bustling city of over a million. Asunción was a backwater. Quite literally. It had been built on the inside of a river bend, so over time the wharves had silted up. This meant that the *Tacuari*, with its ocean-going draft, had to anchor some way out in the stream.

Even so, Eliza's heart must have lifted when she saw the crowds on the quayside. Carlos was so delighted at the return of his favourite son, he had declared a public fiesta and, so as not to displease the old dictator, the entire population of the city had turned out to greet the Hero of Corrientes. The people would have looked strange to Eliza. Paraguayan women wore a long, loose cotton chemise called a *tupoi* with a border of embroidery in black or scarlet, fixed around the waist with a broad sash and with the skirts puffed out by starched petticoats. The men wore embroidered shirts with white fringed cotton kilts, leather aprons, ponchos, straw hats and enormous silver spurs, weighing perhaps two pounds a piece, though few wore shoes. Those that did were called *gente calzada* – 'people with footwear'. The rich favoured patent leather boots and European dress.

For his homecoming Francisco was wearing tight-fitting pastel-coloured breeches, boots with high silver heels, a blue frock coat and an enormous stove-pipe hat. When the crowd spotted him on the deck of the *Tacuari*, they cried: '*Taita Guazu, Caria Guazu*' – 'Great Lord, Big Lord'.

75

But when Eliza appeared beside him the crowd fell silent. Only the López family knew she was coming and nothing could have prepared the people of Asunción for what they saw. Everyone on the quayside had black hair and the women of Asunción wore their hair in two long plaits, sometimes wound around the head or rolled back. The old Spanish style of hair swept back and held in a comb had gone out of fashion when the *peinetas de oro* appropriated the style in Francia's time. By contrast, Eliza's red hair cascaded from her crown in ringlets – a colour and style completely unknown in Paraguay.

Eliza wore a pale lilac *décolleté* gown with a matching bonnet and a lace stole. The dress was cut in the latest Parisian fashion. Draped around her figure and clinging to her hips, nothing could have been further from the style of the *tupoi*. Though the bodice of the Paraguayan chemise was cut low and immodestly loose around the neck, Eliza's *décolletage* was carried almost to the fifteenth-century extreme which exposed the bust completely. It showed off Eliza's high, firm breasts which, unlike those of the brown-skinned women on the quayside, were milky white.

'When she landed in Asunción the simple natives thought her charms were of more than earthly brilliancy, and her dresses so sumptuous that they had no words to express the admiration they both excited,' wrote one observer.

What's more, she was very obviously pregnant.

As the *Tacuari* could get nowhere near the jetty, the overdressed couple had to be helped into a canoe and paddled ashore where, flanked by the Presidential guard, three coaches waited. In the first was Carlos López with his ceremonial sword on his lap and a huge hat on his head. In the second was his wife Doña Juana and their daughters Inocencia and Rafaela, dressed in black shroud-like gowns that were stained with sweat under the armpits, while the third carriage sagged under the combined weight of Benigno and Venancio, bulging out of their tropical suits.

Francisco took Eliza's arm, helped her up the steps on to the landing stage and presented her to his father. Eliza smiled and held out a gloved hand. The old man grunted something unintelligible. These were the only words he would ever address to Eliza. Then he ordered his coachman to drive on. The escort that followed kicked up a cloud of red dust, which covered Francisco and Eliza with smuts. Then without a word to her son or Eliza, Doña Juana screamed for her coach to drive on. It took off with such a lurch that Eliza's lilac dress was splattered with horse dung. Benigno and Venancio followed smirking, refusing even to acknowledge the presence of their brother.

This snub was a huge setback to Eliza. She was not used to being treated this way. Although she had been a courtesan in France, she would only have been looked down on by provincial people. In Paris, she mixed with princes and dukes. Who was this tin-pot dictator and his overweight family to look down on her? She was British, educated, cultivated and sophisticated. They were little more than savages.

In fact, Eliza was not impressed by the Paraguayan people in general. Few showed any inclination to work. Young women preferred to spend their time dancing while the men sat around sucking *yerba maté*. The cult of the Virgin – whose effigy often seemed as coquettish as Eliza herself – must have seemed to her Protestant eyes little short of idolatry. The priests were ignorant and immoral. And everybody – both men and women – smoked. The children started as soon as they were old enough to walk. Both boys and girls ran around naked until puberty. They had no toys and never played, preferring to smoke cigars and gamble like their elders. One visitor to Asunción around the time found a group of children burying a live baby in a hole in the street, while two or three of their companions – who, at five, considered themselves too old for such childish entertainment – looked on smoking. Worse, after centuries of tyranny and the Jesuits, the Paraguayans were gentle and submissive, hardly the people who build great empires.

The city itself was no more impressive. Its one-storey adobe buildings were as blood-red as the soil. Most had no windows and little furniture. The Paraguayans had not flattened the land they were built on, so nothing aligned and the whole town looked as if it was going to slide down the hill into the river. The house Francisco gave Eliza on Calle Independencia was typical. Its rooms all opened out into a large courtyard, but there were no connecting doors, so to go from one room to the next, you had to go outside. It was next door to a jail and Eliza found that her servants locked her door at night in case anyone escaped; the heavy iron gratings on the windows would have made her feel as if she were in prison.

The streets were not paved and turned to a sea of mud in wet weather. The upper reaches of the town were cut by ravines that had been filled in half-heartedly. When it rained they became a raging torrent. All the rubbish that had collected in them was washed out into the streets and it became impossible for anyone even to visit their neighbours.

To Eliza's eyes, this was no imperial capital. Asunción needed to be transformed, the way Baron Haussmann was transforming Paris for Napoleon III. Fortunately, there were men who could effect such a transformation in Paraguay at the time. William Whytehead, chief engineer of state, was building an arsenal with a team of British craftsmen. Another English engineer, George Paddison, was building Paraguay's first railway. His architect Alonzo Taylor was designing the terminus, while other Englishmen were in Asunción to build new docks. At Eliza's prompting Francisco came up with an ambitious programme of urban modernisation, which he presented to his father. And Carlos, who still considered himself a progressive, approved. Within weeks of Eliza's arrival, Asunción had become a building site.

Unfortunately Francisco had neither the character nor the application of a Haussmann or a Wren. He was impatient and would start one project, then move on to another before it was finished. Along with the arsenal and the railway station, work on a splendid new Presidential palace, a new customs house, a cathedral, a post office and a complex of government offices built along an esplanade was begun, but they were only to be completed long after Francisco had fallen from power and Madame Lynch had fled from Paraguay.

Apart from Francisco's vacillating temperament, development was dogged by another handicap. Although a talented group of Englishmen drew up the plans, the labour force was unskilled. Francisco pressed boys between the age of six and ten into service. It was 'a sad sight to see the little fellows made prematurely old by labour to which they had been condemned,' Ambassador Washburn noted. 'They were constantly watched . . . and appeared like worn-out gnomes in whom all hope was so utterly extinguished that they never ceased for a moment in their labours.'

These wretches were paid just six or eight cents a day, which was scarcely enough to buy food. So it was hardly surprising that the poorly constructed railway station crumbled while it was being built and the half-finished customs house was demolished by a hail storm.

Eliza also proposed that Asunción have a public library. She liked to read and thought that her future subjects might also benefit from the habit. However, since Carlos had re-opened the elementary schools, most of the locals assumed that what was taught there was all they would ever need to know. According to George Masterman, a young doctor who arrived in Paraguay in 1861 and later became Chief Apothecary to the army, no one was ever seen reading in the library. This might have been because the only books available were impenetrable works of theology. Later, Francisco found a use for these volumes. During the war, they were cut up to make cartridge cases and rockets.

'I saw them one day serving thus a folio Hebrew Bible, with an interleaved Latin translation,' wrote Masterman, 'a most South American mode of diffusing the word of God.'

Nevertheless Eliza conjured up even more ambitious plans. She insisted that no self-respecting imperial capital could be without an opera house. Carlos was against the idea – who wanted to listen to opera in the middle of the jungle? But Doña Juana and her daughters were all for it. They thought that it would be the perfect place to by seen by society and they talked Carlos round. An Italian architect was employed and construction began on a scaled-down replica of La Scala. Unfortunately, the maestro did not know how to build a roof. The opera house was not completed for almost a century and, until its first operatic production in 1955, the only creatures that sung there were parrots. While the opera house was perhaps Eliza's greatest imperial folly, Francisco himself had even more grandiose architectural ambitions. He began planning the replica of Napoleon's tomb which, one day, would house his own remains.

Francisco did manage to complete a new house for Eliza and one for himself. For the sake of decorum they had to be seen to be living in two separate establishments. However, when she gave birth to their son Juan Francisco – known as Pancho or, more commonly, Panchito – this fiction was harder to maintain, so Eliza persuaded Francisco to build her a country home in the village of La Recoleta, near to the *quinta* of the López family, in the faint hope that one day she would be accepted by them.

Her ostentatious new home did little to help her cause. Designed by Eliza herself, this pink and white marble palace was the first two-storey building in the country. A visitor said that it was as if Madame de Pompadour's Petit Trianon had been transplanted to Paraguay. A vaulted carriageway led into an inner courtyard where two sweeping staircases rose up to the country's only balcony, overlooking an orange grove. It was there that Eliza played at being Marie Antoinette.

'The luxury, elegance, variety and dignity of its furnishings makes its reputation as the rendezvous of foreign visitors,' gushed a Buenos Aires newspaper. 'Many of Madame Lynch's brasses and porcelains are museum pieces and the French tapestries and Oriental rugs are distributed with excellent taste in a manner to delight the eye.'

Paraguay had seen nothing like it. Eliza became an icon of chic in the region. French and English novels became fashionable among the literate of the three capitals of La Plata and, although *El Semanario* remained silent, the Argentine newspapers raved about her.

'It is enough to see her ride by, gracefully and easily, firmly seated and handling her spirited horse with all the coolness of a woman who has overcome fear, to realise that she is like the women riders of gay background, whom one has read about, who ride daily in Regent's Park and the Bois de Boulogne,' said one.

The 'gay background' is a reference to Eliza's former profession. From around 1825 until the 1950s, a 'gay woman' meant a prostitute. Although they tut-tutted, the people of the region took a perverse pride in fact that La Plata boasted a woman so arrogantly capable of withstanding their disapproval. Here was truly an independent woman. No other woman from Asunción would dare go on a shopping expedition to Buenos Aires on her own. Eliza did. And it won her the respect of Francisco.

'In public and on occasions when Madame Lynch was not present, López always referred to her as he would refer to any distinguished lady of culture and great beauty, never as a personal possession of his own,' wrote Argentine journalist Héctor Varela.

Nor did she eschew the company of other men.

'She was ever civil to her bachelor fellow-countrymen,' wrote Sir Richard Burton, 'but the peculiarity of her position made her very jealous of wives who, in the middle classes at least, are apt to be curious about "marriage lines".'

Burton also remarked that: 'Her manners are quiet, and she shows a perfect self-possession.' But he also noted a trait that would manifest itself when, as consort of Francisco, she came to power. 'She is said to be, when offended, very hard,' Burton wrote, 'and to display all the *férocité des blondes.'*

Even though Eliza had moved out of town, no secret was made of the fact that she was Francisco's mistress. The first straight road in Paraguay was built to connect his house in Asunción to Patiño, her country residence. With a fresh mount, he could be in her bed in half an hour. Nor was her influence over him any the less. One can easily detect her hand in the decor of Francisco's official residence.

'His house is on the corner of the Market Plaza and differs from the other houses in Asunción in that it is low and of recent construction,' wrote one newspaper. 'It seems quite spacious and is painted yellow according to the current style. The drawing room furniture would be perfect in Paris. López has gilded furniture, silk curtains, chiffoniers and cabinets of exquisite workmanship inlaid with ivory, mirrors in Florentine frames, paintings of distinction, rare bronzes and porcelains. His is the residence of a well-travelled man with a taste for good living.'

The piece goes on to describe his elegant attire, that

'might have come from Bossi or Gaumy' – the leading stores in Buenos Aires. Francisco plainly encouraged visits from journalists who could write such gushing copy. One presumably well-oiled correspondent wrote: 'In manner, General López is very affable. He was in a jovial, light mood all evening and talked interestingly of world affairs without dwelling too long upon matters which might be controversial.'

However, something altogether darker lurked below the surface. One night in December 1857, Héctor Varela dined with Francisco and Eliza, and, after he had consumed nine glasses of sherry, Francisco's conversation turned to politics and war.

'I shall never be able to return to Europe because my destiny is completely linked with that of my people,' he told Varela. 'My worthy father is old and suffers from a chronic malady which, because of his advanced age, will cause his death. His wish and that of my countrymen is that I should succeed him. On the day that this happens, I will do that which he had not wished to do in spite of my counsel. I know that Brazil and you Argentines covet Paraguay. We have here sufficient means to resist you both, but I do not believe in waiting for you to make the attack. It will be I who shall make it. In other words, on the first pretext that they give me, I will declare war on the Brazilian Empire and the Plate Republics who, if they continue to live in distrust of each other, will have to unite in order to fight me.'

Francisco believed that Brazil and Argentina had already drawn up a secret treaty. The US State Department thought so too. Under its provisions, Argentina had ordered 4,500 cavalry lances, the principal weapon of its gaucho army, and had agreed to send men over the border into Paraguay if war broke out with Brazil. Brazil was also making warlike preparations and Francisco predicted that, as Uruguay was in a state of almost constant civil strife, any outbreak of hostilities would engulf the entire region.

Although Francisco feared attack, any war would clearly not be entirely defensive. Privately, Francisco argued that, geographically, Asunción was ideally suited to being the capital of South America. It had the most stable government in all of Latin America. Since the Spanish had been ejected in a bloodless coup, Paraguay was the only country in the region that had not had a revolution, nor even the threat of one. With its treasury full with the profits of the trade in *yerba maté*, it had the gold reserves to establish a banking system. And there was plenty of room for expansion. Francisco had watched enviously while the Brazilian Empire, under Pedro II, had devoured large tracts of land to the north.

Soon after she moved into her candy-floss palace, Eliza found that she was pregnant again. And she was clearly not pleased. She went riding a lot in the hope of inducing a miscarriage. But on 6 August 1856 she gave birth to a daughter, named Corina Adelaida. It was said that, once the child was born, Eliza's feelings about her new motherhood changed and when Corina died six months later she was heartbroken. A maid sewed a pair of gauze wings on to the child's dress before she was laid to rest in the cemetery at La Recoleta. However, the verse Eliza had so lovingly inscribed on Corina's gravestone, not far from where Eliza herself now lies reads:

Ere sin could blight or sorrow fade
Death came with friendly care
The lovely bird to Heaven conveyed
And made it beossom [sic] there.

According to the inscription, the author was one 'B.M.' But family members have maintained that this should read 'J.M.' – for John Milton.

Having lost her second child, the christening of her first became a priority. As Eliza was unable to marry Francisco, having him publicly acknowledge the child was her only possible long-term hold over him. Francisco was regularly seen around Asunción with other women and it was no secret that Juana Pesoa, one of the spoils of war that he had brought back with him from Pilar after his victory at Corrientes, and their two illegitimate children, Emiliano and Adelina, lived in some style in a town house Francisco had given them. But Eliza seems not to have been jealous. Far from trying to end the relationship between Francisco and Juana, Eliza seems to have encouraged it. Juana had another son by Francisco in 1860 and, after her death in 1870, Eliza adopted Emiliano, Juana Pesoa's only child to survive the war.

Francisco's infidelity clearly did not unduly concern Eliza.

'Although he was unfaithful to her, with any woman who took his fancy for the time,' wrote Cunninghame Graham, 'she knew he never would forsake her, for he relied upon her knowledge of the world to deal with consuls, ministers, and in general with the outside world, a world of which, brought up as he had been, he was quite ignorant.'

Eliza may indeed have encouraged him to take other mistresses to keep him out of her bed. She found pregnancy a burden. She would even procure for him, assuring the families of potential lovers that they would be taken care of when Francisco came to power. This was, perhaps, something Eliza had borrowed from the Empress Josèphine, who performed the same task for Napoleon. The Empress Eugénie was equally tolerant of Napoleon III's peccadilloes. She was kind, even generous, to her rivals, as a means of maintaining a certain amount of control over her consort. For Eliza, this was essential. As she could not marry Francisco, she vetted other candidates to make sure they had no intention of marrying him either. She would brook no challenge to her position as the next First Lady of Paraguay.

Naturally, there were plenty of people prepared to extend Francisco sexual favours in the hope of preferment. Pedro Burgos, a judge from Luque who had been a favourite of Carlos's, had a tall, good-looking young daughter and paid for his position in Francisco's new administration with her virginity. His subsequent reward was to be arrested, starved and tortured to death. What happened to his daughter is not known for certain but Washburn speculated: 'She may have expired like a hundred thousand others in the wilderness, or may have been one of those unhappy wretches whose sufferings have been such that, on being rescued from the power of López, the very instincts of modesty had been almost destroyed.'

With López Eliza had another advantage over other women – her children.

'He was extremely fond of Mrs Lynch's children,'

wrote Francisco's military engineer Colonel George Thompson, who was close to the family throughout the war, 'but not of his other ones, of whom he has a number by different women.'

Francisco certainly doted on young Panchito and groomed him for the succession. But Francisco was a man with a mercurial temperament. Who could tell when his feelings might change? So, soon after the death of their daughter, Eliza persuaded Francisco to announce the birth of their son publicly. He did this with a hundred-and-one-gun salute. This caused the collapse of eleven buildings in downtown Asunción, including five that were under construction as part of Francisco's urban development scheme. One field gun which had not been properly cleaned backfired, killing half the battery and putting the rest in hospital.

Francisco then announced that his son was to be baptised in the as-yet unfinished Catedral de la Encarnación in Asunción. The López ladies were furious. It was unheard of to have the *nietos bastardos* recognised by the Church. Carlos forbade the christening and his brother Basilio, Bishop of Asunción, issued an edict threatening excommunication to any priest who baptised the boy. Even Francisco's lifelong friend and tutor Padre Maiz refused to perform the ceremony, even in secret.

Eliza then threatened to have the boy baptised, like herself, as an Anglican. But as the Church of England had not reached Paraguay, to do so she would have to leave the country. Francisco begged her to stay and she was reluctant to go. By leaving Paraguay, even for a short time, she risked losing everything. But, ever resourceful, Eliza came up with another plan. She found a venal, incompetent priest named Manuel Antonio Palacios, said to be a man of 'very limited education' with 'a sinister and forbidding appearance'. Ambassador Washburn added that he had 'never been accused of a good act'. Palacios was such a bad priest that the previous bishop had banished him to a remote village where even the Indians mocked his ignorance of the scriptures. Once when Panchito was playing with a model of Noah's ark, Eliza noticed that a figure representing one of Noah's three sons was missing and chided the boy for losing it. Palacios, who was walking by, raised his hand in benediction and said: 'Pray do not scold the dear child, Madame. There could not have been three figures, for Noah had only two sons, as all the world knows their names are Cain and Abel.'

Although Palacios was afraid of defying his bishop and risking the wrath of Carlos, Eliza gave him a fist full of silver and promised to make him bishop when Francisco came to power if he would baptise the child. But first, he had to take a bath and shave.

Fearing his father's displeasure, the only person who now stood in the way of the baptism was Francisco himself. So Eliza began to pack. She knew that Francisco's spies reported back to him on everything she did. The moment he heard she was packing he rode out and told her that he was not going to let her leave the country. He would use force if necessary. Francisco was a violent bully, who would use any means to get his own way. But Eliza was not intimidated. She knew how to handle him. If she wanted to leave the country all she had to do was turn to Carlos. He would be only too eager to ensure her safe passage out of Paraguay, with an armed escort if necessary.

Realising that he had been outmanoeuvred, Francisco backed down. He consented to see Father Palacios, who had been cleaned up a bit by then. Even though he was shaky on theology, Palacios was an accomplished sycophant and he told the Hero of Corrientes that he would one day be the saviour of his country. Clearly, Palacios was Francisco's kind of priest.

For the ceremony, Eliza had an elaborate christening gown made, though Panchito was now two and rather too large to be carried to the font. Francisco insisted that the whole of Asunción society, including the diplomatic corps, attend the christening. Clearly fearing Carlos's wrath more than Francisco's, none of them turned up. The only people present were Eliza's Guaraní domestic staff.

While Francisco's public acknowledgement of his son secured her position, everything she now did seemed to be calculated to alienate Francisco's family further. She was seen around Asunción in the latest Paris fashions which showed off her magnificent figure to maximum advantage. The López women could not compete and the aristocratic ladies of Asunción would cross themselves when *la ramera irlandesa* rode by in her imported coach-and-four.

Not that they were really that prudish. It was not uncommon for unmarried young Paraguayan women to find themselves pregnant, even in the best families. Their offspring were accepted as 'children of the air'. What shocked Paraguayan society was that, while bearing Francisco's children, Eliza was still married to someone else. Writing of the sexual mores of Paraguay at the time, Masterman said: 'It is somewhat ungenerous to speak of the morals of one's friends, so I will only say that incontinence before marriage is not looked upon there as a serious fault, but I never heard of a faithless wife the whole time I was in the country.'

The women of Asunción dismissed Eliza as *La Vincha*, 'the headband' – possibly a reference to the fancy gold hair combs that the *peinetas de oro* wore. By contrast, the men were only too eager to suck up. As Francisco would one day be President, their livelihoods depended on it. Despite their wives' protests, they turned up to Eliza's elegant soirées, where she treated them to their first experience of piano music. She brought a breath of European sophistication into their Latin American back-woods and few seem to have been able to resist flirting with such a beautiful woman. All their wives could do was seethe. They were clearly outshone by her beauty and, despite their aristocratic pretensions, none could match the 'Irish whore's' European poise, grace and cultivation.

One of Eliza's most attentive courtiers was Colonel du Genie Enrique – though he also styled himself François – von Wisner de Morgenstern, a 65-year-old Hungarian who routinely wore the uniform of the Hungarian hussars, complete with embroidered silk frogs and astrakhan collar, despite the heat. Tall and mustachioed, he had left the court in Vienna after a homosexual scandal and had been a soldier of fortune before fetching up in Paraguay. For him, Eliza's palace was a little haven of the old world and Francisco could hardly object to his presence there as he clearly had no interest in women.

As well as being Eliza's constant companion, von Wisner became an important adviser to Francisco and encouraged him in his imperial ambitions. As Eliza grew tired of Carlos's longevity, von Wisner advised that, if Francisco and Eliza were to build an empire in South America, they had better begin by making Paraguay a power in the region. This could be done with diplomacy as well as force. As Carlos grew older and wiser, he had managed to stay out of the region's wars, apart from the odd border skirmish with the Brazilians. But civil war was still raging in the Argentine. At von Wisner's encouragement, Francisco put himself forward as a mediator at the very moment Argentina's seven-year civil war was won. After a ten-day peace conference, the warring factions signed a fourteen-point accord and Francisco was acclaimed as the hero of the hour. He was paraded through the streets of Buenos Aires to a military march composed in his honour. Flowers and confetti were thrown at his head, while *porteñas* threw themselves at his feet, and he was presented with an illuminated scroll proclaiming him the 'saviour of Argentine blood'.

This moment of triumph was followed by a humiliating anticlimax. Just as Francisco pulled out of Buenos Aires on board the *Tacuari* on his way home, a squadron of the Royal Navy's South Atlantic fleet hove into view and seized the Paraguayan steamer with Francisco on it. Although this was a flagrant act of piracy, it was justified on the grounds that James Canstatt, a British subject, was still languishing in a Paraguayan jail, unjustly accused of planning to assassinate Carlos. The Royal Navy said it would hold the *Tacuari* until Canstatt was freed. Meanwhile Francisco had to make his way home overland. *El Semanario* played down the unfortunate incident. When Francisco finally reached Asunción, it declared 'peace in our time' and, once again, Francisco was proclaimed a national hero. Eventually, Carlos had to release Canstatt and his 'co-conspirators' and pay out considerable reparations. Only then was the *Tacuari* returned.

Francisco's diplomatic triumph had put him back in favour with his father and he seized the opportunity to start building up the army. More arms and munitions – including ten of the latest Whitworth guns – were ordered from England. A vast military training camp was set up at Cerro Leon, a beautiful valley about 50 miles to the east of Asunción. Francisco had 30,000 men under arms there, with a further 17,000 at Encarnación, 10,000 at Humaitá, 4,000 at Asunción and 3,000 at Concepcion. Eliza also showed an interest in the build up of the army. A mile from Cerro Leon, she built a cool, windowless summer house, the Casa Blanca, decorated with tiles imported from Marseilles.

In Asunción she busied herself on the cultural front. She brought over M. de Cluny, an old friend from Paris, to open an Academy of Music and French Language and Literature. In an attempt at populism, the Academy threw open the doors of high European culture to the local Indians. Unfortunately, the Guaraní seem to have preferred their native folk songs to Bach and Beethoven, and showed no more inclination to learn French than they had previously shown to learn Spanish. M. de Cluny soon returned to France, where he evidently felt his talents could be more usefully employed.

Eliza also tried to woo the upper classes by opening a finishing school. She summoned two of her fellow *filles de joie* from Paris, Mesdames Luisa Balet and Dorotea Dupart, to teach the young ladies of Asunción etiquette and deportment. But the matrons of Paraguay would have walked through the streets naked rather than put their daughters in the hands of these two old slappers. Luisa and Dorotea returned to Paris to resume their former calling. Mme Laurent Cochelet, the prim and *provinciale* wife of the French Ambassador, was so appalled at the disrepute Eliza was bringing to French culture that she prevailed on her husband to try to have her deported.

Eliza's next project was the establishment of a National Theatre and she brought the Spanish novelist and playwright Ildefonso Bermejo over from Madrid to run it. The López ladies quickly appreciated the possibilities. The National Theatre's performances at the new – though still roofless – opera house would be gala events where they could be seen by the populace. They soon convinced Carlos that every self-respecting country should have a National Theatre, run by the government, and seized control of it from Eliza. Instrumental in this coup was Mme Cochelet, who persuaded Señor Bermejo's wife, the not inappropriately named Doña Pura, that she should have nothing to do with *la ramera irlandesa* and prevailed on her husband to do likewise. Eliza left cards, but they did not call. Consequently, the credit for founding Paraguay's National Theatre went officially to Mme Cochelet and *La Presidenta* herself, Doña Juana.

Eliza was not the sort of woman to take this lying down and she struck back. If Sr Bermejo's company was truly to be a National Theatre, she argued, then all its employees should be Paraguayan and she prevailed upon Francisco to persuade Carlos, who did not like Spaniards anyway, to ban the import of any more foreign actors. As no Paraguayan had ever seen a play, much less acted in one, this more or less guaranteed disaster.

For months beforehand there was only one topic of conversation in Asunción society – the National Theatre's debut production. For the occasion Señor Bermejo had written a Paraguayan epic called *La Maldonada* – 'The Wicked Lay Sister'. Set at the time of the conquest, it told the story of a virtuous Spanish woman, played by Doña Pura herself, who was saved from the savage Guaraní by befriending a lion – a version of the story of Ruiz de Galan tying a woman to a tree to be devoured by wild animals. All Asunción was expected to turn out for the first night and society ladies busied their seamstresses running up copies of the dresses shown in the latest imported magazines. Eliza, naturally, intended to outshine them all.

Decorum decreed that Eliza should sit not with Francisco, but alone, while protocol dictated that Carlos and the First Family sit in the Royal Box. But Eliza was not to be upstaged. She persuaded Francisco to have the boxes redesignated so that the Royal Box was stage right, rather than in the centre of the circle. When the Presidential party arrived, they were ushered around to a box at the left of the circle, only to find a dazzling Eliza already sitting in the centre box with everyone's eyes upon her. Sr Bermejo was already in his lion's costume; it was too late to protest. Héctor Varela witnessed the scene.

'On the opening night of the new theatre, the high society of Asunción attended,' he wrote. 'In the box of honour, the broad-faced and corpulent dictator sat with his equally corpulent wife and two obese daughters decked out like Bavarian eggs. Next to them sat the sons of the dictator, General Francisco López and Colonel Venancio López . . .' Or 'Baron von Wisner' in some versions (he seems to have been promoted for the occasion). 'But seated in the centre box, gorgeously dressed and displaying many jewels, was Madame Lynch. Even a famous courtesan such as Cora Pearl fell short of awakening in the ladies of the Faubourg St Germain the jealous envy that Madame Lynch, more resplendent and enticing than I have ever seen her, awakened that night in the ladies of Asunción. The gentlemen all watched her with respectful admiration, while the ladies gave her hostile looks, whose meaning could not be misinterpreted.'

Varela seems even more taken with the imposing figure of President López:

'One rarely sees a more impressive sight than this great tidal wave of human flesh. He is a veritable mastodon, with a pear-shaped face, narrow forehead and heavy pendulous jowls. During the entire performance, the President ostentatiously wore an enormous and atrocious hat, quite appropriate to him and equally suitable for either a museum of curiosities or for the Buenos Aires carnival. Throughout the evening, which seemed to last an eternity, I watched López for a sign of any impression produced upon him by seeing a play for the first time in his life. It was like watching a stone in a field. At the end of the tedious proceedings, without any display of either approval or disapproval, the old monarch of the jungle glared momentarily at Madame Lynch and rose and left, followed ponderously by his wife, his daughters and the soldiers of the praetorian guard.'

As for the play? 'The performance of the actors, as well as Señor Bermejo's play, can be dismissed in one line,' said Varela. 'It was as ridiculous as President López's hat.'

While for Eliza the evening was a triumph, for

Bermejo and his wife it was a humiliation and they fled back to Europe. Even though Eliza had enjoyed one more victory over the López ladies and the women of Asunción, Varela was filled with foreboding.

'I was struck by the deep dislike and rancour that all Paraguayan women showed towards Madame Lynch due to her handsome physique, superior education, modishness and elegance,' he wrote. 'Particularly they found her role in Asunción society mortifying and humiliating, and they hated to think how much more prominent her position would occupy when Francisco López succeeded his father.'

Eliza made one last attempt to ingratiate herself with the ladies of Asunción. The occasion was a boat trip up the Paraguay River. During his time in Paris, Francisco had invited Napoleon III to send immigrants to Paraguay. In due course, 500 arrived. Not only had they suffered terribly on their passage from Bordeaux, when they arrived in Paraguay they found the land they had been given for their colony, New Bordeaux, quite impossible to cultivate. Nevertheless the founding of the new and immediately failing colony was thought to be an appropriate occasion for celebration.

By this time Carlos was ill, so responsibility for the arrangements fell to Francisco. Unaware that the colony was already a fiasco, he organised a trip to New Bordeaux. The entire diplomatic corps along with Asunción's leading citizens would travel there on horseback, while the ladies would go by steamer. The French Ambassador's wife, Mme Cochelet, was to be guest of honour on the boat trip, while Francisco designated Eliza as its hostess. This was more than the ladies of Asunción could bear.

When the women arrived at the rotting quay in their carriages, Eliza could be seen sitting under a canopy to the right of the gangway. Mme Cochelet – who referred to Eliza as 'that devious Irish slut' – ascended first, followed by the waddling figures of Doña Juana, Inocencia and Rafaela. They pointedly ignored Eliza. Many of the other ladies of Asunción society followed suit and those who spoke to her, did so only once. By the time the steamer pulled away from quayside, Eliza was red-faced and fuming.

In her last desperate attempt to win over the ladies of Asunción, Eliza had laid on a sumptuous meal. It was served on her finest silverware and choice pieces from her collection of Sèvres and Limoges china. She served roast turkey, baby lamb and suckling pig, with succulent fruits and vegetables, ice cream in the colours of the French tricolour and fine imported wines personally selected by Baron von Wisner. She even provide *sopa paraguaya* and *yerba maté* for those with more parochial tastes.

As this lavish meal was being laid on a table on the deck, the ladies of Asunción crowded around. Eliza, as hostess, moved forward to preside, but the ladies would not let her through. She had been in Paraguay for seven years by then. All that time they had treated her as a pariah. They had snubbed her at every opportunity and publicly insulted her and her children. This was the last straw. She ordered the captain to stop the engines and drop anchor. Then she got the crew to throw every scrap of food overboard and kept the ladies of Asunción moored mid-stream for ten hours, perspiring in the blazing sun with nothing to eat or drink.

When they heard of the day's events, Francisco and

von Wisner found the entire fiasco terribly funny, but Eliza was not amused. Later she would take an even more terrible revenge on those who dared to look down on her.

❧ 7 ❧

Coming to power

Although he had been a military adventurer when he first came to power, Carlos López had mellowed with age. In his twilight years, he said that he would rather lose half his territory than go to war – a wise approach, as half of Paraguay was a wasteland not worth defending. However, by 1862, thanks to Francisco, Paraguay had the largest standing army in the region. It was six times the size of the US Army before the Civil War. Of a population of around a million, 80,000 were under arms. Under Francia, Paraguay's forces had never amounted to more than 5,000. Slowly, it dawned on Carlos that Francisco's military build-up might not be intended to be solely defensive in nature. But it was too late. Carlos was already bed-bound with dropsy.

Although Carlos no longer had the strength to restrain Francisco as his Minister of War, Carlos could still influence the choice of his successor. Under the constitution he himself had written, the President could name a Vice-President who, in the event of his resignation, incapacity or death, would rule until a Congress could be convened to elect a successor. Carlos conspicuously failed to name Francisco Vice-President. But Francisco was not about to be cheated of his birthright. When the old dictator was on his deathbed, he turned up in full dress uniform with his personal cavalry escort. These were known as the Black Tails or Monkey Heads because of the monkey tails that decorated their brass and leather helmets and the long black horses' tails that hung down to their waists from the back. They wore scarlet tunics and white trousers and were viewed as the smartest troops in South America. This show of strength was said to be Eliza's idea.

In his dying days, Carlos seemed to have come to favour his youngest son Benigno, who was both less prone to violence and less ambitious. This engendered an intense jealousy between the two brothers, especially as Benigno was Carlos's natural son while Francisco was the bastard son of Don Lázaro Rojas. Eliza can certainly have had no time for Benigno. It was he who had informed Francisco's family of her relationship with Francisco and turned them against her before she even arrived in Asunción. Benigno was there at the deathbed but, according to Padre Maiz, the López family confessor, Carlos's last words were addressed to the beribboned Francisco.

'There are many pending questions to be settled,' said the dying man, 'but settle them with the pen rather than the sword, particularly with Brazil . . .'

Padre Maiz was administering extreme unction when the old man slumped back in the arms of Benigno.

'Is he dead?' asked Francisco.

Carlos's personal physician Dr William Stewart said that he was.

When Eliza heard the news, it is said, she cried: '*Vive l'Empereur!*'

With his father dead, Francisco surrounded the house with his Black Tails and the army was ordered on to the streets. He then forced Chief Justice Pedro Lescano, Carlos's most trusted adviser, to hand over the key to the vault that contained his father's private papers. Then Francisco entered the vault, alone, to read his father's will.

It was rumoured then that a codicil to the will named Benigno Vice President, or that Carlos stipulated a triumvirate to take over the reins of power. We shall never know. Francisco emerged triumphantly and announced that, at last, his father had appointed him Vice President – though he showed no one the will to prove it. He would act as interim President and, on that authority, he immediately arrested Lescano, Padre Maiz and Benigno for conspiring against the constitution.

As a member of the family, Benigno was banished to a *quinta* in the interior where he was kept under house arrest – although he was later to suffer imprisonment, torture and execution at Francisco's order. Lescano and Maiz were tried by a military court and jailed. Lescano, who was 60, did not survive long. He was tortured and left out in a muddy field day and night until he died of exposure. After he was dead, Francisco's smiling police chief played a cruel trick on Lescano's wife. He told her that her husband had been freed. She could visit him in hospital and take care of him there. But when she turned up, she found her husband laid out for a post-mortem. He then went to a pauper's grave alone in a rough cart. None of his relatives dared attend the burial.

Padre Maiz was younger and stronger. Although he was renowned as a saintly man he was tortured relentlessly until he confessed every sin of hypocrisy, vice, heresy and lewdness. 'It was said that this priest, who had been considered so immaculate, so pure in his walk and conversation, was the greatest hypocrite and libertine in Paraguay,' wrote Washburn, 'and that when brought before the tribunal he confessed that for many years he had been given up to debauchery and had been the first to lead astray scores of innocent young women.'

His full confession was published in *El Semanario* on 17 November 1866. In it he admitted numerous, though ill-defined, crimes and thanked 'the very God of Heaven and Franciso Solano López who occupies His place on earth' for saving him. 'Francisco Solano López is for me more than any other Paraguayan a true Father and Saviour,' he said. After three years of the most appalling treatment, Maiz was released. His conversion was so thorough that he went on to become Francisco's chief torturer. So it is all the more surprising that, 53 years later, in his memoirs *Etapas de Mi Vidas*, Maiz admitted that there had indeed been a conspiracy. As Francisco's tutor, he had known the dictator from an early age. Later when Francisco was a swaggering young officer, Maiz had seen how readily he abused his position as a military commander, brooking no hint of opposition, and feared what he might do once he was given unlimited power as President.

'For this reason, I desired a constitution that would deprive him of absolute powers and that might place a restraint on his arbitrariness,' wrote Padre Maiz, who suggested writing a new constitution, based on that of the United States, establishing the independence of the legislative, executive and judicial branches. For these revolutionary thoughts, he claimed he was denounced by a fellow clergyman, Eliza's favourite Palacios. Paraguay only adopted a constitution that separated legislative, executive and judicial powers in 1992.

How Eliza reacted to Francisco's savagery towards Lescano and Maiz is not recorded, but Cunninghame Graham gave her the benefit of the doubt.

'Till they arrived in Paraguay she probably was unaware of his cruel character, and when she learned of it, most likely cared nothing for it,' he wrote. However, he also suggested that she was unscrupulous enough to make use of it to maintain her influence over him. And, after all, Maiz was one of the priests who had refused to baptise Panchito.

Although Francisco was now in power, under the constitution his father had written, he had to call a Congress to elect a new President – or, as no one would dare to stand against him, confirm him in office. Even so he took great care to make sure that no one was selected who might not favour his election. Before the Congress was convened, López demanded to see the list of delegates put forward by the 92 *partidos*, or electoral districts of Paraguay. In each *partido*, the local police chief, judge and parish priest chose the delegate. One of the delegates selected was a wealthy landowner named Manuel Rojas who had suggested that, once the Congress was convened, it might review the constitution and introduce clauses that would limit the powers of the executive. His name was struck from the list of congressmen. He fell from favour and died, during the subsequent war, a common soldier in the trenches.

While the Congress was sitting, Francisco also took

the precaution of having his soldiers drill outside Government House. Even so, one delegate had the temerity to suggest that, on certain points, the constitution was somewhat ambiguous. Francisco, who sat as the chairman of the Congress, immediately rose to his feet and declared that even the suggestion that there might be something wrong with the constitution was an insult to the memory of his dead father who had written it. The delegate slunk back to his seat. He was later arrested, imprisoned and executed for having 'conspired to subvert the legal and constitutional process'.

After that López decided that there had been quite enough debate. He was eager to proceed to the election of the new President. Don Nicholás Vasquez, the Minister for Foreign Affairs under the old regime, who had sworn undying allegiance to Francisco before Carlos's body was even cold, duly put forward the name of General Francisco Solano López as the choice of the people. But before the Congress could move to a vote, Don Florencio Varela, the richest man in Paraguay outside the López family, rose and confessed that he was a little confused. Although, he said, the Hero of Corrientes was plainly the man for job, he pointed out that the constitution specifically prohibited the Presidency being handed from father to son. Vasquez leapt to his feet. He said that the constitution was meant only to prohibit the Presidency being handed from father to son if it was done in defiance of the will of the people. As this was plainly not the case, the Congress should not be fettered or restricted in its choice of President. Varela thanked Vasquez for clearing up his confusion on this tricky constitutional point and seconded the nomination of

General López. Francisco was elected by acclamation and the news was conveyed to the people of Paraguay. Many congressmen assumed that the exchange between Varela and Vasquez had been scripted by López to clear up any doubts delegates might have. But Varela found himself stripped of his property. He was arrested and disappeared into jail, never to be seen again.

The Congress voted Francisco an annual salary of $50,000, five times what his father had been paid – though this was academic, as both used the treasury as a personal bank account. Then Francisco announced to the Congress the joyful news that Madame Lynch had just presented him with another son.

'Before I dismiss this assembly,' he said, 'I should like it to be known that it is our pleasure and desire that from this day onwards Madame Eliza Lynch is to enjoy the same privileges as those usually accorded to the wife of a head of state. I have every confidence that my countrymen as well as the diplomatic corps will respect my wishes in this matter.'

When Doña Juana heard the news, she fainted.

The Congress also raised 55,000 pesos to erect a statue of Carlos in the main plaza of Asunción. But after his state funeral was held in the still unfinished Catedral de la Encarnación, his remains were taken from the city and interred at the church of La Trinidad, the López parish church four miles outside Asunción. Merchants and foreign residents were then asked to contribute to the statue of Don Carlos that the Congress had already paid for. It was never built. Nor was the money accounted for. But there was no doubt as to where it went – into Eliza's and Francisco's pockets.

The news that Francisco was now 'Commanding General of the Army Forces and President of the Republic of Paraguay' was conveyed to all the countries with which Paraguay maintained diplomatic relations. Unfortunately, congratulations proved thin on the ground. Queen Victoria was still mourning Prince Albert, who had died the previous year. Abraham Lincoln was busy fighting the Civil War, while Victor Emanuel II of Piedmont and Sardinia had just become the first king of a united Italy. Even those neighbours who should have been interested – Emperor Dom Pedro II of Brazil and President Bartolomé Mitre of Argentina – were too busy squaring off over Uruguay to pay much attention. However, Napoleon III took time from organising his disastrous invasion of Mexico to write:

General,
I have been very touched by your personal letter and its warm recollections of your visit to My Imperial Court.

Believe me, I assure you that I too remember them with pleasure. I have had occasion to appreciate your noble qualities which do you honour and therefore it is with that knowledge that I congratulate your country in electing you to safeguard her destiny.

It has filled me with great pleasure to look with admiration at the remarkable progress which Paraguay made under the rule of your illustrious father, may he rest in peace, and I have no doubt that under your wise and patriotic direction, your country will continue her progress along the path of civilisation.

In expressing my cordial best wishes for your personal happiness and for the dignity of your office, it pleases me to offer you my personal esteem. In so far as I can, I pray to Almighty God to bless and preserve you.

Given by my hand in the Palace of the Tuileries,

Your good friend,

Napoleon

1 January 1863

Francisco and Eliza must have been delighted. Here was the Emperor of France writing to López as an equal. They could hardly have asked for a better omen. After all Louis-Napoléon had been elected President of the Republic before becoming Second Emperor, while his illustrious uncle had been First Consul of France on his way to the imperial throne.

Within a month of Francisco's accession, more than 1,000 prominent Paraguayans had either fled the country or were in prison. 'The only offence so far as I know that is charged against the prisoners is that they preferred someone else for President,' wrote Washburn, 'and this in most countries would not be considered a capital crime.'

But was López really in command of Paraguay? Cunninghame Graham certainly believed that Eliza was the real power behind the throne. Examining their folie à deux in his book *Portrait of a Dictator*, Graham said: 'Both were unscrupulous. Both had talents of a certain order, but certainly obstinate though he was, he was entirely dominated by his clever, beautiful and unscrupulous mistress. Money and personal aggrandisement were the ultimate aims of both of them.'

Graham also suggested that other uniformed dictators, such as Antonio López de Santa Anna, who had ruled Mexico twenty years before, were too wild and uncivilised to be influenced by a woman like Eliza. López, by contrast, came from a race who were gentle, sensual and indolent.

'Vanity and sensuality, mixed with a touch of cruelty, joined to great obstinacy, seem to have been the chief ingredients of the character of Madame Lynch's lover,' he wrote. 'She took full advantage of them all, using them for her own ends, and for the ruin of the country that an unlucky fate delivered into her hands.'

Eliza's closest confidant, Baron von Wisner, became Francisco's Lord Chamberlain. Meanwhile Eliza assembled her own imperial entourage. Two young ladies from the most distinguished families of Asunción, Doña Dolores Carisimo de Jovellanos and Señora Juliana Echegaray de Martínez, were chosen as ladies-in-waiting. Along with Doña Isidora Días, Eliza's Mistress of the Robes – presumably a full-time job – they were the leading society gossips and effectively ran a network of spies for Eliza.

Despite his limited grasp of scripture, Padre Palacios became Bishop of Asunción, in fulfilment of Eliza's promise. He was also in the business of spying and, under Palacios, there were to be no secrets of the confessional. In the official diocesan history of Paraguay, historian Antonio Zinny says of Palacios: 'Even though he was of benign appearance, he was of perverse character, never looking anyone in the face . . .' But he knew which side his bread was buttered. '. . . His sermons before *El Supremo* López the Second were the most complete blasphemy and altogether dedicated to flattery.' From the moment he was appointed bishop, Palacios rarely left López's house and ate with Francisco and Eliza every day.

Don Vicente Barrios became López's first Minister of War and Don Saturnino Bedoya became Chancellor of the Exchequer. To ensure their loyalty, these two unfortunate young men had been forced to marry Francisco's rotund sisters. Both would die at Francisco's order. The rest of the cabinet was filled out with toadies and men too old to be any threat. Don Carlos Sánchez, who had been in government since Francia's days and was known to be a man without ambition, became Vice-President, while 65-year-old Don José Berges, a former Ambassador to the United States, was forced to become Foreign Minister, a deeply unenviable job.

'He must be both the slave and spy of an imperious, selfish and brutal master,' wrote Washburn. 'He also knew there was but one step from refusal to imprisonment. He was compelled to treat with the representatives of foreign nations in personal interviews in which questions would arise that he could not even discuss without danger of incurring the anger of his master.'

What is more, Eliza effectively usurped his position. Ambassadors arriving in Asunción had to present their credentials at Patiño, her pink palace outside the city. When Senhor Vianna de Lima, the Brazilian Minister, neglected to pay his respects to Madame Lynch, Francisco refused him the use of a carriage normally accorded to a visiting diplomat. The same treatment was meted out to Edward Thornton, who had been the British chargé d'affaires in Buenos Aires when the *Tacuari* was seized. When Thornton visited Asunción, he had to make his way to Government House on foot while being jeered by a crowd. When he finally presented his credentials, he was left standing throughout the entire interview.

'Though the government of the elder López was a despotism, that of his son is indescribably worse,' Thornton wrote in a despatch to the then British Foreign Secretary Lord Russell. 'The new President is already developing into a tyrant so vain, arrogant and cruel that there is no misery, suffering or humiliation to which all within his power will not be exposed . . .'

Thornton went on to describe the conditions in Paraguay: 'The prisons are filled with so-called political prisoners, many of them of the best families. The President looks into and directs everything. Not a man in the Republic from the ministers downwards would refuse to perjure himself on the order of the President. No one is allowed to marry without His Excellency's permission . . .'

Much of Francia's system of repression had been revived: 'His Excellency's system seems to be to depress and humiliate; if a man shows a little more talent, liberality or independence of character, some paltry excuse is imme-diately found for throwing him into prison. The judges are unpaid and are the most servile instruments of the President.'

And Thornton warned Russell not to think that change was imminent: 'The great majority of people are ignorant enough to believe that they are blessed with a President who is worthy of adoration. The rule of the Jesuits, of the Dictator Francia, and of the Lópezes father and son, have imbued them with the deepest veneration for the authorities.'

Thornton estimated that there were only perhaps three or four thousand people in the country who opposed the tyrant. But they did not trust each other enough to form any sort of opposition.

'I do not believe that there is any man who would dare to confide his feelings with regard to the government to his brother or his dearest friend, lest he be denounced,' Thornton wrote.

But there was another way to keep people's minds off politics – sex: 'Anxious as the President is that his fellow citizens should not trouble themselves with political matters, he cares little how much they may be addicted to vices of all kinds, and the immorality that pervades the country is extreme. His Excellency shows but a bad example; besides a number of his countrywomen who have yielded, perhaps most reluctantly, to his desires, there is an Englishwoman, calling herself Mrs Lynch, who followed him from Paris in 1854 . . .'

Thornton dismissively referred to Eliza as 'the Paraguayan Pompadour', though he recognised her as the power behind the throne: 'This woman has been living nearly ever since in Asunción in comparatively speaking the greatest splendour. She certainly possesses considerable influence over the President, and her orders, which are given imperiously, are obeyed as implicitly and with as much servility as those of His Excellency himself. I need hardly tell your lordship with what profound and bitter hatred she is looked upon by the native ladies.'

He refused to pay court to her – which must have been all the more wounding to her as she was proud to be a British subject. In response, López harassed Thornton by arresting British subjects and refusing to pay the British engineers he had recruited to work on the railway and in his armaments factories. Thornton advised all British subjects to leave Paraguay, then left himself.

Although Washburn was later to suffer at López's

hands, he was initially more kindly disposed towards Francisco than Thornton was, spotting in him 'an ambition to be something more than a petty despot'. Indeed, Francisco began a loan scheme for native-born Paraguayans who needed money for 'enterprises of general utility', dropped import duties on machinery and tools, and provided a government subsidy for the cultivation of cotton with an eye to taking over the markets that the United States had supplied before the outbreak of the Civil War in 1861. But the signs of his true nature were already showing. Francisco played the race card. In editorials in *El Semanario* he hinted that he intended to rid Paraguay of any trace of Spanish blood, conveniently forgetting his own Spanish heritage.

The wives of the diplomatic corps were also obliged to make an appearance at the pink palace. Eliza personally poured a cup of the finest coffee for Mrs Washburn, the New Jersey-born wife of the US Ambassador. Others were invited around for afternoon tea, English-style. Even Doña Juana, Inocencia and Rafaela showed up and offered their apologies for not having called sooner. Eliza did not remark that they had had eight years in which to do so. Only Mme Cochelet refused to pay court.

Eliza's genteel visitors were perhaps pleasantly surprised that they were not greeted by a scarlet woman fresh from the *trottoirs* of Paris. Instead, they found a cultured woman who spoke English, French, Spanish and Guaraní fluently. She was a charming hostess and a devoted mother. But her beauty inspired jealousy and her sophistication made them feel parochial. Behind her back they tore her to shreds and every word of their backbiting was reported back to her by her web of spies.

Eliza staged a series of ten-course dinners and dazzling balls. An invitation was a command to attend and guests had to pay a 'subscription', though Paraguayan merchants were compelled to supply the food and drink for free, driving many of them out of business. Eliza served *haute cuisine* that was not at all to the taste of most Paraguayans, who preferred the more familiar – and stodgy – fare of *sopa paraguaya* and *chipá*, a savoury doughnut. She insisted that women dress in the latest European fashion with stays, rather that the *tupois* they preferred, and they had to keep their shoes on when dancing, although they preferred to kick them off. However, these social occasions were a chance for the women of Paraguay to show off their jewellery. Paraguay was awash with jewellery at the time. Beautiful pearls, gemstones and plate had been brought there by the Spaniards and valuable pieces had been handed down from generation to generation. Even quite poor women possessed precious bracelets, earrings and necklaces. They invested any money they had in personal adornment. Often it was their only luxury.

At these occasions Eliza would be seen to outshine everyone, dressed in white satin with a coronet on her head, while Francisco would appear decked out in one of his ostentatious uniforms and the Presidential sash. At balls held in El Casino Nacional – the National Club – in Asunción, Francisco and Eliza would be enthroned at one end of the ballroom and the quadrille was danced diagonally across the room so that no one turned their back on them. Choirs would sing odes in Francisco's praise. Dozens of young women – including recently discarded mistresses – would step forward one at a time, each bearing a crown of laurel leaves and proclaiming Francisco to be 'the greatest, the bravest, the best of mankind'. Their eulogies were approved beforehand by Francisco himself and were often written by Colonel Coriolano Marquez, a former henchman of Rosas who had escaped a death sentence in Argentina for numerous atrocities, prior to embarking on this literary career. He was later arrested, tortured and executed along with a number of other Argentine soldiers of fortune who made the mistake of rallying to the Paraguayan cause.

Often the family and friends of those attending Eliza's balls were rotting in Francisco's jails. Washburn tells of one unfortunate woman who was forced to sing the praises of Francisco when her husband had been jailed and loaded with fetters only weeks before, for what offence it is unclear. He died just two days before she was required to join in the glorifying of the man responsible for her husband's death.

At the height of the season there was a masked ball. The costumes were assigned by Eliza. Doña Juana had to appear as the goddess Diana, complete with bow and arrow. In nineteenth-century Paris, the huntress was often depicted bare breasted. It is not recorded how the ample Doña Juana coped. The generously proportioned Inocencia and Rafaela were commanded to appear as 'two emaciated Guaraní maidens'. It is hard to see how they could have been convincing. Mme Cochelet, the French Ambassador's wife, suffered an even greater humiliation. She was forced to appear as Queen Victoria, in her widow's weeds. However Washburn, a New England puritan, refused to dress up, incurring Eliza's anger. Francisco, naturally, was dressed as Napoleon, while

Eliza herself, decked in gold and pearls, appeared as Elizabeth I modelled on Gower's Armada portrait. This was thought to be thoroughly appropriate. After all, were she Empress of South America in her own right, Eliza would indeed have been known as Elizabeth I.

Of those who attended the balls, Washburn reckoned, by the end of the war, none of the men, just one in twenty of the women and only one of the 45 foreigners listed on the 'subscription list' would survive. 'Many were flogged and executed, others expired under torture or from drudgery and starvation in the camps, and many died of exposure, hardship, and privation in the mountains to which they had been driven by the same remorseless despot who had forced them to chant his praises and crown him with laurel while yet they had homes and a hope of deliverance from his terrible power.'

In fact, laurel crowns were later rejected as suitable headgear for López because they were worth nothing – even though a design produced for Francisco had little flowers made from clusters of diamonds between the leaves.

What Eliza did not know at the time was that Francisco was planning to abandon her. Just as the Emperor Napoleon had dumped his Josèphine for an advantageous marriage to Marie-Louise, daughter of the Habsburg Emperor Francis I, Francisco was planning to dump Eliza. He had written to Dom Pedro II, Emperor of Brazil, asking for the hand of his daughter Princess Isabella. This was part of Francisco's imperial strategy. The diplomatic traffic of the time was full of rumours of change in the system of government in Paraguay. Francisco was aware that his friend Napoleon III wanted

Latin America to follow Continental models of monarchical government, rather than the democratic model of the United States. At that time, French troops were in control of Mexico City and Archduke Maximilian of Austria was preparing to leave Europe to become Emperor of Mexico under Napoleon III's sponsorship. López knew that he would be more likely to get himself taken seriously as an emperor if he was recognised by the only emperor in the region, Dom Pedro of Brazil. There could be no more public way of doing this than by marrying his daughter. López even boasted that Pedro II had urged him to call himself *Francisco Primero* – Francisco the First – though scurrilous writers dismissed him as López II.

In fact, as the son of the King of Portugal, Dom Pedro was outraged that an upstart like López had the pretensions to aspire to marry a Braganza. After months of silence, Dom Pedro wrote back saying that the Infanta was too young to marry. To add insult to injury, he announced shortly afterwards that she was to marry her cousin, the Comte d'Eu, a prince of Orleans and a member of the old French Bourbon royal family.

López was furious. He became determined to marry Eliza and to legitimise Panchito as heir to the López dynasty. He petitioned the Pope to have Eliza's marriage annulled on the grounds of non-consummation. However as López had installed Eliza's dubious choice as bishop, expropriated church funds and suborned priests to violate the confidentiality of the confessional, his pleas to the Vatican, unsurprisingly, fell on deaf ears. Nevertheless, the new Bishop of Asunción announced from the high altar of the still-to-be-completed Catedral de la

Encarnación that the Lynch children were to take the surname López. Eliza celebrated by commissioning plans for a new palace, next door to Francisco's and just as splendid, in downtown Asunción, while Doña Juana took to her bed for a month.

Dom Pedro's snub greatly strengthened Eliza's position and it cannot have been difficult for her to manipulate López's bruised ego. Eager to get his own back, López began looking for an opportunity to move against Brazil. He did not have to wait long. On 14 October 1864 Brazil invaded Uruguay on the pretext of intervening in an uprising there which was being backed by Argentina. For years a civil war had been raging in Uruguay between factions known as the Blancos and the Colorados. Guerrilla armies of gauchos would sweep across the pampas drafting men at bayonet point. Anyone who resisted would be despatched by a blade drawn across the throat – an action known in Uruguay as 'playing the violin'.

The latest round of fighting had begun in April 1863, when the Colorado leader General Venancio Flores set off in a small boat from the gasworks in Buenos Aires to bring down the Blanco government in Montevideo. Once the fighting was under way, the Brazilians rode in, hoping to take Uruguay back into the Brazilian Empire – it had been part of Brazil twice before. The Uruguayan government appealed to López for help and their Ambassador in Asunción, José Vásquez Sagastume, oiled the wheels of diplomacy by plying Eliza with expensive gifts. At Eliza's behest, López made a formal protest to the Brazilian Ambassador in Asunción. But then López made a serious error of judgement. Instead of aligning himself with the powerful General Urquiza, Governor of the Argentine state of Entre Rios and long-time rival of General Mitre in Buenos Aires, he began to negotiate with Mitre, who was Flores's sponsor. These attempts at arbitration were ridiculed in the Argentine press, who said that López should not meddle in the affairs of countries that were far more civilised that Paraguay. Asunción, the Buenos Aires papers said, was a collection of wigwams, Francisco was an Indian chief and Eliza his squaw. These insults incensed Eliza and she urged López to attack Brazil.

Francisco was certainly ready for war. The Paraguayan Navy now boasted a dozen gunboats – two purpose-built in England, the rest part-converted paddle-steamers. Military engineer Colonel George Thompson had been brought in from England to complete the defences at Humaitá, which was vaunted at the 'Sebastopol of South America', and shore batteries had been constructed along the Paraná. Thompson was a favourite of Eliza's and she sought out the company of other British compatriots. The Englishman William Whytehead ran Paraguay's arsenal. Carlos's physician Dr Stewart, a Scot who had served in the Crimea, had become Chief Surgeon of the Army and George Masterman, another Englishman, was now Apothecary General. Their services were in demand as López was drilling his men so hard that some died from over-training – training *à la* López involved frequent beatings and the use of the stocks. George Paddison had completed the first stretch of railway to Villa Rica, ready to shuttle troops from Cerro Leon to Asunción, while the German Baron von Fischer-Treuenfeld had built the first telegraph system in South

America, enabling López to communicate with his troops in the field.

Congress stumped up a further $5 million for armaments. Francisco's agent Don Candido had been sent to France to buy 60,000 rifles, 100,000 cases of cartridges, 42 cases of bayonets, equipment of every description for a modern army – and more fancy uniforms. He also visited Prussia to acquire the latest in machine-gun technology. Meanwhile the trusted Don Felix Ejusquiza had been appointed commercial attaché to Buenos Aires to ease the passage of matériel. He was also commissioned to buy a new landau and yards of muslin for Eliza.

In preparation for war, all civil development work was stopped. Describing Asunción on the eve of war, Sir Richard Burton wrote: 'Public conveniences are nowhere; the streets are wretched; drainage not been dreamed of; and every third building, from chapel to theatre, is unfinished. The shops are miserable . . . The barracks and churches, the dungeons and the squares for review are preposterous . . . The lieges [that is, López's vassals] must content themselves with the vilest ranchos, lean-tos and tile roofs supported, not by walls, but by posts.'

Burton was well aware of where the money had gone: 'A large and expensively built arsenal, riverside docks, a tramway and a railway, have thrown over the whole affair a thin varnish of civilisation; but the pretensions to progress are skin deep.'

He could perhaps have mentioned that, as a result of Francisco's ambitious redevelopment project, the streets were now at least cobbled.

With Eliza urging Francisco to go to war, no one could stop him. Domestic opposition was not a concern. Those who were not in jail had fled. By 1864, it was claimed, a quarter of the population of Paraguay were in exile; there were enough men in Buenos Aires to form a regiment of Free Paraguayans when the war came. But those who remained in the country seem to have been fiercely loyal. Although Francisco's troops were not paid and had to live by stealing or requisitioning food from farmers with government IOUs that López had no intention of honouring, they knew that they were being led by a modern-day Alexander. *El Semanario* told them so. When he visited his men, he joked with them in their native Guaraní and hinted that he would liberate them from the yoke of the Hispanic aristocracy.

Families with members in Buenos Aires were pressed into writing letters to *El Semanario* condemning their relatives. López even forced his mother to write a long letter condemning her beloved Benigno, who was still in internal exile.

'If my son, Benigno, persists in his misguided way, he will receive the malediction of all his fellow citizens, and of his afflicted mother, who will, against her wish, be obliged to curse him,' her letter read.

Meanwhile Eliza dedicated herself to building morale. She decided to build her own Longchamps on a patch of stunted tropical vegetation called Campo Grande. There each Sunday primitive two-horse races were held where the riders battled it out with whips. When Masterman attended the races there, he wrote: 'An hour or more was lost in wrangling and mutual abuse before one could be decided . . . There was little betting or excitement among the crowd.'

That year the celebrations for the President's birthday

stretched out over two weeks with a series of balls, river trips, railway excursions – which Francisco loved – fire-works and 'bull-fights', though by all accounts these were dull affairs. Instead of bulls the oxen they used were so tame they could not be provoked into charging even by the numerous pricks and tormenting of the cowardly matadors.

Black-faced clowns mingled with the crowds at these events. The crowds threw money at them, knowing that they were actually Francisco's secret police in disguise. It was rumoured that Eliza demanded ten per cent of their takings. Attendance at Eliza's celebratory balls was made compulsory for the aristocracy. When one girl begged to be excused because her father had died, Eliza said: 'That is no novelty; everyone's father dies eventually.'

Bands roamed the streets and played outside Eliza's house. Every evening there were bonfires in the plazas. People gathered in large numbers and danced until late at night 'to testify to their joy and their love for the great López,' according to Washburn. Sentries were posted to prevent women going home even when they tired. When one woman complained that it was hard to dance on an empty stomach, she was punished with a hundred strokes of the cane. Others were banished to the interior for speaking out. Although no food was provided, wine and *caña* – the local firewater – were laid on and, as one foreign observer remarked, the drunken Paraguayans 'actively engaged in raising the birth rate'.

All this was paid for by merchants and foreigners who had to purchase 'subscriptions' and pay punitive taxes. Even political prisoners were forced to contribute.

'Everything is calculated to dazzle and please the

masses,' Washburn wrote in his dispatches. 'The lower classes have been indulged in a manner they never dreamed of before.'

But Washburn was pessimistic: 'I fear lest I may have occasion to write another dispatch ere long that will be a dark chapter in the history of Paraguay,' he wrote.

At a thanksgiving service, Bishop Palacios gave a sermon claiming that Francisco ruled by divine right. Citizens owed him unquestioned obedience. Even an innocent man condemned to death should go to the gallows without protest. On hand were a number of political prisoners who were forced to pray for their jailer.

Francisco and Eliza seem to have been too busy enjoying themselves to pay any serious attention to planning the conduct of the war. A sensible strategy would have been to back the Blanco government in Uruguay against Flores, join forces with General Urquiza in Entre Rios and bring down Mitre in Buenos Aires. Brazil would then have been isolated and Paraguay would have become the regional power broker. Instead, López was distracted by a lucrative prize that steamed into view. In November 1864, the Brazilian steamer *Marquez de Olinda* chugged up the Paraguay river. It was carrying the new Governor of Matto Grosso, the Brazilian state that lay to the north of Paraguay and could not easily be reached by land from Rio de Janeiro. With him he had a shipment of gold with which to fund his administration. However, López did not seize *Marquez de Olinda* when she docked in Asunción. That would have been too easy. Instead, he let her sail off up river and, when she was almost over the border into Matto Grosso, he sent the *Tacuari* after her. The ship was seized and the gold was used to buy army supplies waiting in Montevideo. The boat itself was pressed into service in the Paraguayan Navy, and the Governor and the ship's crew were thrown into jail. Washburn urged López to release them, pointing out that holding them would unite the people of Brazil and turn world opinion against him. López took no notice. His captives died in prison from torture and starvation. Not one of them saw Brazil again.

It was said that the idea of seizing the *Marquez de Olinda* and its cargo of gold was Eliza's, dreamed up with the Uruguayan Ambassador Vásquez Sagastume, who was now paying nocturnal visits to her pink palace.

❧ 8 ❧

IMPERIAL AMBITIONS

Eliza was now almost thirty and still had no imperial crown on her head. She urged Francisco to press home his advantage and invade the outlying provinces of Brazil that were cut off from Rio and the coast.

Still without a declaration of war, López attacked Matto Grosso and boasted to the American Ambassador over a sumptuous dinner that the Brazilians would not dare fight back. On 14 December 1864, 5,000 men, under the command of Francisco's brother-in-law General Barrios, boarded five steamers and three schooners in Asunción, and headed up river to Corumbá, the capital of Matto Grosso, urged on by Francisco's parting words.

'Soldiers,' he said, 'my endeavours to keep the peace have been fruitless. The Empire of Brazil, not knowing our valour and enthusiasm, provokes us to war. This challenge, by our honour and dignity, we are bound to accept in protection of our dearest rights.' Throughout the war, López maintained the fiction that it was Brazil who had started the war, not Paraguay. Even so, it was widely acknowledged that López was an effective orator, especially when it came to inspiring confidence in his troops and their contempt for the enemy.

The Brazilians were taken completely by surprise. They had no inkling of Francisco's intentions. Nor could they defend themselves. Their forts were designed to defend them from marauding Indians and the guns' fixed positions pointed out over the Chaco. Corumbá was defended by just 200 men. Barrios could have stood off and battered them into submission with the 68-pounder guns they had towed up the river on barges. Instead, Barrios and his officers got drunk and, with no discernible plan of attack, he led a charge that was repulsed with a great loss of life. However, the following day, hopelessly outnumbered, the Brazilians evacuated the fort and the rest of the province fell without a shot being fired.

López had promised the American Ambassador that Paraguay would show itself to be a truly civilised country and abide by the rules of war – the first Geneva Convention that had been proposed earlier that year. A proclamation to this effect, signed by López, was printed up and copies were scattered where the enemy troops would find them in the hope that they would desert. But Francisco's promises were empty. Brazilian prisoners of war were slaughtered and their ears were cut off. Men of property were stripped and tied naked to gun barrels in the hot sun until they revealed the whereabouts of their valuables. Corumbá was sacked and its women raped. Barrios himself shot a father who tried to protect his daughter from his advances. Some women were taken back to Asunción (where they were later reduced to begging in the streets) along with all the cannons the Paraguayans could strip from their mountings. The two sons of Baron de Villa Maria, the wealthiest landowner of the province, were killed, but the Baron himself escaped with a jar full of diamonds. It took him a month travelling on foot, guided by the stars, to reach Rio de Janeiro and inform the Emperor that he had lost his richest province. Until then, Brazil had not even known it was at war.

In Asunción, people danced in the streets – St Vitus's dance it was mockingly called in Buenos Aires. On the Campo Grande a military review was held to celebrate the great victory of 5,000 men over 200. López appeared on horseback flanked by his sons in cadet uniform, while Eliza stayed under the shade of a ramada for four hours as 12,000 soldiers marched past in the dust. They wore scarlet tunics, white trousers and black caps like those of the French Imperial Guard, but no shoes. Even upper-class Paraguayans had to discard their footwear when they joined Francisco's barefoot army.

At the height of the celebrations, Eliza was presented with the patent of nobility, looted from the hacienda of Baron de Villa Maria – it later adorned the wall of her ante-room – while a string of Brazilian ears was ceremonially hung around Francisco's neck. Later, Eliza suggested that the ladies of Asunción might like to celebrate Francisco's victory over the Brazilians by begging him to accept a flag embroidered with gold, diamonds and rubies, and hung from a silver staff with mountings to match. Francisco was so delighted by his victory that he allowed Benigno to return from internal exile to take over as Admiral of the Fleet.

If López had been a wiser man he would have stopped while he was ahead. As there was no easy overland route from Rio it would have been difficult to retake the Matto Grosso if López had concentrated his troops there. The only way the Brazilians could get enough soldiers to the Matto Grosso to take back the province was by river. Even to attack Paraguay they would have had to ferry troops hundreds of miles up the Paraná river, through Argentine territory. Its traditional rival, Argentina refused to back Brazil despite being offered all sort of inducements. Indeed, Argentina was eager to stay out of any war between Brazil and Paraguay and hoped to profit from staying on the sidelines.

But López was not a wise man. He was hungry for more territory and sent the troops he had just reviewed to take Brazil's southernmost province, Rio Grande do Sul. To get there, his army would have to cross Argentine territory. Francisco asked Argentina for permission. It was refused. Nevertheless Francisco planned to march across the sparsely populated Argentine province of Misiones into Rio Grande do Sul. From there he could move on into Uruguay to support the Blanco government. With the support of Urquiza in Entre Rios to his rear, Buenos Aires would be able do nothing but make loud protests.

It was then that the Argentine newspaper *El Siglo* - 'The Century' – published a far from flattering biography of Eliza. Furious, she urged Francisco to attack Argentina directly. So on 14 April 1865 – the day John Wilkes Booth assassinated Abraham Lincoln – López overran the Argentine city of Corrientes without a shot being fired. In the process he seized two Argentine steamers – the *25° de Mayo* and the *Gualeguay*. These two unseaworthy boats, one of which was the former Royal Mail packet *Camilla*, constituted Argentina's entire Navy.

López was very conscious of the criticism he had received internationally for attacking Brazil without a formal declaration of war. So this time he had taken the precaution of convening a Congress to make a formal declaration of war on Argentina. The following day, 19 March 1865, the declaration was gazetted in *El Semanario*. However the declaration did not reach Buenos Aires until 35 days later, nine days after López had overrun Corrientes. By that time, the *Esmeralda* had sailed up from Buenos Aires with a cargo of munitions, along with Eliza's new landau and her muslin, and the commercial attaché in Buenos Aires, Ejusquiza, had withdrawn all the Paraguayan gold reserves held in Argentine banks.

The Argentine government could scarcely believe that, having taken on the mighty Empire of Brazil, López wanted war with Argentina too. Eliza urged Francisco to march on down through Entre Rios, with the connivance of Urquiza, and attack Buenos Aires to defend her honour. If he overthrew the unpopular dictator Bartholomé Mitre he would be greeted by the Argentinians as a liberator. But Francisco's maltreatment of the Argentine prisoners of war captured at Corrientes put paid to that. When an Argentine named Ramon Capedevila, a long-time resident in Paraguay, tried to help them he was arrested. His wife bribed Eliza to intercede for him and he was released. But then she thought better of it. Capedevila was rearrested and found that his wife's efforts earned him a beating and two extra sets of fetters. The hide he lay on was taken, so he had to sleep on the ground. He was tortured and, eventually, executed, and his wife and four young children were driven out into the cordilleras. The wives and children of Argentine soldiers captured at Corrientes suffered the same fate.

When the Argentinians heard of the treatment of their compatriots, they united behind Mitre. A crowd stormed to his house demanding war. He addressed the mob.

'Gentlemen,' he said, 'after the provocation and insult to our flag by the tyrant of Paraguay, your Governor can only tell you that proclamations and manifestos will be translated into deeds. In twenty-four hours we shall be in the barracks, in a fortnight in Corrientes, and in three months in Asunción.'

Mitre's speech was greeted with great cheers and excitement spread through the city. A performance in the music hall was brought to a halt. *Porteños* took to the stage to make speeches supporting the war, while the words 'In three months in Asunción' were projected on to the curtain behind them. The Paraguyan attaché Ejusquiza was arrested, bailed, then arrested again the next day. Meanwhile, a little to the north in Rosario, in Cordoba province, the Paraguayan Consulate was looted and Francisco's portrait was seized, used for target practice, then thrown in the river. López would later condemn this misuse of his picture as an atrocity. Even General Urquiza, a potential ally of Paraguay and a supporter of the Blanco government in Uruguay, was moved by popular anti-López sentiment and was forced to back Mitre. The whole country rallied behind the Buenos Aires government, a rare thing in Argentina.

Argentina and its traditional enemy Brazil were now united in a common cause. In Uruguay, the Blanco government, which had been holding out for help from

Paraguay, fell; its military leaders were summarily executed and their bodies mutilated. The new Colorado government in Uruguay under General Flores was now beholden to both Argentina and Brazil and had no reason to be sympathetic to López as he had backed the Blancos, with words if not deeds.

On 1 May 1865, Argentina, Brazil and Uruguay signed a secret treaty, called the Treaty of the Triple Alliance. In it they promised 'not to lay down their arms, unless by mutual consent, until they had abolished the present government of Paraguay'. They specifically declared war on the tyrant López rather than Paraguay itself. This secret treaty was not secret for long. A Uruguayan official showed it to the British chargé d'affaires in Montevideo, who sent a copy to London. There it was read to a closed session of Parliament – but the next day it was all over the papers.

In the Treaty, the Allies made it clear that the war had been provoked by Paraguay. To this day, Brazilians, Uruguayans and Argentines refer to the war as the Paraguayan War, while Paraguayans call it the War of the Triple Alliance. The responsibility for provoking the war remains a matter of passionate debate in Paraguay. Some claim that war had been inevitable ever since the country had been cut off from the sea; others that Brazil and Argentina conspired to dismember Paraguay, that they aimed to destroy the country completely, but left the rump we see on maps today to disguise their intentions in the eyes of the world. There may be some truth in this. Brazil had a greater military presence in the Matto Grosso than was strictly necessary for its defence and a border dispute had been outstanding since 1858. The Argentines had always been jealous of Paraguay's railways, shipyards, arsenals and telegraph system, which were all considerably more advanced than those of the Confederation at the time. This was because the wealth of Argentina had been expended on numerous civil wars, while Paraguay had long been at peace. Its finances were healthy through the profits of the *yerba maté* trade and, when the Paraguayan dictator wanted something, all he had to do was order it from England. But then, the Brazilians were armed by the British too. There is even a theory that Great Britain was behind the war, signing a secret treaty with Argentina over the ownership of the railways.

However, George Masterman, who was in Paraguay at the time and a regular guest at the Lynch-López household, had no doubt where the blame lay. In his book about his experiences entitled, with masterful understatement, *Seven Eventful Years in Paraguay*, he wrote: 'In Paris he [Francisco López] remained for some time, and from thence he imported two novelties – a French uniform for the officers and his mistress; the latter the most fatal step in his life. That lady occupied a very prominent place eventually in Paraguayan affairs, and, I believe, by her evil counsels was the remote cause of the terrible war which has utterly depopulated the country.'

Masterman is also clear about how Eliza did it: 'A clever, selfish and most unscrupulous woman, it will be readily understood that the influence she exercised over a man so imperious, yet so weak, so vain, and sensual as López was immense. With admirable tact, she treated him apparently with the utmost deference and respect, whilst she could really do with him as she pleased and virtually was ruler of Paraguay.'

Masterman also identifies her motives: 'She had two ambitious projects: the first, to marry him; the second to make him "the Napoleon of the New World". The first was a difficult one, for her husband as a Frenchman could not sue for divorce; but should the second succeed, it would not be very hard, perhaps, to obtain a dispensation, and her equivocal position would be exchanged for a secure one. Therefore she gradually and insidiously imbued López with the idea that he was the greatest soldier of the age, and flattered the vain, credulous, and greedy savage into the belief that he was destined to raise Paraguay from obscurity, and make it the dominant power of South America. It was necessary for the realisation of this ambitious project that a war on the grand scale should be undertaken; and with neighbours so encroaching as Brazil, so turbulent and lawless as the Argentine Confederation, it was not difficult to find a pretext for hostilities.'

Later Masterman mentioned that, when he looked back on that period of his life, despite all the appalling things that López did – and Masterman himself suffered torture at the Francisco's hands – he could almost pity him. He believed that Francisco was as 'plastic as wax' and that if he had but one 'trusted counsellor who would have developed the good in him, rather than the evil, he would have made a zealous, but weak ruler'. Masterman believed that, in those circumstances, the people of Paraguay would have benefited materially as they had under his father Carlos. 'But such a mentor could not be found in Paraguay.' Instead 'the ambitious and unscrupulous woman he made his chief confidante, proved to be his greatest enemy, and her evil counsel made his desire of military glory, which might have been but a passing whim, the ruling passion of his life.'

Sir Richard Burton, te British representative in São Paulo, also blamed Eliza. In his book *Letters from the Battlefields of Paraguay*, he wrote: 'Madame Lynch must be somewhat ambitious. It is generally believed that she in company with Bishop Palacios, a country priest, and with a Hungarian refugee, Colonel von Wisner de Morgenstern worked on President López and persuaded him that he might easily become Master and Emperor of the Platine Regions.'

No less than López, Eliza exercised dictatorial powers in Paraguay. Two young Frenchmen who 'applied ugly words to Madame Lynch, were at her instigation arrested . . ., thrown into prison, and compelled to beg their bread on the streets'. She had another Frenchman jailed for saying she wore a wig.

Cunninghame Graham, who live in Paraguay before the war and visited again immediately after it, wrote: 'All those who knew her at the time seem to have had no doubt of her intention to push López into the position of the first ruler in South America, to make her fortune, and to retire to Paris to live upon what she had wrung from Paraguay. It was not certainly a great ambition, but natural in her case. Had López followed her advice, the precious pair might have become important figures on the boulevards of Lutetia [the Latin name for Paris], and nobly alternated with the Kings of Patagonia, Presidents of Cappadocia and the rest of the strange, motley crowd of flesh flies, who had their little hour, and then fell back into the mud from which they had emerged, during the Second Empire.' Indeed, the Emperor of Brazil ended up there.

But before Eliza could live it up on the streets of Paris on what she had wrung from Paraguay, more of the comic opera had to be played out.

Within hours of the Triple Alliance being made public, Francisco convened another Congress. On 5 May 1865, this promoted López to the rank of Marshal – *Mariscal* – of Paraguay. Eliza begged him to take the rank of Emperor there and then to ally himself with the great monarchs of Europe. But Francisco was more concerned, for the moment, to garner the support of the republics of the New World. There was still a chance that Chile and even the United States might come to his aid. However, he did establish the Grand Cross of the Paraguay National Order of Merit. This medal could only be conferred on hereditary rulers or sovereigns for life, not presidents. López was head of the order and it was widely understood that, when the war was over, he would do as Eliza told him and have himself formally crowned Emperor. As it was he was already having himself proclaimed *Francisco Primero* in the countryside.

'It is almost a pity that López never had himself crowned,' wrote Cunninghame Graham. 'Madame Lynch would have made quite a creditable Empress "*de la main gauche*". The stocky little half-breed in some *opéra comique* uniform bedizened with orders of his own bestowal and his demi-rep Empress, with her good looks and Parisian experience, would have provided a theme that to do justice to would have required an Offenbach.'

The intention was clearly there. With the rank of *Mariscal* came a wreath of gold oak leaves similar to that worn by Napoleon at his coronation, a gold-hilted sword and a $30,000 marshal's baton. Congress begged him to accept a massive pay rise. A law was proposed 'prohibiting him from exposing his precious life in the war' and government employees had a whip-round to buy him some gold ornaments studded with precious jewels and a solid gold equestrian statue. Eliza then proposed that the ladies of Asunción might like to hand over a tenth of their jewellery to help the war effort. These should be accompanied by an adulatory speech, saying to Francisco: 'Take my jewels, and realise your sacred thought.' However, most of the jewellery, it was said, ended up, 'in, if not on, Madame's chest'. Naturally Eliza took great pleasure in depriving the women who had looked down on her for so long of their finery.

In recognition of her fund-raising efforts, Francisco suggested that Congress send an agent to Paris, via Bolivia, to buy a coronet of brilliants studded with pear-shaped diamonds reminiscent of Empress Josèphine's crown. They approved the purchase with a unanimous vote. Unfortunately, when the coronet eventually arrived, along with a plaster cast of Napoleon's crown that Francisco had ordered, it was impounded by customs in Buenos Aires.

When Sir Richard Burton heard about the crown, he dismissed it as a *ruse de guerre*. But then he saw it for himself in a warehouse in Buenos Aires along with furniture Eliza had ordered – £400-worth destined for a single room. It consisted of 'fine solid curtain hangings, showy chairs, white, red, and gold, and tinsel chandeliers, with common cut glass and white paint showing under the gilding'. This too revealed Eliza's imperial pretensions: 'It bore the arms of the Republic,' said Burton, 'but it was evidently copied from the Tuileries.'

Armed with all the powers of a Napoleon to prosecute the war in any way they saw fit, Francisco and Eliza dismissed the Congress indefinitely. For good measure they had the new Uruguayan Ambassador arrested, tortured and executed. Later the same fate befell the envoys of rebel factions from Argentina, who had at one time sought to ally themselves with Francisco, along with the Spanish Consul captured at Corrientes.

Although Paraguay now stood alone against three of its four neighbours, the situation was not yet hopeless. López had been preparing for war while the Allies had been squabbling among themselves. While Paraguay had between 80,000 and 100,000 men under arms, the Allies only had 40,000 – 3,000 from Uruguay, 12,000 from Argentina and 25,000 from Brazil. But the Allied armies were volunteers of fighting age who were fit and well equipped. Francisco's army boasted 50-year-old men, fourteen-year-old boys and even many cripples. Although every Paraguayan soldier had a smart French-made uniform, only 40 per cent bore firearms. Some were so old that they still carried the manufacturing marks of the Tower of London, whose armoury had been destroyed by fire in 1842. Most had been badly misused. Men were issued with a few rounds of ammunition to shoot game. But they would cut up the lead bullets to make shot to hunt duck, which stripped the rifling from the barrel. The rest were armed with home-made lances and knives. Colonel Thompson pointed out that it would have made more strategic sense to send half the men home to till the fields and prevent the starvation that eventually overtook the country.

Moreover, Paraguayan cavalry lances were at least a

foot, and sometimes three feet, shorter than those of the Allies. And Paraguay artillery was so antiquated that Sir Richard Burton speculated that López had 'acquired all the old smoothbores which had previously decorated Montevideo street corners as trash receptacles'.

'They were like the guns which do duty as posts on Woolwich Common,' said Thompson. Nor were the gunners well trained. 'Neither the riflemen nor artillery of Paraguay were ever taught the use of the graduated sights of their arms, but they elevated their guns up pointing them so many yards above the mark, according to its distance.'

Even then, they were better marksmen than the Brazilians, whose tactics, according to Thompson, 'consisted in firing whenever they have any guns to fire with, whether or not they see what they are firing at, no matter whether they killed friend or foe, or both together – which last is generally the case'.

The Allies had the added disadvantage of being hopelessly disorganised. The Brazilian generals resented taking orders from the Argentinian General Mitre who headed the Allied forces. He was more of a scholar than a soldier – he had translated Dante's *Inferno* into Spanish and wrote a biography of General Belgrano. And he was hopelessly over-optimistic. The war that he said would be over in three months, lasted five years. But then López also predicted it would be over in three months, though obviously with a somewhat different outcome. And between the two of them, they managed to lose some 50,000 men – civilians as well as troops – to disease and starvation before the first major battle.

On the diplomatic front, Paraguay was lagging way

behind the Allies. López had turned the western world against him by flouting the rules of international law and going to war without a formal declaration. If Paraguay had gone to war to defend Uruguay from Brazil, López would have gained much international sympathy for siding with the underdog. As it was, he had manoeuvred three powerful neighbours – two of which were traditional rivals – into declaring war on him. In other circumstances he could have expected help from Britain or France, but he had alienated both nations by maltreating their citizens and harassing their ambassadors.

López also had no clear strategy. As his aim was to be Emperor of the River Plate, Thompson urged him to march his army south from Corrientes as far as Entre Rios, where the maverick Governor Urquiza would have joined him. Eliza also urged him to go south and take Buenos Aires where the newspapers had insulted her. This could indeed have been a winning strategy. 'López would have been victorious for he would have instantly appeared before Buenos Aires or Montevideo, and, by threatening bombardment, compelled them to make terms with him,' said Masterman. And once he controlled the Paraná all the way down to Buenos Aires, it would have been nearly impossible for the Brazilians to attack him.

'As things turned out, he looked very small to the Allies,' wrote Thompson subsequently.

But while Eliza was angry with Argentina, López was mad with Brazil, and he was wedded to his plan to invade Rio Grande do Sul. He sent 12,000 men under the formidable ladies' man Colonel Antonio Estigarribia across the Paraná river at Encarnación into Misiones.

And another 25,000 men under General Wenceslao Robles made a sweeping movement across the province of Corrientes. Both headed for the Brazilian border. On 3 June, Robles reached the small town of Goya where, in the house of a Señor Delfino, he came across a new piano, which he sent back to Eliza as a present in an effort to ingratiate himself. It did no good. Robles was a cruel and ruthless torturer and his ability to extract 'confessions' from Francisco's enemies gave him an influence over López that rivalled her own. The gift of a piano was not going to save him from his fate.

With the Paraguayan Army on its way to Rio Grande do Sul, Paraguay was vulnerable to attack from the river. Brazil assembled a fleet of twenty purpose-built gunboats with more than enough firepower to knock out the 90 guns at Humaitá. The Brazilian sailors said that the Paraguayans would abandon their fort when the flotilla came into sight. Despite this boast the Brazilians were over-cautious. The fleet hung around in Buenos Aires for weeks, then ten war-steamers crept gingerly up the river, taking 42 days to cover 600 miles. And once they were in sight of Corrientes, though out of range of the Paraguayan guns, they proceeded to blockade the river.

López suddenly realised how vulnerable he was and hatched a daring plot. He would send his fleet of paddle-steamers down the river and seize the Brazilian flotilla. This time López wanted some of the glory for himself so, on 2 June 1865, he issued a proclamation.

'Citizens,' it said. 'The course of the war in which our Fatherland is engaged no longer allows me to continue the self-sacrifice of absenting myself from the seat of war and from my companions in arms. I feel the necessity of personally participating in the fatigues of the brave and loyal defenders of our country. On separating myself momentarily from the bosom of the Fatherland, I carry with me the sweet satisfaction that the general administration of the State will be carried on with loyalty, devotion and patriotism.'

López was to leave Asunción with the fleet on 8 June. The entire population of Asunción turned out, fearing that it might be construed as an unpardonable affront if they stayed away. They waited on the quayside the whole afternoon, then at sunset López arrived in his carriage with Eliza. Washburn noted: 'Some slight attempts at a cheer of *viva* were made.'

HMS *Doterel*, which was in port, manned her yards to salute the hero as López went on board the *Tacuari* as the fleet sailed out that night. But López was not really going into battle. Congress had passed a bill prohibiting him from risking his life. So at Humaitá, he disembarked.

As he saw off the fleet down the river into battle, he was asked: 'What shall we do with the Brazilians? Shall we kill them?'

'No,' said López confidently. 'Bring me some prisoners.'

The attack was to be commanded by Admiral Pedro Mesa who, it was said, had only one merit that would have commended him to Julius Caesar – he was fat. Indeed he was fat, old and sick, and 'as ignorant of naval warfare as a Guaicuru Indian' – a tribe who lived far from the river in the Gran Chaco. The fleet was to leave Humaitá at midnight and catch the Brazilians unawares at dawn. But they had only just started downstream when one of the gunboats ran aground. Trying unsuccessfully to dislodge it delayed the strike force. Instead of taking one hour, it took three to reach Tres Boccas and the Paraná river. So by the time the armada arrived at the blockade, the sun was already up and the Brazilians could see them coming. Instead of turning and running back to the safety of Humaitá, the Paraguayan fleet swept on down river. The plan was to sail past the Brazilians, turn and attack. It was misconceived. First it gave the Brazilians a chance to get up steam. Then the Paraguayans had difficulty finding a place wide enough to turn around. Meanwhile a second Paraguay gunboat was put out of commission, this time by a shore battery, and a third was beached on a mud flat.

The only place where the fleet could turn was in the mouth of the Riachuelo, a small tributary on the Corrientes side of the river. By the time they reached it, the Brazilians were on top of them. The Paraguayans started firing on the lead ship, but managed to do more damage to their own boats with friendly fire. The Brazilians were no more effective at naval warfare than the Paraguayans and the Brazilian ships rammed into each other. In the confusion, a Paraguayan boarding party managed to seize a Brazilian vessel. Now they had their chance to seize the whole fleet. Admiral Mesa gave the order to break out the grappling irons – only to discover that they had left them behind in Asunción. A burst of fire sent the Paraguayan boarding party leaping into the water and the Brazilian fleet, now under the command of an Italian engineer who just happened to be on board, turned their fire on them. It was only thanks to the quick thinking of *Tacuari*'s English engineer John Watts that four Paraguayan boats escaped. They were all more or less disabled, but fortunately none of them at been hit by the Brazilian 150- and 120-pounder guns. This is because the Brazilian guns could not be depressed enough to make them any use in close combat; some of the Brazilian cannon balls were found five or six miles inland. Some Paraguayans swam for the shore to escape across the Chaco. The Brazilians sent an armed boat to kill them, but instead the Paraguayans killed its crew, seized the boat and escaped. The Brazilians also tried to set fire to the *Paraguari*, a war steamer López bought in England for £50,000. But it was made of iron and would not burn. The Paraguayans managed to tow it away. It came in useful later in the war as scrap when iron became scarce.

Mesa himself had been shot in the lung by a musket ball. When news of the defeat reached López, he flew into a rage and sent a message telling Mesa that he had better die of his wounds, otherwise he would be shot for incompetence. Obligingly, Mesa expired on receipt of the message. For saving the remnants of the Paraguayan Navy, Watts was awarded the lowest order of the *Légion d'Honneur*. Three years later, he was arrested, tortured and shot as a traitor. Those who had distinguished themselves in battle on the Brazilian side fared rather better. The Italian engineer responsible for the Brazilian victory was awarded 500 ounces of gold and the rank of lieutenant-colonel, while the Brazilian admiral who was supposed to be in charge of the action – but, in fact, got drunk and hid in his cabin throughout the entire battle – was made a baron. In any other country, Thompson pointed out, he would have been court-martialled for cowardice – as well as for allowing the remaining

Paraguayan steamers to get away without even attempting to pursue them. This contrasting pattern of recompense and punishment was to continue throughout the war. Dom Pedro gave those who disgraced their flag with acts of cowardice or stupidity rich rewards, while Francisco rewarded loyalty and bravery with imprisonment, torture and death.

This defeat led Eliza to arrange a new round of fund-raising balls, where men were to pay a 'subscription' and women were to hand over more of their jewellery. Of course, none of their contributions helped the war effort in any way. With the river blockaded, the money and jewellery could not be used to purchase munitions abroad and, domestically, López simply took anything his army needed without compensation. But as the alternative was pay up or go to face jail, many began to lodge their valuables with the American Ambassador for safe-keeping, rather than let Eliza get her hands on them.

The setback at Riachuelo was a huge blow. Had the Paraguayans succeeded in seizing the Brazilian fleet, they would have controlled the river all the way down to Montevideo. Brazilian troops would not be able to get up the Paraná to attack them and they could have dictated terms to Buenos Aires. But instead, Paraguay was now cut off from the sea and open to attack. Undaunted, López continued with his grand strategy to seize Rio Grande do Sul, but this plan also began to unravel.

Robles was probably the most effective general in the army and, when he heard of the navy's defeat at Riachuelo, he realised that Paraguay was now wide open to attack from the river and made the sensible strategic decision to fall back to defend his homeland. But neither

Eliza nor Francisco were prepared to countenance. Eliza discovered that Robles had received several letters from the enemy and alleged that he was considering an offer from Mitre that would have given him command of the Legion of Free Paraguayan dissidents that were assembling in Buenos Aires under Colonel Decoud. López sent Barrios to arrest Robles. He was brought back to Humaitá in chains and he and his staff were shot as traitors.

Meanwhile Estigarribia had swept on through Misiones unchallenged. In the process, he had outrun his supply train, which got lost because none of the drivers knew the roads or could read a map. Determined to seize Rio Grande do Sul and march on Montevideo, Estigarribia crossed the Uruguay river into Brazil at São Borja with the bulk of his army, leaving 2,000 men under his second-in-command Major Duarte on the right bank to protect his rear. They marched down opposite banks maintaining communication by canoe. On 6 August 1865, Estigarribia took the important Brazilian town of Uruguayana, while Duarte took Yatai on the opposite bank. Suddenly Duarte found himself under attack by a combined force of Brazilians and Uruguayans and the 2,000 men under his command were quickly reduced to 300. He sent a desperate message to Robles, pleading for help – not knowing that Robles was in no position to lend him any assistance. Worse, the message fell into Allied hands. In it Duarte mentioned that López had ordered that all Allied prisoners were to be killed. This sealed his fate. He and all his remaining men were massacred. The news pleased Francisco. The Allies now knew that Paraguayans would fight to the last man.

When Estigarribia had tried to retreat across the Uruguay river to relieve Duarte he had found his way blocked by four Brazilian gunboats under the command of Admiral Tamandaré. Then the Comte d'Eu, the son-in-law of the Emperor of Brazil and Francisco's rival for the hand of Princess Isabella, arrived bringing the Allied strength up to 30,000 men. The Paraguayans were hopelessly outnumbered, but when the Allies offered them the chance to surrender, Estigarribia replied with a long and lofty letter that began:

> Viva La Republica de Paraguay
> Your Excellencies, the sacred ensign of liberty
> will not be besmirched by me. Perish the thought.
> Although my bones and those of my heroic
> legionnaires should find their only sepulchre
> among the ruins of Uruguayana, our spirits free
> and proud shall soar aloft . . .

He went on to accuse the Argentinians of starting the war by blackening the name of the government of Paraguay in the Buenos Aires newspapers.

The following day, the Allies offered him a second chance to surrender, reminding him that their aim was to free the people of Paraguay from the tyranny of López and enumerating their by now vastly superior forces. This time Estigarribia replied at even greater length, enquiring how the Allies could say they were going to free the people of Paraguay when Brazil was a slave state – nearly four million African slaves had been taken there, eight times the number taken to the United States. He also drew a parallel with the Battle of Thermopylae, where

Leonidas and 300 Spartans held off a huge Persian army. The story goes that, when a soldier told Leonidas that his enemies were so numerous that their arrows would darken the sun, Leonidas replied: 'So much the better, we will fight in the shade.'

In his letter to the Allied commanders, Estigarribia wrote: 'When you enumerate the number of your forces and the amount of your artillery, I answer your Excellencies: "So much the better, the smoke of our cannon shall be our shade."'

At the third time of asking, Estigarribia had run out of both ammunition and rhetoric, and his army had just eaten their last horse. He surrendered and went to live in Rio de Janeiro where, it is said, his daily expenses were as much as his annual salary under López.

Unfortunately, Eliza had planned a great victory ball to celebrate victory at the Battle of Riachuelo, which had been rapidly rescheduled as a great victory ball to celebrate the capture of Uruguayana. For the event the whole city was decorated with flimsy triumphal arches made from wood and cloth, covered with eulogies to the great López.

'The ingenuity of the people in framing so many expressions on the same barren subject was wonderful,' marvelled Washburn. He listed some of them: 'The great man, the unequalled warrior, the father of his people, the defender of the country, the great pacificator, the promoter of national progress, the champion of independence, the guardian of liberty, the dauntless hero . . .' No doubt much of the irony is lost in translation.

When the news came that Estigarribia had surrendered, Eliza ordered that the information be withheld from the public until after the ball. Eliza and von Wisner even opened the proceedings by proposing a toast to the hero of Uruguayana, General Estigarribia. But López was in such a rage that he refused to attend, so Eliza had an oil painting of the *Mariscal* in his full regalia placed on his throne which men and women had to bow and curtsey to.

This was supposed to be a joyous occasion, but throughout the gavottes and mazurkas, Eliza spotted one of her ladies-in-waiting, Señora Jovellanos, in floods of tears. When Eliza asked her what the matter was, she said that she had just heard that her husband had been killed in battle – in fact, he had just been arrested, but she did not dare say so.

'You should rejoice,' said Eliza. 'It is a great privilege to die for one's country.'

That evening Eliza played the perfect hostess. She extended her hand for every gentleman to kiss and complimented the ladies on their gowns and their jewellery. The women of Asunción had been ordered to wear all their jewellery so Eliza could conduct an inventory. She also had another insult in store for them. At midnight, she stood by the door of the ballroom and personally greeted the *peinetas de oro*, who arrived at her special invitation. When the upper-class ladies expressed horror at rubbing shoulders with common prostitutes, Eliza said that, on such a patriotic occasion, all classes should mingle. Masterman recalled seeing Señora Jovellanos, 'a gentle shy creature', being forced to 'stand with a row of shameless courtesans, marshalled by Mrs Lynch, and sing a "patriotic hymn" in honour of López, whilst her husband lay a prisoner, loaded with irons'. Privately the ladies of Asunción commented that Eliza was merely mixing with her own, but they overlooked that fact that the *peinetas de oro* had often had three or four ounces of precious metal in their golden combs, gold which would soon be lining Eliza's coffers.

Estigarribia's 'victory' could not be kept secret for long. Barrios was now in full retreat with the remainder of Robles's men and Francisco sulked in his room unable to believe that the fortunes of war had turned so disastrously against him. He would not even speak to Panchito, his favourite son. The only way Eliza could get him to snap out of it was to suggest that *El Semanario* print an article condemning Estigarribia as a traitor and claiming that he had 'sold himself to the Argentines for 10,000 pesos'. When the article appeared, there were demonstrations in the streets. Estigarribia was burnt in effigy. His property was confiscated and his family arrested.

Francisco's disastrous strategy had cost the better part of the Paraguayan Navy and nearly 21,000 men. In all, 40,000 Paraguayans had died since the beginning of recruiting and another 10,000 had been taken prisoner. Diarrhoea and dysentery had caused havoc in the ranks and epidemics of smallpox and measles had carried off further thousands. All Paraguay had gained from Francisco's Argentine adventure was the plunder taken from Corrientes and more than 100,000 head of cattle, which had been driven back across the river. Unfortunately the cows were not used to the vegetation in Paraguay, which poisoned them. They died and the vapours given off by their rotting carcasses were thought to have seriously affected the health of the remaining troops.

The Allies could have finished off the Paraguayan Army during Barrios's retreat. But groundless fears of drowning in shallow waters or that the Paraguayans might have fortified the river with hidden batteries prevented them going in for the kill. Meanwhile, *El Semanario* continued its habit of comparing López to heroes of the ancient world. A mischievous American suggested that they add to the list of citations the name Cincinnatus. Apparently no one on the paper knew that Cincinnatus had been appointed dictator of Rome in a time of crisis, defeated the enemy in a single day, then relinquished power and returned to his farm. Not only had López singularly failed to defeat the enemy in a single year, let alone a single day, he was clearly in no mood for giving up power. As one of his biographers put it: 'He never escaped the belief that there were people who had no aspiration in life save that their Emperor ride above their graves.'

And the Emperor was about to announce a stern new policy. At one of the *beso manos* – 'hand kissings' – at his headquarters he warned his staff officers: 'Take care. Until now I have pardoned offences – and take pleasure in pardoning them. But from this day I pardon no one.'

'The expression on his face gave double power to his words,' said an eyewitness. 'As I looked round on the wide circle of officers, bowing low as he left the room, I saw many a blanched face amongst them, for they knew he would keep his word.'

9

QUEEN OF THE SIEGE

Even the great López could not be in two places at one time. He had planned that his move to Humaitá would be brief, so that he could steal the glory for the victory at Riachuelo. But now with the Allied Army standing at the gates of Paraguay, it seemed he was stuck there for the duration. So Eliza in Asunción became Regent of Paraguay.

Her first act as Regent was to publish an announcement in *El Semanario* that the women of Paraguay were to hand over more of their jewellery as a 'testimonial of gratitude for the protection of General López in defending their country against the invasion of a barbarous foe'. Women were also ordered to volunteer for the army – 'to beg permission to take up arms and fight by the side of their brethren'.

'This offer was turned down for the present,' wrote Colonel Thompson. But some twenty girls from the village of Areguá were issued with lances and uniforms consisting of a white dress with tricolour bands and a sort of Scottish cap designed by Eliza. And they went about Asunción singing patriotic hymns.

Eliza visited the primitive hospital in Asunción where

the lucky among the wounded lay two to a bed. Others lay on the floor or huddled under the open colonnades outside. As the war progressed more than 1,000 men were crowded into a hospital designed for 300. Masterman, who worked there, reckoned that 50,000 men died in Paraguayan hospitals during the war. Women who wished to demonstrate their patriotism volunteered as nurses, or were ordered by the police to do so. Pretty sixteen-year-olds were less than useless as nurses, Masterman wrote, but they kept the wounded amused with their flirtations.

Eliza also had to maintain her international profile. Foreign ambassadors were regularly invited to dinner and it was said her palace was the only place in Paraguay where one could enjoy a civilised meal, properly served. Entertaining in such a lavish style did not come cheap, so Eliza went to the treasury where she asked the Chancellor, Saturnino Bedoya, to hand over four crates of gold coins. When Don Saturnino refused, she told him that she knew that he visited Doña Juana's house every afternoon. The López family were plotting against Francisco, Eliza said, and they had been corresponding with the Allied commander General Mitre through the French Ambassador Cochelet.

There must have been some truth in Eliza's allegations as four cases of gold coins turned up at her palace that night. According to the distinguished Paraguayan scholar Dr Cecilio Báez, who was President of Paraguay 1905–6, these crates of money were subsequently loaded onto *La Ardita*, an Italian corvette that had run the blockade, and sent to Eliza's agent, Antoine Gelot in Paris, along with a consignment of jewellery. One can hardly blame her.

Francisco had already smuggled large sums of money out of the country on board the French warship *La Decidée*, in case the war went against him.

As well as shipping money and jewellery out of the country, Eliza was also buying up real estate and, given her position of power, she did not perhaps always have the most scrupulous of ethics in acquiring it.

'Madame Lynch, foreseeing that López must finally be overthrown, had been engaged in buying up a large part of the most valuable property,' wrote Washburn. 'The people who owned it had no alternative, when she offered to purchase it, but to accept her terms. She invariably paid in the paper money of the country, which would be of little, if any, value should López be overthrown, and of which she had an unlimited supply by order of her paramour. When she made an offer for a house or other building, the owner dared not refuse it, for he knew she had both the power and the will to punish him for a refusal; and hence all those bargains were in fact nothing more than a confiscation of the property for the benefit of Madame Lynch, for which in turn she gave them, in charity, just what she pleased.'

Such things had been going on since Carlos's days. He would simply call in the deeds of any property he coveted and have them invalidated. And under Francisco the property of all political prisoners and deserters, real or surmised – and often that of their relatives – was forfeit to the state.

Eliza quickly became the world's greatest woman land-owner with more than 22 million rural acres and 26 valuable urban properties to her name. In her own defence, Eliza said that she bought up the property because Benigno had dumped all his real estate on the market and she feared a collapse. She also said that she gave the owners a receipt and her pledge that they could have their property back after the war for exactly what she paid for it, without interest – as if anyone would dare ask.

Under Eliza, Paraguay became a kleptocracy. Horses and cattle were taken. Houses were ransacked, and the people robbed of their bedding, their clothes and their cooking utensils. And while everyone knew that their goods went to swell the private fortunes of Francisco and Eliza, they were forced to say that they were contributing willingly to the war effort.

An even more shocking charge was laid at Eliza's door. In the village of Caacupé some 40 miles from Asunción, there is a church which is home to a famous statue of the Virgin. In the latter part of the eighteenth century, the daughter of the local district chief fell ill. The child's mother prayed to the Virgin and vowed that, if the child recovered, she would give the Virgin a valuable bracelet. This crude bribery seems to have worked. The child recovered and the woman handed over the bracelet. Mothers of other sick children followed suit, plying the Virgin with expensive jewellery. When news of the miraculous recovery of ailing offspring reached the ears of the Bishop of Asunción, he made a pilgrimage to Caacupé, whereupon the Virgin performed a miracle for him. He then issued an episcopal letter accrediting the cult of the Virgin of Caacupé and, by the 1860s, people had been loading the statue with valuable jewels for more than 80 years. According to Washburn, there were several well-authenticated cases of persons whose offer-ings were of inferior quality 'being taken, soon after

1. Eliza Alicia Lynch

2. Francisco Solano López

3. López (right) and
Napoleon III in Paris, 1853

4. López with his oldest
son, Juan Francisco, known
as Panchito

5. Disembarkation at Buenos Aires
6. The unfinished cathedral of Nuestra, Señora d'Asunción, 1869

7. The Palacio di Gobierno, Asunción, where war was declared on Argentina on March 18th 1865

8. López' palace, a military hospital during the war. The building was demolished in 1936

9. Colonel Venancio López, Minister for the Army and Navy

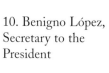

10. Benigno López, Secretary to the President

11. Grand Military Polka 'November 10th', composed in homage to López'
mediating mission to Argentina, 1859

12. Brazilian Emperor Pedro II and the Empress Ysabel

13. Argentinian General Bartolomé Mitre before the Battle of Pavone
14. Mariscal Luis Alves de Lima e Silva, Duke of Caxías

15. Colonel
Antonio de la Cruz
Estigarribia

16. Colonel
Francisco Wisner
de Morgenstern

17. Colonel Julián Godoy

18. Prince Gaston d'Orléans, Comte d'Eu

19. G.F. Masterman

20. Diploma awarded to Dr William Stewart for his services to Paraguay

21. The *Tacuari*
22. Humaitá, at the end of the eighteenth century

23. Paraguayan soldiers in the trenches at Tuyutí
24. López visits the heros of Tuyutí

25. The bodies of the Paraguayan dead after one of the battles of the War of the Triple Alliance

26. Paraguayan woman with her child after the war, as represented in *Harper's Weekly*, 1870

making them, with some terrible calamity'. So it was widely known that the jewellery adorning the Virgin of Caacupé was of the highest quality.

When Eliza became aware of the custom, she entered into a theological discussion about the Virgin of Caacupé with Bishop Palacios. In the eyes of the Lord, she proposed, glass had the same value as diamonds. Palacios agreed that the Heavenly Father was not concerned with 'temporal things of this nature'. So Eliza reasoned that if the jewels at the shrine of Our Lady of Caacupé were replaced with paste it would make no difference to God. Even Palacios was shocked at the suggestion that valuable jewellery should be replaced with worthless paste as people had sacrificed their jewels as a token of their faith. But Eliza pointed out that it was spiritual rather than material value that concerned the Kingdom of Heaven and Palacios was forced to concede the point.

Eliza then made her own pilgrimage to Caacupé. In the church there, she found the statue of the Virgin covered, it was said, from head to foot in diamonds and every kind of precious stone. 'Her diadem alone, not unlike the crown of the Andes, was worth a king's ransom,' read one account. 'Pendants hung from her ears, her fingers were stiff with rings and row after row of priceless pearls had been placed around her slender neck by the devout pilgrims who, when unable to attach another pearl to her person or ornament to her dress, had laid offerings at her feet so that she stood in a sea of jewels.'

The Virgin was guarded by a solitary hermit, said to be a leper, and it was the custom for the faithful to ask the Virgin a question. She answered with either a nod or a shake of her head; to achieve a desired response it was found to be best to give the leper a silver dollar.

Palacios paid the leper, while Eliza asked the Virgin whether she was willing to give up her jewels for the sake of Paraguay. Apparently there was a slight pause before the Virgin nodded her head. Was she willing to give them up to ensure peace? Eliza asked. Again the Virgin nodded. Then Eliza asked whether they were going to win the war? The Virgin made it clear that she, for one, was on Francisco's side.

Eliza then stripped the statue of its jewels. In their place she swathed the Virgin in the Elizabeth I costume she had worn to her fancy-dress ball. When Pope John Paul II visited Caacupé during his trip to Paraguay in 1988, he could not have failed to notice something strange about the Virgin's attire. Elizabeth I may have been the Virgin Queen, though there are good reasons to doubt her chastity, but she was, famously, a Protestant.

Eliza's apologists insist that the story is not true. They maintain that the habit of making offerings of jewels to the Virgin of Caacupé did not begin until after the war, though according to Ambassador Washburn it had been going on for nearly a century by the time he arrived in Asunción. Even if Eliza did take the jewels, her defenders say, it would have been for the war effort, not her own personal gain. But even though money and jewellery could be smuggled out of the country, no arms or materiel could come in through Argentina because of the Brazilian blockade and, according to a British visitor to Paraguay at the time, 'trade with Bolivia is insignificant owing to the almost insuperable difficulties of communication'. Indeed, the trade was discouraged. One of

López's torturers Captain Adolfo Saguier said that both Bolivian traders and soldiers from Bolivia who entered Paraguay to fight on Francisco's side were 'sacrificed'.

With a comfortable retirement now assured, Eliza packed up her clothes, linen, china, jewellery and her Pleyel piano and set off for Humaitá, which was being bombarded by Brazilian ironclads at the time. When she arrived, Francisco demanded to know what she was doing there as she was supposed to be running the government in Asunción.

'The seat of government is wherever you are,' Eliza is said to have replied.

Although Humaitá was vaunted as the 'Sebastopol of South America', Sir Richard Burton was not impressed – though, admittedly, when he arrived there the Brazilians had blown up the citadel. Its strength lay, not in its fortifications, but its position. It lay on the outside of a tight bend in the river so that the fire from its batteries could be concentrated on any boat trying to take the turn. The bank there was twenty to thirty feet high, with swamps both upstream and downstream of it. However, though it effectively stopped the Brazilian ironclads sailing up the river to Asunción, they could stand off out of the range of the Paraguayan guns and bombard the fort at will.

Although Francisco's military headquarters were officially in the fort at Humaitá, he spent his time at Paso Pucú a few miles inland and safely out of range. His house there was also protected by a huge earthwork constructed by Colonel Thompson. At Paso Pucú, Francisco and Eliza still maintained decorum by living in separate establishments – though this may also have been to enable Francisco to entertain other mistresses. Eliza moved in next door and planted geraniums in flower beds bordered with white-washed pebbles. She also established a cemetery on the hills above the fort for the thirteen Englishmen who died in the Battle of Riachuelo and, although she was surrounded by death during the bombardment, it is said that she put fresh flowers on their graves every day.

Eliza also did a little humanitarian work at Humaitá. When General Díaz had his leg amputated by Dr Frederick Skinner, she went in her carriage to collect him from hospital. She also collected his leg which was soldered into a little coffin of its own. After a few days, Díaz died and he was sent to Asunción to be buried, along with instructions for the ladies of the town to lay more of their jewels on his tomb. Reading of this in *El Semanario*, Colonel Thompson noted that the article did not say what was done with the jewels afterwards.

Even though she was again pregnant, Eliza seems to have been quite fearless, walking to and fro without a care during the shelling, while López cowered in a shelter. One of the fort's batteries was named after her and, when Burton visited Humaitá, he noted that some of the ladders and walkways of the fortifications were swathed in hides and matting. This was 'an unusual precaution intended to conceal petticoated ankles,' he wrote. 'I was assured that from this point the undaunted Mrs Lynch used to direct bellicose operations.' The hangings were to prevent Francisco's troops from looking up her skirt while she directed the battle. In other accounts it is said that Eliza wore the uniform of a colonel in the Paraguayan Army when she went into action. But if the

Paraguayan troops risked being distracted by her 'petticoated ankles', the sight of her in tight cavalry riding breeches would surely have lost them any battle.

According to Cunninghame Graham, even those people who hated and feared Eliza and dismissed her as Madama Lynch or Madama Lavinche 'could not withhold their admiration for her good looks, and for the courage she showed when under fire'. Washburn also testified to Eliza's courage, in contrast to that of López, writing that she, 'in time of battle would expose herself where the danger was greatest'. But he also accused her of encouraging Francisco's natural cowardice by playing on his fears as a way to increase her influence over him.

In fact, Francisco was in no real danger. Thompson's fortifications had rendered his headquarters virtually bombproof. But Eliza would constantly beg him not to risk his valuable life by exposing himself to the danger of a stray bullet. Occasionally a bullet did hit his house at Paso Pucú, but any hole was quickly filled and whitewashed over to maintain the impression that the house was invulnerable.

Eventually, when a piece of shell fell on the roof of his house, he had an armoured casemate made – a nine-foot box of ironwood covered with nine feet of earth and more ironwood – where he could live during the shelling. His horse was saddled each day before dawn in case he had to flee. Its gold saddle-cloth was turned inside out and López gave up wearing fancy uniforms, wore a straw hat and banned his escort from wearing their flashy brass helmets, in case they drew the attention of snipers.

It was lucky that Eliza had a cool head to take command in the heat of battle. One day, when they were expecting an attack, López simply fled at daybreak leaving no orders and abandoning Eliza and the children. She had to go looking for him. She found him at about midday, cowering behind a hill. But while they were talking, two bullets came within about a mile. López thought they were aimed at him and he fled once more.

'He possessed a peculiar kind of courage,' said Thompson. 'When out of range of fire, even though completely surrounded by the enemy, he was always in high spirits, but he could not endure the whistle of a ball.'

When López fled from the slightest danger, his whole entourage had to flee with him as 'it would have been construed as worse than treason for them to show less fear than their chief'. And it was not just gunfire that frightened him. Although he could ride well from a young age, when he grew older and fatter he traded in his cavalry charger for a docile horse which rarely broke into a gallop. And he would not walk up the gangplank of a steamer without a trusted officer on each side of him to prevent him falling in the water. Those who saw his short steps and frightened looks said they would have shamed a woman of 80. This was not the story the Paraguayan public heard though. *El Semanario* consistently praised López for his valour, his generalship and his sacrifices, and said that the Paraguayan people could never pay the debt they owed him for daily leading his legions into battle and exposing his life to constant danger.

Eliza's dire warnings eventually engendered in the already unstable López a paranoia worthy of Dr Francia.

'With her at his side ever whispering that he was in great danger, that his enemies were plotting his destruction,' Washburn wrote, 'it is not strange that he was constantly haunted with the fear of treachery and assassination.'

López already had systems in place to feed his paranoia. Along with Palacios's priests, who reported what they heard in the confessional, Francisco had inherited a vast network of spies from Dr Francia and his father. Every third man spied on his neighbour and was given the authority to shoot them on the slightest suspicion of treason. Many took the opportunity of shooting their neighbour before they were shot themselves.

Fearing enemies all around him, López strengthened the double cordon of sentries around his house to a triple cordon. But he then became convinced that his own guards were plotting against him. One evening, as Colonel Thompson and a number of other officers were waiting to see López, Thompson exchanged a few words with the sergeant of the guards. Soon after the other waiting officers were arrested. Later, one of Francisco's aides-de-camp came to Thompson and said: 'His Excellency sends word to you to write down all the conversation you had with the sergeant of the guards and bring it tomorrow.'

Thompson did as he was told, but discovered that, by then, the sergeant of the guards was already dead and the rest of the guard had each received a hundred lashes. When he asked why, Thompson was told that the sergeant had been implicated in a plot to murder López. Thompson was bemused; all the sergeant had said to him was: 'Does Queen Victoria wear her crown when she goes out for a walk?'

According to Dr Stewart, López also believed that enemy agents were entering his camp dressed in women's clothing to poison him and his officers. While such conspiracies were plainly fanciful, no one dared contradict Eliza when she told tales of treason and assassination, only too aware of the risk of being denounced as an accomplice of the conspirators. But even if there were no direct attempts on his life, López cannot have been popular in Paraguay. 'I lived there so long that I got the confidence of quite a number of Paraguayans,' Washburn told the US House Foreign Affairs Committee later. 'They thought that I was a safe person to talk to. They told me that there was the most universal hypocrisy there; that there was not a man, woman or child who would not be delighted to know that López was forty feet under the ground.'

One of the reasons that López was so unpopular was that, while his troops starved, Eliza continued to maintain her lavish table. Regular dinner guests included Colonel Thompson, von Wisner, Bishop Palacios, General Barrios, Dr Stewart, Masterman and sometimes even Ambassador Washburn. These dinner parties were nervous affairs because of the constant shellfire, while despatches from the front were delivered to the dinner table. Eliza's presence was also unsettling. Dr Stewart wrote to his family in Edinburgh: 'Nobody felt at ease in her presence, despite her great beauty.'

Although Eliza tried to maintain culinary standards, Francisco did not go in for fancy food. Instead, he tucked into enormous quantities of 'rank and greasy food' – so much of it that Washburn speculated that López was more likely to die in bed from overindulgence than on the field of battle. Eliza also kept a good cellar, stocked with foreign wines and ale for her English visitors. But Eliza herself had more expensive tastes. Masterman said that she 'gave capital dinner parties and could drink more champagne without being affected by it than anyone I have ever met'. López drank claret and brandy. At dinner, he would keep the best wine for himself, serving inferior vintages to everyone else. And after dinner he would treat his guests to a drunken sing-song. Between meals he swilled brandy around his mouth to dull the pain of his rotten teeth and diseased gums, then spat it out on anyone who happened to be in the way. But as time went by he would swallow it down. In drunken rages he would then order torture and executions. Later, when he sobered up, he would rescind the orders, often to find that it was too late.

Again responsibility for this was laid at Eliza's door. Cunninghame Graham wrote: 'All those with whom I spoke in those far-off days who had known Madame Lynch testified to her ability, but were all agreed as to the evil influence she had on López, flattering his vanity, encouraging him to drink, and pushing him to enterprises that, with her knowledge of the world, she must have known were far beyond his power, and ruinous to a small country such as Paraguay.'

According to Thompson, at the beginning of the war López only drank at mealtimes. But as the war dragged on he would call out for glasses of port throughout the day. But when a soldier asked for a little brandy to give him courage before going into action, López told an officer to take him outside and kill him. The man duly had his head cleaved in two with a sword.

Although the Brazilians bombarded Humaitá with up to 4,000 shells a day, most of them landed harmlessly in the fort's earth ramparts and many failed to detonate.

The Paraguayans were soon low on ammunition as Mr Whytehead had committed suicide and the arsenal had become a shambles. At one point the only response the Paraguayans could make to the Brazilian bombardment was a short blast on their horn-like *turututús*. But Eliza proposed an idea. She persuaded López to offer a mugful of corn to anyone who collected an undetonated Brazilian shell. This was clearly an irresistible offer to starving troops and their camp followers. Unfortunately, many shells went off some time after they landed. Many Paraguayans, mainly the wives and girlfriends of the soldiers, were killed trying to recover them. Later, troops learnt that it was easier and safer to take shot from their own guns and claim the reward.

Otherwise the shelling had little effect as the Brazilian ironclads preferred to stay well out of range of the Paraguayan guns. Their only visible target was the spire of the church. Even then the Brazilian gunners were wildly inaccurate. One day a furious bombardment succeeded in killing only one aged cow. The man responsible for this inept performance was Admiral Tamandaré. He was to be loaded with honours by Pedro II and thanked personally by the Emperor for his valiant service – even though, as Thompson pointed out: 'His incapacity and his inertness cost the Empire many millions of dollars and many thousands of lives, and he left López stronger than he found him.'

However, even this wasteful expenditure actually worked to Paraguay's disadvantage. While Francisco had a full exchequer and nowhere to spend it, Brazil had to borrow to finance the war. She ran up such debts in Europe that her creditors could not afford to let the Allies lose. This was another reason no major power came to the aid of Paraguay. It was said that Brazil was like a man who had begun to dig a well, thinking that the water table was just a few feet below the surface but, when he found it was not, continued digging so that he did not waste the effort he had already put in.

As control of the river was key to the outcome of the war, the Paraguayans tried to retrieve some of the boats they had lost by sending barge-loads of men down the river at night. They would dress in white and paint their faces so the superstitious Brazilians would take them for evil spirits. Eliza always saw off these raiding parties personally, giving the departing soldiers cigars and other presents. When one such party recovered the hulk of a gunboat, López hailed it as a great victory. This gave the Paraguayans the courage to stage a daring canoe-borne attack on the Brazilian Navy. Eliza told the departing men to 'go and bring me back my ironclads'. The raid was unsuccessful and 200 men were lost.

The *Gualeguay*, one of the Argentinian boats seized at Corrientes, was sent out to harass the Brazilian fleet every afternoon. López would watch – from a safe distance – with a telescope and the little ship's antics amused him greatly. This went on for three weeks until the *Gualeguay* was sunk. While López sank into a deep depression, Eliza went to commiserate with the friends of the crew who had lost their lives, though they were stoical.

'We are sad for them,' said the dead men's comrades. 'Tomorrow they won't be having a good laugh at the *macacos*' – or monkeys, as the Paraguayans dismissively referred to the Brazilians.

Although the Paraguayans were proud of their racially

mixed background, there was a strong racial element to the war. Brazilians, both black and white, were referred to as 'cambas' – the equivalent of 'niggers'. Indeed, as the war went on, the complexion of the Brazilian Army changed. After 1867, when news reached Rio de Janeiro that cholera had killed over 13,000 men and 50 were employed full time burying the dead, the enlistment of free men ground to halt. African slaves were impressed into the army. López considered sending a slave army against him a deliberate insult, but *El Semanario* made much mileage out of it. Each time fresh recruits arrived, it was said that the Brazilians sent back the chains for the next batch of 'volunteers'.

While the Brazilian Army became increasingly black, the Paraguayan Army had only one black officer – and then only briefly. As a sergeant he had been sent out on a raiding party to the Allied camp and told to bring López back a trophy. He returned with nine Allied heads which he piled at López's front door. In recognition of this, he was promoted to ensign – the lowest commissioned rank – and sent into every action afterwards, effectively ensuring his death.

After failing to capture the Brazilian fleet, twice, López tried to blow it up. An American named Krüger and a Paraguayan who learnt engineering in London named Ramos fashioned some crude torpedoes, but only succeeding in blowing up themselves and killing the crews of their boats. Not one to be discouraged by the huge loss of life, López had more torpedoes fashioned by some English engineers. These were to be laid by Jaime Corbalàn, the son of one of the oldest families in Asunción who had been drafted into the army. He was to carry the missiles downstream in a canoe and detonate them in the middle of the Brazilian fleet. But as soon as Corbalàn was out of range of the Paraguayan guns, he surrendered to the Brazilians – 'to escape the tyranny of López,' he said.

His family had already suffered at Francisco's hands. His aunt, recently widowed at the time, was accused of saying something disrespectful about López. She was a quiet and timid woman and no one who knew her believed the charge. Nevertheless, she was confined to a dog kennel for six weeks with a sentry standing outside the door day and night.

Jaime Corbalàn's uncle, a priest, spent many years in jail before being executed in 1868. Jaime's mother Señora Oliva Corbalàn then bought a house from Eliza, which Eliza sold because it was too close to the *calabozo* and the screams of the prisoners disturbed her. But Doña Oliva put up with that in the hope of catching a glimpse of her brother and reassuring herself that he was still alive.

When her son surrendered himself and his torpedoes to the Allies, Doña Oliva was pressed into writing an article in *El Semanario* denouncing him. Her other two sons were sent to the front. One died from his wounds; the other from cholera. Then Doña Oliva was stripped of all her possessions, including her clothes, and exiled with her four daughters to the Chaco, where she died. One of the daughters went mad; the others were reduced to begging, slavery and prostitution.

Even at Humaitá Eliza kept up morale among the officers with dances and balls. And for the troops she organised a magic lantern show. She had ordered the apparatus from Paris before the war to amuse her children. Unfortunately the instructions that were to follow were held up in the Brazilian blockade. Nevertheless Colonel Thompson and George Masterman managed to rig it up and the troops were ordered to turn out for the show. They stood in a courtyard, clearly bemused, as coloured etchings from the *Illustrated London News* showing 'The Bay of Naples by Moonlight' or '*Un Chasseur d'Afrique* engaging ten Arabs at once' flashed up on an old sheet. Some of the slides showed scenes from the recent Franco-Italian campaign and Thompson, who was introducing the slides, tried to liven up the proceedings by misrepresenting the scenes, describing them as 'The Battle of Copenhagen, between the Persians and the Dutch', 'The Capture of the Jungfrau in the Final Charge at Magenta' and 'The Death of General Orders at the Moment of Victory'.

In the midst of the show, López was heard to say: 'Ah! That was a terrible affair – "The Field of Trafalgar after the Battle, showing the Mamelukes Removing the Wounded".'

'What Christian humanity, sire,' responded Bishop Palacios, without irony.

When the light from the screen illuminated Palacios, Masterman saw him stuffing a handkerchief into his mouth to try to stifle his laughter. What particularly amused Palacios was the picture of a dwarf whose nose gradually swelled to phallic dimensions. Then, when the Bishop's own nose got in the way of the lantern light and its elongated shadow was thrown across the screen, the troops reacted for the first time. They burst into laughter. López, it was said, laughed so much that tears ran down his face.

Palacios was less amused by the balloons the Brazilians deployed to try and discover why they were making so little impression on the Paraguayan defences. These came from France and cost $15,000 each. Secured by ropes, a spotter would be raised 300 feet into the air. Palacios was terrified because he believed the flying objects to be supernatural. When the first balloon caught fire, he rejoiced that it had been stricken by the hand of God. When a second disappeared into a passing cloud, he declared that it was unnatural for men to be given a glimpse of the hereafter before their time. However, his flock took no notice of their Bishop's dire pronouncements. They had an altogether more robust response. Contemporary etchings show the Paraguayan troops dropping their pants and mooning at the Brazilian aerial spotters. López ordered fires to be lit, obscuring the fort with smoke and suffocating the balloonists. That put paid to the experiment. Meanwhile the Frenchman in charge of the first balloon was arrested by the Allies for attempting to set fire to their powder magazines and sentenced to death. Palacios himself fell from favour, despite being a one-time dinner guest with Eliza and Francisco, when Pius IX issued a papal bull putting the See of Asunción under the authority of Buenos Aires. If a Churchman could not handle Church business, what good was he? López reasoned. Palacios was arrested, tortured and shot.

An Allied army of over 60,000 men now massed on the Paraguayan border. They were held at bay by batteries of dummy guns hastily rigged up by Colonel Thompson. All Francisco's military advisers urged him to stay within the walls of Humaitá and fight a defensive action. Even when the Allies had crossed the Paraná, they would then have to negotiate the marshland known as the Estero Bellaco that lay to the south of the fort. And the *macacos* feared the cholera and malaria that lurked there almost as much as they feared the Guaranís who were masters of swamp fighting. But stoked up by Eliza, López was in the grip of Napoleonic delusions and was determined to attack. To build up the strength of his army, he drafted all males between nine and 60. Women were left to plough the fields and work the slaughterhouses of Asunción, though the fruits of their labour were seized to feed the Army. The only men seen in the city were the police who were there to arrest any women who complained about the shortages or hardships, or who said they wished the war would end.

When the Allies crossed the Paraná, López hurled an army of 24,000 at the invaders, lead by the Fortieth Battalion. López had put all the sons of the aristocracy into this single battalion. Fearing treachery, he gave them no weapons and no training, and they had to lead the charge barefoot and unarmed. In one stroke, Paraguay shed the last of its Spanish blood. Only two of the Fortieth Battalion survived to be captured, and one of those died soon after. Those who had been slaughtered were denounced as traitors and their property confiscated.

El Semanario boasted that 971 Allied soldiers were killed and 3,000 thousand wounded in the Battle of Estero Bellaco. The newspaper did not say that the action was a complete fiasco. The truth was that López was no Napoleon. He had no understanding of the importance of the lie of the land. His plan of attack called for his troops to take the enemy by surprise at dawn. But they had found themselves in a pine forest which they had had to hack their way through with axes. They reached the enemy at midday, long after Allied scouts had seen them coming. Six thousand Paraguayans died and 350 were captured. The 7,000 wounded made it home, it was said, wearing looted uniforms with their pockets full of gold, which Eliza swiftly changed into paper currency.

The paper could also boast that only one Paraguayan officer had been killed by the enemy – and that was because he was old and so fat he could hardly walk. But in fact, López had emptied his dungeons of officers whom he had jailed on various whims since he had been elected President, demoted them to sergeant, freed them from their shackles and sent them out to fight. All of them were killed.

General Barrios, who had led the charge, was another casualty. When the action failed to push the Allies back across the Paraná, he was arrested. Terrified of torture, he attempted suicide. When he survived, he was tortured so brutally that he went insane. When his wife, Doña Inocencia, cursed López for his cruelty, she was savagely flogged, forced to write a denunciation for the newspaper and imprisoned – even though she was Francisco's own sister. Eventually Barrios was shot while his wife and sister looked on.

Although defeat in the Battle of Estero Bellaco lost López half his army and helped lose him the war, it put the fear of God into the Allies. 'Officers from the Allied camp wrote from the battlefield that the carnage had been something frightful as no human power could make the Paraguayans surrender and then, every single individual would rather fight on, with certain death before them,' wrote Colonel Thompson in his book *The War in Paraguay*.

Thompson himself was in awe of the Paraguayan troops. 'A Paraguayan soldier never complained of an injustice and was perfectly contented with whatever his superior demanded – if he was flogged, he consoled himself by saying: "If my father did not flog me, who would?" Everyone called his superior officer his father and subordinate his son.'

A corporal was allowed to give any man three lashes with a stick. A sergeant could give twelve and an officer as many as he liked. Such floggings were commonplace. A girl from Corrientes who had been brought back to Paraguay with the army, was caught trying to escape, and was given 60 lashes in public on her bare flesh, Thompson noted, 'which was considered a very good joke'.

This casual brutality was part of the system López had adopted at the beginning of the war and which almost guaranteed that he would lose. His men were trained to be mere machines and do whatever they were told, without a thought for their own lives – so they never acted on their own initiative. They were to fight desperately whatever the odds and never surrender – so they often sacrificed themselves needlessly. Meanwhile López remained safely in his headquarters in a central position where he could keep an eye on his subordinates in case they were plotting against him, so he never understood what his men were going through and his officers were too terrified to criticise his more deranged orders or even make suggestions. In the field, every soldier was responsible for the conduct of at least five others. If any man lagged or faltered, it was the duty of the two men either side of him to shoot him, or be shot themselves. The non-commissioned officer set over them was responsible for the behaviour of them all. If one of them escaped, he would be flogged or shot when the battle was over, while defeated units were regularly decimated and their officers shot. Consequently, good men and battle-hardened troops were disposed of. Francisco's system was a very efficient meat grinder that would eventually consume the entire male population of Paraguay and fill the country with piles of corpses.

After the Battle of Estero Bellaco, the Allies had the grisly chore of clearing up the battlefield. They buried their own dead, but heaped up the Paraguayan corpses in huge pyres, alternating layers of bodies and layers of wood, 50 or 100 bodies to a pyre. But when they lit the pyres, the bodies were so lean that they would not burn. When Thompson returned to the battlefield six weeks later he saw that the bodies had not decomposed. Instead they were 'completely mummified, the skin having dried on the bones, and the bodies looking tawny and thin'.

Terrified of the fanatical enemy they found themselves up against, the Allies halted their advance. This gave Colonel Thompson time to construct a new line of defence downstream from Humaitá on the 30-foot cliff at Curupaity. Meanwhile López cleared the hospitals of the walking wounded. Six weeks later, he fielded a rag-tag army of 20,000 and hurled them at the Allies, causing 5,000 casualties for the loss of 2,500. This was hailed as a great victory and gave time for Colonel Thompson to have trenches dug 3,000 yards downstream from Curupaity at Curuzú.

By this point the war was being conducted with unprecedented savagery. Paraguayan boy soldiers were told to slit the throats of the wounded. Brazilians suspected of being spies were thrown alive into the cages of hungry jaguars. Allied officers who escaped that fate were driven ahead of the Paraguayans when they advanced, as a human shield. Not that the Allies behaved any better. Paraguayan prisoners of war who did not 'volunteer' to fight against their own side were shot.

When the Allies attacked Curuzú, the small garrison there killed thousands and sunk an ironclad. But eventually, in the face of overwhelming odds the Paraguayans withdrew. López, who himself had fled to the safety of his bombproof earthworks at Paso Pucú, was furious. He had every tenth man shot in front of the whole battalion. Officers drew straws. Those who drew the short straws were demoted. The rest were shot.

Although the Paraguayans were gradually being pushed back, the Allies found fighting from trench to trench, in a way that would only become familiar in Europe 50 years later in the First World War, was so costly that López figured he could sue for peace on favourable terms. He sent a note to General Mitre requesting a truce.

On the morning of 12 September 1866, López rode out in full-dress uniform with a new kepi and gloves. He wore a grenadier's patent leather boots and gold spurs in imitation of Napoleon. Over his uniform he wore his favourite poncho, made of scarlet cloth lined with vicuna, with a golden fringe around the edge and a high collar magnificently embroidered in gold. By this time he had put on so much weight that he filled the entire back seat of his American buggy. He was accompanied by twelve-year-old Panchito dressed in the uniform of a colonel in the Paraguayan Army.

Two hundred yards from the enemy lines, López got out of the buggy and struggled to mount his favourite white mare, which was so completely covered with silver trappings that they formed a coat of mail. He was so afraid of being shot he had an escort of 24 cavalrymen huddled around him like sheep and a battalion of riflemen hidden in the undergrowth nearby. Halfway to the meeting point, he came over faint and had to be revived with brandy.

While López could have been dressed for one of Eliza's fancy dress balls, Mitre turned up to the meeting in a baggy old suit and a battered black broad-brimmed 'Jim Crow' felt hat. This was Mitre's trademark and the badge of his party, and was known in Buenos Aires as '*El Sombrero Mitre*'. The two presidents saluted each other with unsheathed swords and dismounted. Some chairs had been placed in a jungle clearing and the two of them sat and talked for five hours. Francisco argued that enough blood had already been spilt to wipe out their mutual grievances. Mitre pointed out that, under the terms of the Triple Alliance, to make peace López had to be removed from the government of Paraguay. He would have to abdicate and go into exile in Europe. If he did so, it was made clear that it would be made worth his while financially. López agreed, then stipulated that he must be allowed to return to Paraguay after two years. According to one account, Mitre was about to concede this point too, when López changed his mind again. He wobbled drunkenly to his feet and cried: 'I will never yield an inch of this sacred soil nor forsake Paraguay unless I die.'

The two presidents exchanged riding crops and toasted each other's health in brandy. They parted amicably, though Panchito hurled a torrent of abuse at the departing Mitre. López, Thompson said, looked 'very black' after the interview. Over dinner Eliza consoled him, though she was very cross with Panchito for his rudeness. She considered his outburst a sign of ill-breeding. Meanwhile Mitre sent a report back to Buenos Aires saying: 'López has returned to his base to fulfil his destiny as *el verdugo de la Patria*' – the hangman of his country.

Mitre had not entirely given up hope of making peace though. There was still a possibility that López might agree to his terms and he did not resume the bombard-ment of Humaitá. However, during the armistice, two of Mitre's aides-de-camp and a couple of men from the Paraguayan Legion who were fighting on the Allied side had crossed the lines to take *maté* with the Paraguayan advanced guard. They were seized. The aides-de-camps were jailed, and later died of starvation and ill-treatment. The Paraguayans were flogged to death and the bombardment resumed.

From then on Mitre became the devil incarnate in Francisco's twisted mind. He had a patrol of Guaranís racked because they would not say that they had seen Mitre's body dead on the battlefield. Two Argentine deserters were flogged until they 'admitted' they had smallpox and had been sent by Mitre to infect the Paraguayan ranks, then they were flogged to death. López denounced Mitre daily in *El Semanario*, often in the most scatological terms. Almost every week the paper announced that Mitre was dead, though he lived for another 40 years.

Francisco's hysterical rants against Mitre did not abate even when he no longer faced him across the lines. Mitre's 'three-month' war had already lasted a year-and-a-half when a revolt broke out in Argentina and he had to go home to quell it. He was replaced as commander of the Allied forces by the Marquis of Caxias, a Brazilian.

With Mitre out of the way, Eliza encouraged Francisco to sue for peace once more. The American Ambassador Charles Washburn was asked to act as a peace envoy. He was summoned to Humaitá where he was persuaded to affirm the principle that every nation had the right to chose its own government. In a preliminary letter to Caxias, he said that insisting Mariscal López resign as a precondition of peace was the equivalent of asking Dom Pedro to abdicate his throne or President Mitre to renounce his presidency. This annoyed the Allies, who retaliated by holding up Washburn's provisions and mail that came in from Buenos Aires. A copy of the letter containing this diplomatic gaffe was then published in *El Semanario*, hopelessly compromising Washburn. It was a ruse to embroil the United States in the conflict. Eliza and Francisco still had hopes of recruiting the United States onto their side as the US Navy's South American Squadron had run the blockade, at Washburn's insistence, when he returned from home leave in September 1865. What they did not know was that the incident had caused a rift between the Navy and the State Department, sparking a Congressional enquiry that went on long after the war was over. To ingratiate himself further with Washburn, López had the landlord of the Ambassador's residence jailed, so that Washburn would have to pay no rent.

Though the odds were now stacked against him, Washburn made a genuine attempt to meditate. He went to see Caxias, who mentioned the old Portuguese saying, 'always provide a golden bridge for a fleeing enemy.' By this he meant that, if López were to leave Paraguay, the Brazilians would make it worth his while financially. When Washburn returned to the Paraguayan lines, he mentioned the 'golden bridge' to López. Francisco replied – surely to Eliza's horror – that he was not interested in money. He said that he would never leave Paraguay. He would stay there and fall with his last guard. His enemies should only have the satisfaction of seeing his tomb. He did not want to be a South American hero like Simón Bolívar or General Belgrano. He wanted to be a Washington or a Lincoln – and if his whole people had to die to achieve his grandiose ambitions, that was the way it would be.

To Washburn this talk was demented. He pulled out all the stops to persuade López that the Allies were in an overwhelming position. He told him of the great style in which the Marquis of Caxias was living and how his men enjoyed fresh meat from the markets of Montevideo. He gave López an accurate map that the Brazilians had made of his defences to show him how good their intelligence was and he warned him that General Osorio was about to cross the Paraná at Encarnación with 10,000 men. In response, López pointed out some minor mistakes on the Brazilian map and boasted that Osorio would be cut to pieces in the narrow gorges of the eastern part of the country, inland from Encarnacion. So Washburn appealed directly to Francisco's Napoleonic delusions, pointing out that the French Emperor was no less honoured for having died in exile on St Helena, but this only convinced López that the American Ambassador had turned against him.

ᨢᤦ 10 ᨢᤦ

THE CHARM OFFENSIVE

By this time, Uruguay had dropped out of the war and Argentina's participation was strictly limited, but Francisco's habit of jailing foreigners for no discernible reason prompted the navies of Britain, France, Italy and the United States to join the Brazilian blockade. It was clear to Eliza that what was needed was a diplomatic charm offensive. The foreign ambassadors that López baited were plainly reporting back to their governments terrible things about the situation in Paraguay – in other words, the truth. So foreign naval officers from the blockading fleets were invited to Paso Pucú. They were treated to a lavish meal served by the beautiful Eliza herself. Then they would be allowed to visit compatriots, who had themselves been fed well beforehand and were interviewed within earshot of Francisco's secret police.

'The very men who would gladly have given anything they had in the world to get away from Paraguay would not dare to express a word of discontent, or hint at a wish to return to their native land,' said Washburn.

After these interviews, the naval officers would accept a 'trifling present' from Eliza's own hand before leaving the country. Apparently 'a good dinner, a ring, a towel of

Paraguayan manufacture or a *tercia* of *yerba* was sufficient for them to betray their trust and leave their countrymen to be tortured and executed'. The naval officers reported that they had seen no sign of want or suffering in Paraguay and that none of their compatriots wished to leave. Newspapers throughout the world carried stories saying that Francisco Solano López was a wise and just ruler – and that stories of his cruelty were merely Allied propaganda.

'It is a singular fact that every naval officer who went though Francisco's encampment came away a friend, apologist, and defender of the tyrant,' wrote Washburn, 'while all who went in a diplomatic capacity afterwards represented him to their governments as a monster without parallel.'

Laurent Cochelet and his wife were in this second category. Mme Cochelet had been a long-time enemy of Eliza and the situation for Mme Cochelet had been exacerbated after the colony at New Bordeaux collapsed. The colonists died from starvation, heat exhaustion and Indian attack. Those who tried to flee the colony were beaten, tortured and put to death by Francisco's soldiers. Cochelet protested, but López ignored him. Von Wisner had told him that Napoleon III was too involved with his half-baked scheme to make the Austrian Archduke Maximilian Emperor of Mexico to concern himself with the fate of a few hundred French colonists. López then started harassing Cochelet by arresting and mistreating other French citizens and holding the Ambassador virtually incommunicado. For over a year, López would have nothing to do with the French Ambassador. Conse-quently no one else dared speak to him – though many were accused of receiving letters smuggled in in Cochelet's diplomatic bag.

When Washburn returned from leave, he urged López to let the Cochelets leave. Eventually a French warship turned up at Humaitá to collect them. But López delayed its departure for nine days, while M. and Mme Cochelet were held in a room within the line of fortifications under constant bombardment by the Brazilians in the hope that a stray cannon ball might finish them off. To López's chagrin a shell fell on the house and exploded in the middle of the room where they had been imprisoned, the day after they left. They had nearly suffered the death penalty for an offence that was not tolerated in Paraguay: snubbing Madame Lynch.

When Cochelet reached Paris and reported the true state of affairs in Paraguay to Napoleon III – including the fact that a number of French citizens were at risk of being murdered if they were not rescued – the Emperor refused to believe him as his testimony was so much at variance with the reports he had received from others who had visited Paraguay recently. There were over 100 French citizens still living in Paraguay at the beginning of the war; only three survived.

M. Cochelet was replaced by M. Cuberville who, according to Washburn, 'at once became the apologist and flatterer of López and Madame Lynch'. He became a regular guest at Eliza's dinner table and used his diplomatic pouch to smuggle Eliza's booty through the blockade to her bank in Paris.

Inside Paraguay the Brazilian blockade was taking its toll. There were increasing shortages of even basic necessities such as salt. All sorts of ingenious substitutes were tried, including boiling leaves and mixing them with ash. None worked and lack of salt cost thousands of Paraguayan lives during the war.

Soap was made from animal fat and wine was fermented from oranges – though the latter was not a great success, as the result was undrinkably sweet. Baron von Fischer-Treuenfeld, the director of the telegraph company, found a way to make paper out of *caraguata*, a kind of native pineapple, and ink was made from berries mixed with powder from the arsenal. All the guns and other military hardware were made by English engineers, most of whom had never done that type of work before. They even had to build their own machine tools to make the guns with. To make gunpowder, they had to extract saltpetre from urine and rotten meat, and sulphur from iron pyrites – fool's gold. This was all the harder because López apparently took fool's gold to be the real thing. He was deeply suspicious of the foreign munitions workers and frequently jailed them for stealing what, in irrational moments, he took to be precious metal.

Hides were stretched over drums, beaten and scraped to make clothes for the troops. This worked well enough until it rained. The skins shrank and then became so stiff that the wearer could not bend his arms or legs. The newspapers in Rio de Janeiro reported that these strait-jackets were a new instrument of torture designed by Eliza herself. Apparently, naked prisoners were dragged up on to the roof of the prison, where executioners forced them into Eliza's fiendish shrinking clothes.

'These garments,' read one account, 'are cut from green hides and so designed that they conform tightly to the lines of the body. As they dry out under the sun, the hides contract and tighten, squeezing the body of the poor wretch under torture like the coils of a boa constrictor . . . but more slowly and less mercifully. With devilish ingenuity, this woman has learnt to cut the garments so that the maximum pressure can be brought slowly and crushingly to beat upon any pre-determined part of the body.'

This report was either entirely fanciful or the clothing so lethally effective that no account has survived by anyone who was forced to wear it.

Aubusson carpets from the ballroom of the Casino Nacional in Asunción were cut up to make ponchos. There was, however, no shortage of cotton. But, as one historian has pointed out, what was the use of having fresh underwear when you are starving?

Cholera swept through the population with over 50 deaths being reported daily. López himself was stricken – not with the disease but with the fear of it. He became quite mad and forbade anyone to use the word 'cholera'. Instead the men called it 'chain' – each man who fell was one more deadly link. Dr Stewart prescribed Francisco a bromide to calm him, but López refused to take it and accused the doctor of trying to poison him. This may have indeed been the case. With no quinine left in the country, doctors were instead prescribing arsenic as a cure for malaria. Stewart was arrested for conspiring against López by excusing too many sick men from service. So when López eventually collapsed with a fever, no one knew what to do. Eliza was in Asunción, organising the slaughter of animals, agricultural production and the construction of roads with her all-women work details. She had to be informed but the commanders at Humaitá dared not use the telegraph in case the news of López's illness got out and spread alarm. Panchito had to ride from Humaitá to Asunción to tell her. Eliza rushed back on a river steamer. She nursed Francisco day and night, sleeping on the floor at his bedside as his house was rocked by the bombardment. She mopped his brow, changed his sheets and hung up eucalyptus leaves to keep the mosquitoes away. No one else was allowed in the room. Eventually the fever broke and, when Francisco pulled though, he had a gold medal struck with the profile of Eliza on one side and the words *Defensora Paraguensis* on the other. It was the highest order in the land.

Francisco and Eliza then returned to Asunción for a *Te Deum* to celebrate his birthday and his survival. The High Mass thanking God for Francisco's deliverance from the cholera was held in the still unfinished Catedral de la Encarnación.

'The worm-eaten cathedral looked as if it were about to cave in with the weight of the throng which included strays dogs and baskets of live chickens,' wrote one chronicler.

Eliza outshone the ladies of Asunción in a simple black mantilla, while crippled veterans cheered Francisco. A crowd of women, including a dozen past or present mistresses, read speeches praising Francisco, kindly prepared for them by the government. Afterwards, in the unfinished shell of his palace, Francisco was given a diamond-hilted sword with St George and the Dragon picked out on the guard in jewels and gold scabbard, a golden inkstand and a book containing the adulatory speeches with gold covers a quarter of an inch thick. This was presented by a delegation that included his brother-in-law, the Chancellor Saturnino Bedoya. But once the ceremony was over, Bedoya was promptly arrested for robbing the Treasury. Rafaela begged Eliza to save her husband. This missing money had been given to Eliza and Bedoya pleaded with her to tell the truth.

'Nobody likes to hear the truth, Don Saturnino,' Eliza is reputed to have said.

No one would listen to Bedoya when he claimed that Eliza had taken the money from the Treasury because Eliza had taken the opportunity to tell López that Bedoya was involved in a plot to assassinate him and replace him as President with his brother Benigno. Bedoya was tortured, but his spine was broken and he died mercifully quickly. This infuriated López who was denied the pleasure of tormenting his brother-in-law further and said that, had he known his brother-in-law was dying, he would have had him shot for the sake of appearances. Benigno and Rafaela were then arrested, beaten and jailed. Now both Francisco's sisters had been widowed by his reign of terror, flogged and imprisoned. Everyone who had anything to do with the Treasury was arrested, tortured and shot, so Eliza's secret was safe.

Then came the news that the Brazilians had retaken the Matto Grosso. Over a period of two years, they had gone to extraordinary lengths to infiltrate men overland. The Brazilians had even armed the Indians with rifles, but instead of using them to fight they shot game. Nevertheless, when the Brazilians attacked, the Paraguayans were ordered to fall back. Five thousand Brazilians then marched on Paraguay, believing that López had no forces in the north. But they were struck down with cholera. A few hundred men López sent up the river seized their supplies and despatched those who had survived the epidemic. Perversely López kept this great victory to himself. The Paraguayans then retook Corumbá, but lost it again. López made much out of this defeat, claiming that the expedition's leader, Lieutenant-Colonel Cabral, had sold the town to the enemy and that he and his priest had been butchered and eaten by the Brazilians for their treachery.

In August 1867, shortly after Eliza and Francisco returned to Humaitá, the secretary of the British Legation in Buenos Aires G. Z. Gould arrived on board HMS *Doterel*, once again to check on the welfare of British subjects in Paraguay. Gould was particularly concerned because the contracts of most of the Englishmen working in Paraguay had long since expired. López insisted that all the British men in his service were happy and did not want to leave the country. And he spent the rest of the interview picking up on errors in the French Gould used in his diplomatic notes, rather than addressing their substance.

Eliza turned all her charm on Gould. He had been told to expect to meet a common prostitute, but found to his surprise that she was a cultivated woman. She invited him to dine in an effort to convince him that there were no shortages in Paraguay. It was said that he was won over by a plum pudding made by Eliza herself.

In fact, Gould was not deceived. In his official despatch, he wrote: 'The whole country is ruined and all but depopulated. The cattle in most of the estates have entirely disappeared. The slaves, of whom there were still 40,000, have been emancipated, the males sent to the army and the females, with other women, forced to work in gangs for the government.'

Gould continued: 'Many estates have been altogether abandoned. The scanty crops raised by women are monopolised for the supply of the troops. The women have been obliged to part with all their jewels and gold ornaments, this extreme measure being called a patriotic offering on their part.

'Three epidemics, measles, smallpox and cholera, besides privations of all sorts, have reduced the population of this unfortunate country by more than a third. The mortality amongst the children has been dreadful and both scurvy and itch are very prevalent.'

He went on to report on the military situation: 'The Paraguayan forces amount altogether to about 20,000 men, of these 10,000 or 12,000 are good troops, the rest mere boys from twelve to fourteen years of age, old men and cripples, besides 2,000 to 3,000 sick and wounded. The men are worn out with exposure, fatigue and privations. They are actually dropping down from inanition [starvation]. They have been reduced for the last six months to meat alone and that of a very inferior quality. They may once in a while get a little Indian corn; mandioc and salt are so scarce that I fully believe these are only served out to the hospitals. There must be, from what I saw, a great scarcity of drugs and medicines, if not a total want of them for the sick, whose number is rapidly increasing. The horses have nearly all died off and the few hundred which yet remain are so weak and emaciated they can scarcely carry their riders. The draught oxen are in a dreadful state and cannot last much longer. The cattle are dying very fast from want of pasture. Many of the soldiers are in a state bordering on nudity, having only a piece of tanned leather around their loins, a ragged shirt, and a poncho made of vegetable fibre.'

Gould estimated that Paraguay had lost 100,000 men, 80,000 of disease alone. However, Masterman, who was in a better position to know, reckoned that some 200,000 men passed through the army.

As an astute diplomat, rather than a naïve naval officer who could be charmed by Eliza, Gould was not permitted to speak to any of the British subjects López was holding, with the exception of Dr Stewart, who was considered to be too valuable to be left in chains. Before the interview, López warned Stewart to be very careful what he said. Gould was not to know that most of the British wanted to leave the country. However, in the end, López did allow Gould to leave with the widows and children of three English mechanics who had died in the service of Paraguay.

In an attempt to ease the situation, Gould offered to make another attempt at mediation and, after consider-able toing and froing, an eight-point peace plan was drawn up. This stipulated that Allied forces would with-draw from Paraguayan territory, while Paraguayan forces would withdraw from Brazilian territory. Prisoners of war would be exchanged. The integrity of Paraguay would be recognised by the Allies. Any outstanding territorial disputes would be settled by the arbitration of neutral powers and the Parguayan Army – or what was left of it – would be disbanded. The eighth and final clause read: 'His Excellency the Marshal President, at the conclusion of peace, or the preliminaries thereof, will retire to Europe . . .' on board HMS *Doterel*, it was implied.

Gould presented the peace plan to the Allies. But before they had time to respond, it was repudiated by López. There is some dispute as to why. *El Semanario* said that the eighth article, stipulating that López would abdicate, had been added by the Allies. Ambassador Washburn said that Gould drew up the peace plan without reference to Francisco and Luis Caminos, Francisco's secretary, wrote to Gould telling him that it had 'never been assented to by López'.

According to Colonel Thompson: 'The real reason why López refused the terms which he had previously accepted was that, while Mr Gould was in the Allied camp offering them, he received news of a revolt in the Argentine Confederation, which he expected would force the Allies to make peace with him on any terms.'

There is another story. In his book *Eliza Lynch: Regent of Paraguay*, Henry Lyon Young suggests that López had drawn up the peace plan without Eliza's knowledge. When she found out, two days after Gould had taken the prosposals to Caxias, she was furious with López. In his presence, she summoned Caminos and dictated a new eighth article saying that the best guarantee for the future of Paraguay was to let 'Marshal López follow the lot which God has in store for the Paraguayan nation . . .'

It continued: 'The Republic of Paraguay will never stain its honour and glory by consenting that the President and its Defender, who has fought for its existence and made countless sacrifices should descend from his post, and still less that he should suffer expatriation from the scene of his heroism and sacrifices.' According to Young, while she dictated this despatch to Gould, Francisco's eyes welled with tears and he mumbled: '*Mi destino. Mi destino.* I bow before my destiny.'

Thompson suggests that when López favoured running away it was Madame Lynch who steadied his nerve. And Cunninghame Graham wrote: 'There is little doubt that although López was as obstinate as a male mule, as ran the saying, and certainly imbued, if not with patriotism, at least with a certain pride in his own country, he was entirely underneath the thumb of the designing woman whose education was superior, and will stronger than his own.'

It cannot have been difficult to persuade the paranoid dictator that he would not be safe in exile abroad. Thousands of Paraguayans, whose families he had persecuted and killed, had fled and would be only too happy to revenge themselves on him whether he were in London, Paris or New York.

Besides, the military situation was far from irretrievable. On 31 August 1867; *The Times* of London reported: 'After a campaign of two years the Allies held but about nine square miles of Paraguayan territory, a space hardly more than sufficient to contain (were they laid side by side) the bodies of those who had perished from sickness and wounds during the attempts to gain possession of it. A report on the military operations which was transmitted to the Foreign Office of London in April states that the Allies could not then place in the field more than 32,000 effective men, a fifth of these being three months' recruits; [however] the whole number of the troops of López was supposed to be reduced to about 20,000, and they were suffering great privations.'

But what impressed *The Times* correspondent was the

'real devotion to the service of López, which is said on all sides to be beyond the powers of belief of those who have not witnessed it'. The article goes on to say: 'The devotion of the Paraguayans to their leader – whether inspired by love or terror is not clear – almost surpasses belief. They have been repeatedly cut down at the very muzzles of the guns which they have been madly endeavouring to drag by main force out of the embrasures. It is, however, confidently asserted that they have never been able to withstand in the open field the bayonet charges of the Brazilian infantry, and that of late they have shown signs of discouragement.'

Nevertheless, according to *The Times* the Paraguayans simply refused to surrender, however impossible their position. They regarded their President-General with something little short of religious awe and received his civil and military orders in a spirit of unquestioning obedience.

'Whatever the faults or deeds of cruelty that may be urged against López,' said *The New York Times*, 'it is impossible to maintain that he rules by mere arbitrary power or terrorism. No personal government based on such a foundation could have stood the strains to which that of López has been subjected. It is to be hoped that the time for mediation cannot be far off. The Allies must see the impossibility of achieving their object without simply destroying the Paraguayan race from the face of the earth. And even supposing that they are prepared to attempt and able to accomplish this, the blood and treasure which they would have to expend would be utterly out of proportion to the stake at issue.'

But in fact the time for mediation had passed.

Thompson, rather closer to the action than the newspaper correspondents, described the rejection of Gould's peace plan as 'horrible selfishness . . . perhaps without parallel. The Allies were disposed to grant such terms that might have been dictated to them by a conqueror. All he had to do was leave the country with every honour. Instead he preferred to sacrifice the last man, woman and child of a brave, devoted suffering people, simply to keep himself in power a little while longer . . .

'The sacrifices and heroism he speaks of in his [or perhaps Madame Lynch's] letter are all false,' Thompson continued, 'as he never once exposed his person, and he had every commodity and luxury which he could wish for.'

Although López might have been short of courage, humility and selflessness, it was said that he had quite a sense of humour. While no one dared tell a joke in his presence, he liked making them himself – though his wit was black to say the least. When Gould returned from his failed peace mission to Caxias, López played a practical joke on him. With Gould and Commander Michel of the *Doterel* on shore at Humaitá, López had the British ensign lowered. Thinking the British had left, the Brazilians resumed shelling. One shell landed near to Michel, covering him with sand. This incident provided Eliza with a topic for 'excellent after-dinner jokes for some time to come,' according to one dinner guest. Gould, however, was not amused. He suspected that López had been hoping a Brazilian shell would silence him forever.

With his peace plan in tatters, Gould returned to Buenos Aires and the blood bath continued. But

Francisco was fast running out of men – Gould estimated his forces were down to 12,000. So, once they had made one final 'patriotic contribution' of what was left of their jewellery – this time with police assistance – every woman between sixteen and 40 was conscripted. That is, they were forced to beg López be allowed to volunteer.

'The tyrant and his whore have taken our husbands, our sons, our fathers, our jewels, our money, our possessions – what else is there left for them to take but ourselves,' one woman told Ambassador Washburn.

Women were taught to use the lance, though they were never issued with firearms. It was feared that one of them might have been tempted to take a pot shot at Eliza. And under her direction, the ladies of Asunción were assigned 'all kinds of menial labour, to keep the camps in order, to cut and bring wood, and even, towards the war's end, to work in the trenches'.

The Times also reported that women were fighting 'by the side of the men, as the bodies of several have been found among the heaps of the slain'. Some more fanciful accounts of Eliza's life have her riding at the head of a battalion of amazons. Sir Richard Burton heard tales of these amazons, but assumed it was propaganda. Such images were certainly used. Burton saw a Paraguayan cartoon showing the Empress of Brazil reviewing a body of Allied 'soldieresses' preparing for war. He also saw, on the Allied side, 'women – Brazilian mulattresses and Argentine "Chinas" – . . . mounted *en Amazone* . . .

'They distinguished themselves as the hardest riders', he said, 'and it is difficult to keep them out of the fire. They are popularly numbered at 4,000, but this surely must be an exaggeration. It is bad enough to have any at all. Some of them have passed through the whole campaign, and these "brevet captains" must fill the hospitals. My Brazilian friends declared them to be a necessary evil. I can see the evil, but not the necessity. Anything more hideous and revolting than such specimens of femininity it is hard to imagine.'

Given Burton's attitude, it is perhaps not hard to see why he might dismiss the idea of such 'brevet captains' on the Paraguayan side as well.

With or without his mounted amazons, Caxias tried to cut off Humaitá by circling it to the east. But the land was marshy and his troops got bogged down. López chose this moment to attack. Eight thousand Paraguayans stormed the Allies' main camp, throwing the enemy into confusion. Some fled back to the Paraná where officers competed with camp followers for boats to carry them back across the river.

This could have been a major victory for Francisco. Had his forces followed through, they would have forced the Allies out of Paraguay completely. Instead his men stopped to loot the Allies' stores for food and much needed matériel. This saved the Allies from a major defeat. Reinforcements were rushed up and the Paraguayans were forced to retreat. Allied losses were around 1,700 killed, wounded and captured. They also lost stores, munitions and artillery. But the looting did the Paraguayans little good. Many of the Guaranís who had sacked the enemy camp failed to make it back to their own lines. Those who did regretted it.

To prevent the Brazilian ironclads getting up the river, the Paraguayans had strung chains loaded with torpedoes across the river. But the Paraguay was abnormally high in

February 1868 and the Brazilians managed to sail over them. Now they could lay siege to Humaitá from both north and south and López realised that his position there was untenable. On the afternoon of 2 March, he ordered that the prisoners of war be butchered. According to Masterman, between 1,500 and 2,000 were mercilessly put to death. That night López's casemate was dismantled, so that there would be no evidence of his cowardice. Meanwhile he crossed the river to Timbó with 8,000 men. Eliza made the journey with Francisco in a rowing boat. From there they headed north across the Chaco. Eliza travelled in a coach pulled by horses taken from a post house. She and Francisco slept in other post houses along the way. Further on, the road grew more difficult, until it was merely a cart track through swampy woods. They had to make make-shift bridges across swamps and cross rivers in canoes. Eliza's carriage got stuck in mud three-feet deep and had to be heaved out using every horse they had. The men were frequently mired up to their waists in mud. The sick and weak drowned. And many of the artillery pieces that they managed to drag along behind them with superhuman effort had to be abandoned. Despite the conditions, López always made sure that Eliza and the children were well looked after. With his exhausted army sleeping in the open on the grass, he ordered a hut to be built of branches for Eliza and the family. Francisco himself was reduced to sleeping in a hammock. Despite the chronic shortage of rations, Eliza made sure the family ate well and, while the army struggled forward, she and Francisco would take an afternoon siesta under the trees.

Colonel Thompson, who was with the column,

believed that López was intending to march on through the Chaco to Bolivia, then escape to Europe with Eliza. He made no attempt to strengthen the river defences to prevent the Brazilian ironclads reaching Asunción and he had five cartloads of silver dollars brought up from the city. But then, perhaps under the influence of Eliza, he seemed to change his mind.

Benigno López, still regarded as Francisco's most likely successor, was brought from Asunción in chains and kept under guard. The army re-crossed the river. Colonel Thompson built new batteries and earthworks at the mouth of the Tebicuary, the largest tributary to the east of the Paraguay. And López then moved his headquarters four miles up the river to San Fernando. A new telegraph line was laid so that he could relay his orders from safety.

At San Fernando López entertained himself with women, who were kept under guard in a special village built for them. He also enjoyed the comforts of family life and would take his sons fishing in the lagoon in the afternoons. And he occupied spare moments having his most loyal lieutenants tortured and killed.

Around this time López got religion. He had a chapel built in front of his quarters, where he would attend mass each day at noon, sometimes spending three or four hours on his knees, still and silent before the altar. However, his Christian charity did not extend to his mother Doña Juana who visited him there and pleaded for the lives of Benigno and Venancio, who had also been arrested. She also begged him to give up his war against such over-whelming odds and retire to Europe. Instead, López ordered a scorched earth policy. From Humaitá to the

Tebicuary, people were forced out of their homes. Carrying what little they could on their heads, they were driven out into the cordilleras, where most died of starvation and exposure. Their cattle were taken by the army, and their crops and houses burnt, leaving the area in front of the Allies entirely deserted.

While Eliza and Francisco were settling in at San Fernando, the Allies began an all-out assault on Humaitá. The fort was now defended by 3,000 half-starved, nearly naked soldiers manning 15,000 yards of trenches. They were commanded by Colonel Paulino Alén and Colonel Martínez. Both had been given orders to arrest the other if they saw the slightest sign of flagging or any inclination to talk to the enemy. First the Brazilians occupied Eliza's former home at Paso Pucú, then they started an assault on Curupaity. They attacked in force at night, wading through knee-deep mud until they reached the earthworks, where they discovered they had forgotten their scaling ladders. In the disastrous retreat that followed, 5,000 men were killed or wounded.

Realising they did not have the manpower to withstand another assault, the Paraguayans pulled back from Curupaity at night, removing the guns and leaving dummies in their place. A skeleton force marched and countermarched, and occasionally loosed off a few rounds, giving the impression the position was manned by a much larger force. This kept the Allies at bay for more than a month.

Eventually the Brazilians plucked up the courage to attack again and discovered that they had been held at bay by half-a-dozen tree trunks. To add injury to insult, a torpedo the Paraguayans had laid in the river some months before went off belatedly, sinking Brazil's most powerful ironclad, the *Rio de Janeiro*. Even so, things were not looking good for the Paraguayans. Martínez and Alén now faced an army of 30,000 men. They sent a message to López saying that they had eaten their last horse and were surviving by grubbing up the roots of plants. López told them to hold out. They did so for a further three months.

By then, the Paraguayans were so weak that, whenever there was a break in the relentless bombardment, no noise could be heard from the fort. Caxias became convinced that the Paraguayans had abandoned Humaitá, as they had Curupaity, leaving behind dummy guns. He was not going to be fooled again. But instead of sending a reconnaissance party, he threw 10,000 men into a frontal assault. When they were within twenty yards of the fortress, the Paraguayans unleashed a thunderous volley. Two thousand Brazilians died in the carnage – probably twice the number they would have needed to take the position if they had approached more cautiously. But there was no rejoicing inside the fort. The defenders were too weak to cheer.

Although the situation was now hopeless, López ordered that they hold out for five more days, though he sent them no rations. Eventually sent half mad by the hunger, the heat and the smell of rotting corpses, Colonel Alén tried to commit suicide, but succeeded only in damaging an eye. Then with a band of men he escaped out on to the Chaco and made for San Fernando. Those who remained behind at the fort were largely the weak, the wounded, and women and children who suffered terribly under the constant bombardments against which they had no defence. Still Colonel Martínez held out, even firing on the flag of truce when the Allies offered to parley. Finally, at the insistence of a priest, Colonel Martínez surrendered, putting an end to the suffering on 24 July 1868, Francisco's forty-second birthday.

The wounded Alén and the stragglers eventually made their way to San Fernando where they were arrested and tortured. Alén – a long-time friend of Francisco who had travelled with him to Europe – admitted under torture that they had sold the fortress to the Brazilians, then he and his men were shot. Martínez, the man who actually surrendered, was now in prison in Buenos Aires, so he was out of harm's way. But his wife Juliana was Eliza's lady-in-waiting. That did not help her. She was arrested, tortured and suffered 'other indignities not to be described, and the nature of which cannot even be hinted at', according to Washburn. For six months she was tortured and flogged until her body became a 'livid mass' and 'not an inch of skin was free from wounds'. Then she was executed along with Martínez's mother. Under interrogation it emerged that she had received letters from her family in Buenos Aires. This, as far as López was concerned, amounted to consorting with the enemy. It transpired that the letters had been brought into the country in Ambassador Washburn's diplomatic pouch. López had already had his doubts about Washburn. After his visit to Caxias, he had urged López to surrender. He had also sided with Cochelet and had helped him and his wife – Eliza's sworn enemy – to leave the country. Now López began to suspect that Washburn was at the centre of a vast conspiracy against him.

⇠§ 11 §⇢

THE GREAT CONSPIRACY

There was another reason to suspect Washburn. As there was no British representation in Asunción, the American Ambassador had involved himself in the fate of George Masterman. The young English doctor had found himself in one of López's jails. Despite the shortages Doña Juana had managed to make herself ill through overeating. López sent a message ordering two English doctors, James Rhind and John Fox, to visit her at her home in La Trinidad just outside Asunción. But Rhind could not find Fox and delayed the visit, fearing that López would interpret attending the lady alone as disobedience. Doña Juana became impatient and complained to Francisco; both Rhind and Fox were arrested. While they were in jail Masterman had tried to visit them and was found to be carrying letters that had been brought into the country in Cochelet's diplomatic bag. In Francisco's eyes, getting letters from outside the country was a treasonable offence. Masterman was arrested as well and, after being forced to sign a false confession, found himself confined to a small, cold, damp, dark cell infested by spider and scorpions. His fellow prisoners, he said, 'were of all ages, some very old men, others but boys, but all reduced to the last stage of emaciation, mere brown skin and bone'.

All of them had one or sometimes two pairs of heavy fetters riveted on their callused and scarred ankles. One man had three pairs on his skeletal legs.

'Yet these sufferers were not half so wretched as one would have thought,' said Masterman, 'they used to laugh and sing, and have clattering, staggering races in their narrow den.

'Every week or so, one and another of them would be taken out to the patio to be flogged. These were sad days for me. I dreaded their coming, and did not recover my equanimity for many hours afterwards. I think the fact of hearing, without being able see the infliction of the punishments, made them more terrible. To hear the dull, heavy thud of the stick wielded by those stalwart, pitiless corporals, and to know that it was descending on living flesh, quivering in agony, made me faint and sick with horror.'

As a surgeon, Masterman was known to be one of the coolest operators, but the sound of the punishment unnerved him completely. And there was worse.

'Sometimes I heard blows, but frequently the cries of the victim alone told how they were torturing him. One afternoon a poor fellow was *estacado* – horizontally crucified just beneath my window. Never shall I forget what I endured that day listening to his moans and occasional frantic yells and prayers for mercy, and in picturing to myself what he was suffering. After hours of such torments I would see them sometimes led, sometimes carried, back again, pale and bleeding, a piteous spectacle.'

His guard was usually a child who could hardly

shoulder a musket. To escape the cold at night in the corridor outside, in their thin cotton ponchos, they would creep into his dungeon for warmth. The young ones, maybe ten or twelve years old, would cry from the cold and hunger. One sobbing guard whispered: 'I want to go home to my mother. I am afraid of the dark.'

Though these child guards were sympathetic, escape was impossible. Even if you got out of the jail effectively, the entire country was a huge prison. The river was swarming with *guardias*. Any other route would have led through swamps and jungles that were full of rattlesnakes and jaguars, or across the open pampas, where it would have been impossible to escape detection. Anyone who saw an escapee would have to report him – or risk his own skin. Not a single prisoner escaped. Nor, as far as Masterman could discover, did anyone attempt to escape, with the exception of a few Guaicuru Indians.

Rhind and Fox were released after two months, probably with the aid of Eliza, and Washburn hoped that Masterman too would be released, but months went by. He knew that it would be futile to speak to López, as any appeal would enrage him and probably result in Masterman suffering even worse treatment. But it was well known in Asunción that Eliza had the keys to the dungeons.

So Washburn contacted Eliza. His wife was pregnant with their first child and he asked Eliza if Masterman could be released to attend the birth. Eliza, who had herself given birth five times by then, was sympathetic. She used her influence and, after eleven months in total darkness, surrounded by people dying of Asiatic cholera, Masterman was released.

'I left prison sick, weak and half-blind, and so changed that my most intimate friends scarcely knew me,' wrote Masterman.

Masterman went to live at the US Legation where Washburn believed he could keep him safe. At the time, López's men were rounding up all foreigners and the remaining Paraguayans of Spanish blood. They were tortured until they confessed what they had been accused of and implicated others. To escape this fate, foreign nationals, including a large number of the British engineers, merchants and their families, turned up at the American Legation. Washburn tried to protect as many he could, telling the Paraguayan government that the people he was sheltering were in his employ.

His first duty, naturally, was to US citizens and he took in an African-American cook from Washington, D.C., named George Bowen, who caused mayhem.

'I soon found that, instead of getting a diminutive white elephant on my hands, as in the case of Masterman,' Washburn wrote, 'I got a big black one – a fellow who would get drunk every chance he could get and would steal anything he could get his hands on to give to his numerous female friends, of whom he seemed to have almost as many as López himself.'

When Bowen got drunk he would fight with the other servants. This was dangerous as most of them were spies working for López – including a Brazilian who moon-lighted writing letters for López over the signatures of Brazilians who had been captured or killed. These letters were sent to Allied camps and urged their former comrades to desert the ranks of the tyrant Dom Pedro and come to a land flowing with milk and honey – that is, Paraguay.

Eventually, Washburn had to send Bowen away. 'What became of him afterwards I never knew,' Washburn said. His chances of survival were not good.

Another American under Washburn's protection was a young scholar named Porter C. Bliss. He had come to Paraguay to write a book on the Chaco Indians but, when he arrived in Asunción, López commissioned him to write a history of Paraguay. The first volume covered the colonial period up to 1810, seventeen years before Francisco was born. Nevertheless, when López saw that the manuscript made no mention of the great man himself, he flew into a rage. But before he could arrest Bliss, Washburn hired him as his secretary.

James Manlove, from Maryland, also fetched up in the Legation. A former major in the Confederate Army, he had come to offer his services to Francisco. His plan was to assemble a fleet of privateers under the Paraguayan flag that would scour the seas plundering Brazilian and Argentinian vessels. López immediately suspected him of being a spy and threw him in jail. Eliza took pity and sent him beer and other presents. Eventually she used her influence with López to get him released.

However Eliza's sympathies seem to have extended only to English speakers. She did not intervene on behalf of Major Von Versen, a Prussian officer who had been sent to observe the war from the Paraguayan side. No one seemed to take to him. When he first landed in Rio de Janeiro he was jailed on the suspicion that he was going to join the Paraguayan Army as its new commander – the Brazilians feared he would do a rather more effective job than Francisco. When the Prussian Ambassador engineered his release, he headed for Buenos Aires where he was jailed again but, eventually, after the intervention of the Prussian Ambassador there, he was freed on the condition that he went to Chile. True to his word he rode across the pampas to Chile, then returned across the Chaco – a journey of 3,000 miles on horseback. Arriving at the Allied camp in July 1867, he bought the best horse he could and bolted across the lines. On reaching the Paraguayan positions, he was immediately seized, stripped, robbed and tied up, then jailed on suspicion of being a spy. There was no Prussian representation in Asunción and Washburn was unwilling or unable to help. Von Versen spent the rest of the war in a chain gang and was lucky to escape with his life.

The situation in the American Legation in Asunción became even more difficult once the Brazilian ironclads had forced their way past Humaitá. The capital was now open to attack and López decided that, if he could not be Napoleon, he would be Tsar Alexander and evacuate the city. The new capital was to be a small town nine miles to the northeast called Luque. All government records and national treasures were taken there. And Eliza, von Wisner and the children made the move using a convoy of landaus, packed with ball gowns, uniforms, Limoges and Sèvres china, the national archives, church treasures, Eliza's wine cellar and, of course, her piano.

The people of Asunción followed, carrying their meagre possessions in bullock carts or on their heads. They were given just 24 hours to pack up and leave, and did so without a murmur, knowing that any hint of complaint would result in a flogging, fetters or imprisonment. Hundreds were left to die chained to the ground for giving way to expressions of sorrow. Very few of those who left the city would ever return. When they arrived at Luque, they found that there were not enough houses to shelter even a quarter of them. Most camped under trees or in the open air. This was made all the more unbearable as it was the rainy season and seven or eight inches of rain fell almost every day. Food was scarce and medicine non-existent. Soon hundreds were dying from disease and famine.

As the seat of government had moved to Luque, López ordered the foreign ambassadors to move there too. Washburn refused. No accommodation for foreign embassies had been provided at Luque and he felt it was unsafe for those he was housing to leave the Legation. The former President of Uruguay, Dr Antonio de los Carreras, the former Uruguayan chargé d'affaires Señor Rodriguez and the Portuguese Consul Leite Pereira and his wife were now under his protection and would be in danger if he left. And a number of Paraguayans who had been forced to leave the city had lodged what remained of their valuables with him.

If his house was not full enough already, Doña Juana asked for Washburn's help for herself and her two daughters, Inocencia and Rafaela, in the event of a Brazilian invasion. Even Eliza had talked secretly with Washburn about the possibility of finding sanctuary in the Legation. Before she left Asunción, she summoned him to her house. She told him the cause was lost and shed some tears, then asked him if she could lodge her valuables with him for safekeeping. He agreed.

'She was very despondent, and said that she did not know what would become of her,' Washburn said, 'and seemed to be aware that she neither deserved nor could expect any mercy if she fell into the hands of the enemy.'

Eliza then became defiant. She had spent $200,000 – and the untold toil, sweat and blood of thousands of Paraguayans – on her palace, only to see it fall into the hands of the Brazilians. As an Englishwoman, she said, she would seek compensation from the government in Rio. But her greatest regret was she would never see Panchito accede to the throne and her other sons would not be imperial princes.

'She only thought of saving her life and the lives of her children,' said Washburn, 'and escaping with her ill-gotten gains to Europe.'

Within two days of the evacuation order being given, Asunción was deserted apart from the 42 foreigners playing billiards on the large table in the American Legation and the policemen who systematically looted the houses of any remaining valuables.

'It was sickening sight to behold,' said Washburn, 'and a forcible commentary on the beauties of strong government.'

Manlove risked leaving the legation and was arrested. He refused to salute the Captain of Police as he himself was a Major – albeit in the now disbanded Confederate Army – and had to be rescued by Washburn. López retaliated by stopping Washburn's despatches. Later Manlove and Washburn quarrelled and Washburn ordered him to leave the legation. When he did so he was arrested, imprisoned, tortured and, later, shot.

Four days after they sailed over the torpedo-laden chains at Humaitá, a handful of Brazilian ironclads arrived at Asunción. They could have easily taken the city. But instead of landing troops, they began a half-hearted bombardment. Brazilian marksmanship was up to its usual standard. They began by firing too high. Once they had found their mark, they fired too wide. The only damage they inflicted on the city was the destruction of the balcony of the unfinished Presidential palace; the only casualties were two dogs in the market square. The small fort in Asunción returned fire. The defenders were scarcely more accurate and any shots that did find their target were 'harmless as paper pellets against the ironclads'. Once again the ironclads' guns could not be depressed sufficiently to return fire, so the Brazilians sailed off back down the river to proclaim a great victory. By comparison, they claimed, the Battle of the Nile and Trafalgar were mere skirmishes.

The cursory Brazilian shelling convinced everyone that the Allies were about to take Asunción – though, in fact, months passed before they came back. Nevertheless those inside the Legation thought they were about to be relieved. However, they soon found that they were under siege from another quarter. While most of the inhabitants had taken their dogs with them when they evacuated the city, they had left their cats behind – who found the provisions stored at the Legation their only source of food. Of more danger was a tame parrot lodged with the Legation which had been taught to say: '*Viva Pedro Segundo*' – 'Long live Pedro II'. Washburn ordered his secretary to wring the treacherous bird's neck. The other enemy was boredom. Masterman passed the time devouring French and Spanish novels, and was amused to find that the villains were always English.

Washburn was buoyed up by the news that an

American gunboat would soon be tying up at the quayside in Asunción so, when Doña Juana asked him to find out how her other children were faring at the hands of Francisco, he risked a trip to San Fernando. There he found himself greeted by Eliza, who was living in a mud hut.

'She, as usual, was all suavity, and abounding in expressions of interest and kindness towards everybody, even those whom she had instigated López to arrest and torture,' wrote Washburn. She told him that the López family members were all alive and well, and assured him that Francisco would not harm them.

'You know his kindly nature, and how repugnant it is for him to shed blood,' she said.

That evening she invited Washburn to play whist with Baron von Wisner, Colonel Thompson and General Bruguez, who Washburn thought was the 'best fighting officer López ever had' and probably the most loyal. He was later tortured to death.

In Francisco's mind, Washburn's visit brought the great conspiracy sharply into focus. He had been in contact with Doña Juana and showed his concern about Benigno, Carlos López's natural son and Francisco's perceived rival for the post of President. He was also concerned about Inocencia and Rafaela, the wives of Barrios and Bedoya, two convicted traitors, and was the protector of Masterman, Bliss and Marlowe. It was plain, to Francisco, that the ringleader of the great conspiracy was none other than Washburn himself.

The problem remained that the United States was a great power in the Americas and López was afraid to move against Washburn himself, so instead he began to harass the legation. First he demanded that Washburn hand over the Portuguese Consul Leite Pereira, who, he alleged, was guilty of treason for providing food and clothing to Brazilian prisoners of war. Washburn refused and the legation was surrounded. Fearing that he would cause trouble for the other inmates of the legation, Pereira left and was immediately arrested. López then demanded that Washburn hand over the Uruguayans Carreras and Rodriguez. They left voluntarily, knowing they faced torture and death.

The British engineers, merchants and their families also left, hoping that López would show them some mercy. Eliza thought of herself as an Englishwoman and it was clear that she had some patriotic feelings. They were taking a huge risk. According to John A. Duffield, an American who escaped Paraguay when he was taken prisoner by the Brazilians, 600 foreigners were tortured and lanced to death, without trial or explanation of any kind, on the orders of López. Nevertheless a high proportion of those who survived were British.

Finally López demanded that Washburn hand over Bliss and Masterman. Washburn protested that they were members of his staff and were consequently protected by the rules of diplomacy. An argument broke out over the exact circumstances of their hiring. López insisted that they were criminals. They had engaged in a conspiracy to undermine him and bathe the soil of Paraguay in fratricidal blood. Even were that the case, said Washburn, they were innocent until proved guilty. If López could produce evidence of their guilt, he would send them back to the United States and Great Britain respectively where they would stand trial. This was all a game of words. But Washburn knew that if he provoked López into sending soldiers into the legation to take Bliss and Masterman, he and his family would also be taken. So he made a pretence of imprisoning them and locked them in a room in the Embassy. Spies among Washburn's staff reported this back to López. But he was not satisfied, so Washburn gave up the charade. Then one night, at about eight o'clock, Eliza arrived at the legation. She urged Washburn to hand over Bliss and Masterman, insisting that they were implicated in a vast conspiracy. A large number of Francisco's former friends, including Berges, the former Foreign Minister, had also been implicated. His brothers Benigno and Venancio, and his sisters Inocencia and Rafaela were all party to the conspiracy. Even Francisco's mother Doña Juana had been put under house arrest in La Trinidad. She was taken to Luque, where she was forced under threat of death to swear at the altar of the church that Francisco alone was her child and to curse the others as 'rebels and traitors'. Later, though she was over 70, Doña Juana was flogged for her part in the conspiracy. Responsibility for this, too, has been laid at Eliza's door. One of Eliza's first biographers, William E. Barrett, claimed that Eliza had denounced the López ladies because of the indignities they had heaped on her when she first came to Paraguay.

Then the finger was pointed at Washburn himself. Eliza told him that there was no point in his denying his part in the conspiracy. Pereira, Carreras and Rodriguez had confessed implicating him. Washburn protested that they had certainly been tortured and, consequently, their confessions were worthless. According to Barrett, Eliza herself oversaw the torture of the 'conspirators' after the 'black savagery of this country had entered her veins'. But Eliza denied everything.

'There has been no constraint put upon them,' she told Washburn. 'It has all been voluntary. The President would never use restraint, or force them to confess against their will. He is very kind-hearted.'

Washburn's main concern was to get his wife and child out of harm's way. He was waiting to be recalled and he said that Mrs Washburn would like to go to Buenos Aires as soon as possible.

Eliza replied menacingly: 'If she can.'

Madame Lynch repeated this, Washburn noted, 'in a tone that said as clearly as words could say that neither Mrs Washburn nor the child would be permitted to leave Paraguay.'

Washburn believed that Eliza had wanted him to become an apologist for the López regime and to try to persuade the United States to intervene on his side. In this, she had failed. Washburn was well aware that she would report his refusal to Francisco. Indeed, he imagined that she would twist his words – 'as this woman was never known to speak the truth when falsehood would serve her purpose as well,' he said.

The following day, Washburn received a letter from the Paraguayan government telling him that Bliss and Masterman, who were ostensibly still in his custody, were preparing to escape. When he referred to this in his reply, he was thanked for the information and accused of colluding in the escape. He was also accused of possessing incriminating letters. Washburn denied this, but said that he had three boxes given to him for safekeeping by Madame Lynch. They might be full of treasonable papers, he said. He did not know; they had been nailed shut. Actually Washburn suspected they were full of money and jewels. Soon after, Eliza's agent José Solis came to collect them. Both Dr Stewart and Washburn believed that she buried them, somewhere between San Fernando and Villeta, 'the exact point I could not tell within a dozen miles,' said Washburn.

By this time all the civil officers of the state – including the judges, clerks and accountants of various government departments – had been arrested. And only a single foreigner remained at liberty in the entire country – Eliza's agent, the Spaniard José Solis. People were being arrested at such a rate that Aquino, the overweight manager of *El Semanario*, who had spent years glorifying López and his innumerable 'victories', decided to ingratiate himself further by lending the police captain a hand. As a result, he himself was arrested and fetters put around his bulging ankles. Soon after the police captain was arrested as well.

Then the new Foreign Minister Gumesindo Benitez came to the Legation to urge Washburn to confess.

'*Sabemos todo*,' he said – 'We know all.' This unfortunate phase was to be his epitaph. To the paranoid López, it meant that he knew things that he had not told the government. He was arrested, tortured, starved, denounced by his wife and, when he was nearly dead, taken out and shot.

As the killing continued, Washburn, Bliss and Masterman became increasingly convinced that there was no conspiracy. It was all a fiction. If there were one, Washburn argued, after those involved had been 'put out of the way, others who knew nothing about it would be left unmolested. But ... scores of others had been executed for no other reason, as we believed, than to afford a pastime to López.' But he did not believe Francisco to be insane 'for in all matters in which he was uninfluenced by his vanity and his innate love of cruelty, his mind was as clear and logical as ever'. Washburn also considered it a remarkable coincidence that the conspiracy was uncovered after the government blacksmith's shop had turned over its entire production to make fetters – ranging in weight from five to 25 pounds – even though there was a surplus left over from Dr Francia's time. Washburn's conclusion was that not even López believed that there was really a conspiracy against him.

'For my part, I do not believe that there is a conspiracy at all,' said another Englishman who survived the holocaust, 'unless on the part of the President himself and some of his tools to rob foreigners of their money.'

But Washburn's reasoning took a more paranoid turn. He came to believe that the idea of the conspiracy had been invented in the hope of blackening his name in the eyes of other nations so that, in violation of international law, Paraguayan soldiers could enter the legation and seize Bliss, Masterman, himself and his family. As a result he entered into a protracted correspondence with López, answering each accusation point by point in the hope of gaining time. The evidence against him, he said, had been extracted under torture and was so full of inconsistencies that he urged López to publish it in *El Semanario* so the world could see his innocence. Instead, *El Semanario* published a long piece, denouncing the native conspirators as: 'These accused sons of Cain, these reprobates who might have enjoyed the incomparable glory as being natives of the same soil as the GREAT LÓPEZ . . .', while foreigners were denounced as people 'who found on Paraguayan soil what they could not obtain in their own native lands, who were but leeches fattening upon the people's honey, who enriched themselves with the precious fruit of the sweat and the blood of the people, while the people have been consecrating themselves as a whole upon the altars of patriotism, making the greatest sacrifices, and bathing heroically with their blood the tree of liberty, and shielding with their lives the sanctuary of their religion and of their sacred rights. . . .'

The author of this rhetoric was, of course, none other than López himself. He concluded : 'Thanks to God and to MARSHAL LÓPEZ! the Paraguayan people is today cured of the cancer that gangrened its existence. Confidence, tranquillity and fraternity recover their immovable seat among us. Who can conquer us? Nobody! God and MARSHAL LÓPEZ are with us.' What a coupling.

But López was not the only one suffering from delusions of grandeur; nor was Washburn alone in experiencing fear of persecution. All Paraguay was paranoid. None dared say anything against López nor listen to anything said against him, for fear that the other was a spy sent to entrap him. In fact, if anyone had been tricked into listening to even the mildest criticism, it would simply be a question of who denounced the other first. And that was as true among family members, neighbours and friends, as it was between strangers.

In Luque, the people were summoned to protest against traitors and denounce their relatives and friends.

Wives denounced their husbands, and husbands their wives. Before long the denouncers found themselves denounced in their turn and sent to San Fernando for torture and execution, while López spent hours on his knees in church, indifferent to their screams, and Eliza did nothing to restrain him.

In the legation, they no longer played billiards, nor whist nor chess. Five months had gone by since the bombardment of Asunción and it was clear the Brazilians would not arrive in time to save them. Sooner or later, López would send his soldiers in and they would face starvation, exposure, the lash and the rack. They knew that even such brave men as Pereira, Carreras and Rodriguez had been tortured to the point where they had made false accusations. Bliss and Masterman said they would have happily gone to the guillotine instead, while Washburn believed that he faced the prospect of watching his wife being tortured in front of him unless he confessed to being conspirator-in-chief. Dr Stewart had told him so in a letter. By this time, López hated Washburn so much that, when drunk, his rants against the US Ambassador far exceeded anything that he had said against Mitre and were so obscene that 'Madame Lynch would cover her face and pretend to blush at the immoralities of the American Legation', according to Dr Stewart.

Shortly before he was arrested, Dr Stewart overheard Francisco and Eliza discussing their plan. At the first prospect of any rescue of Bliss, Masterman and Washburn, they would send soldiers into the legation. Bliss and Masterman would be arrested. Then 'for the safety of the Republic', Washburn would be taken away and tortured – a prospect López looked forward to witnessing. Meanwhile Eliza would visit Mrs Washburn to express her sympathy. She would tell her that her husband was in no personal danger and would be allowed to leave the country so that he could tell the world of the conspiracy he had planned. All Mrs Washburn had to do was write a personal note to López, admitting that there was a conspiracy. Washburn would then be shown the letter to overcome any 'obstinacy' and would be told that his own torture would cease if he made a similar admission. If he still refused, his wife's back and shoulders would be flayed with sticks in his presence. Washburn and his wife would then suffer an 'accident'. Those responsible would be put to death immediately afterwards. Francisco and Eliza would then publicly express their sorrow at the death of the Ambassador and his wife, claim that they had punished the perpetrators and send the Washburns' child through the lines under a flag of truce with messages of regret. With no evidence directly connecting them with the American Ambassador's death, Francisco and Eliza doubted that the United States would retaliate against them.

Still Washburn strained to give Eliza some benefit of the doubt. 'Madame Lynch was in favour of assassination,' he wrote later, 'and for the credit of her sex it is to be hoped she recoiled from the hideous torture that López proposed both for Mrs Washburn and myself.'

This was a faint hope. Washburn himself recorded that when a man who worked for Eliza was 'suspected of having too great an intimacy with one of her maid-servants, she affected to be so greatly scandalised and shocked that improprieties should be committed in her abode of virtue' that she sent the offender to his commanding officer with a note saying the man should be flogged to death. Colonel Thompson recorded the same incident.

Everyone around her said that Eliza encouraged López in his excesses. She cheerfully denounced those who had looked down on her and had people arrested and killed so that she could rob them of their property. But she, too, must have been afraid. She had many enemies, any one of whom could have named her as a conspirator. Being Francisco's lover was no protection. According to John Duffield, López 'boasts of having ruined hundreds of women; and it is well known that lately he ordered several of these same women to be ignominiously put to death for some trifling word which they said, or were accused of saying'.

But before the Brazilians arrived and Francisco and Eliza put their plan into operation, the American gunboat *Wasp* ran the blockade. Washburn requested passports for himself, his family and the staff of the legation so they could leave. López refused. The commander of the *Wasp*, Commodore Kirkland, then told López that Mr Washburn was a personal friend of the new US President Ulysses S. Grant and threatened to bombard Asunción and destroy López's new palace if he did not allow the US Ambassador to leave. He even carried a revolver with him to one meeting with López, resolving to kill him if necessary. When Eliza pointed out that Francisco could ill afford to fall out with the United States at this point, López gave in. He nevertheless refused to issue passports to Bliss and Masterman. When Washburn and his wife left the Legation on their way to the *Wasp*, Bliss and Masterman went with them but were immediately arrested. They had expected as much but hoped that if Washburn could get away and contact the squadron, help might arrive before they were killed. In the meantime, Washburn gave them permission to defame him in any way they saw fit if it helped them with López. He believed that no one either inside or outside Paraguay would believe a word as whatever they said would have been extracted under torture or the threat of torture.

When Washburn left the Legation, he had to leave behind most of the money and goods that had been entrusted to him for safekeeping; he had no doubt who would benefit from that. When he reached the *Wasp*, he was informed by her captain that López was regarded throughout the United States and Europe as a hero, fighting bravely in defence of his country. Eliza's charm offensive had worked. López was seen as a champion of republican principles, involved in a titanic struggle against monarchy, despotism and slavery, as epitomised by Brazil. This was shocking news. And when Washburn revealed what was really going on in Paraguay, it only confirmed to many what López had been saying – that Washburn had led a conspiracy against him. At the same time the newspapers in Rio de Janeiro, Buenos Aires and Montevideo, assuming what he said was true, denounced him for having failed to conspire against the monstrous López.

❦ 12 ❧

THE END OF EMPIRE

As soon as they left the legation, Bliss, Masterman and
Baltazar, Dr Carreras's black servant, were seized by 50
soldiers. They were marched to the police station,
stripped of their possessions, fettered and thrown into the
cells. This time, Masterman noted, his cell had no
furniture at all, not even a bed. The following morning a
sergeant and two men entered his cell. One carried a
hammer and a small anvil; the other another set of irons.

'The fetters I was wearing were removed, and the
massive bar the man bore on his shoulder was riveted in
their place,' wrote Masterman. 'Two rough iron loops,
with eyes at their extremities, were first placed over my
ankles; then the bar, which was about eighteen inches in
length and two in diameter, was thrust through the eyes,
and an iron wedge, with many a blow of the heavy
hammer, riveted firmly at one end, while a broad knob
secured it at the other. Thus fettered, it was with the
greatest difficulty that I staggered to my feet, and then sat
down again, scarcely able to bear the weight.'

Masterman was then led out to a train of mules where
he saw Bliss and Baltazar also fettered. Once mounted,
they were taken to Villeta, about 35 miles away.

According to Bliss, although he was later tortured, it was nothing compared to the agony they suffered that night. 'The weight of the fetters on my ankles became excruciating torture, until I nearly fainted, but nevertheless was obliged to maintain my position, still without food, or relief, until noon of the next day . . . I fell off several times, and was dragged a considerable distance by the horse I rode.'

Masterman begged the sergeant to go slowly as, 'at every step, the heavy bar swung backwards and forwards, and a jolt was agonising'. But at one point the mules broke into a trot and he fell off. 'I was tied to the girths and, unable to extricate myself, was dragged for some distance head downwards, the mule kicking viciously the while. Fortunately the only damage was a deep cut in the ankle and a few bruises.'

Their destination was now the centre of the Paraguayan defence. After the fall of Humaitá, López had abandoned his makeshift fort at San Fernando, where the river was broad. He withdrew to Angostura, the narrows near Villeta, some fifteen miles downstream from Asunción. There Colonel Thompson began work on a new fort while López, with his usual discretion, established his headquarters six miles inland at Pikysyry, beyond a series of low ridges known as the Lomas Valentinas and well out of range of the Brazilian guns.

For López's growing number of political prisoners, the withdrawal to Villeta was a death march. One of those on it was the architect of Francisco's palace, the Chelsea-born stonemason and builder Alonzo Taylor. He had come to Paraguay in 1858 with his wife and children. Before López became President he and Eliza had treated

Taylor well, so he stayed on. Then when the war started, he found he could not leave. At first he was sent to work in the arsenal, while his wife looked after the widows and children of other Englishmen who had drunk themselves to death on *caña*.

By 1868, he was working in the soap factory at Luque. On the evening of 21 July, he returned to his house at ten o'clock at night. Shortly afterwards a cavalry soldier knocked and told him that he had been ordered to take him to the Ministry of War. Knowing that it was useless to resist, Taylor mounted his horse and went with the soldier. But he was instead delivered to the port where he was put in irons, and placed with eight or nine other prisoners. In the morning, they were put on board the steamer *Salto de Guayrà*. At around eleven o'clock, Eliza and her eldest son, Panchito, came on board with some officers and they started down the river to San Fernando.

'As she left the steamer, Mrs Lynch looked, but she took no apparent notice of me, although she used to be very kind to me, and my daughter was often in her house,' said Taylor. 'I had asked an officer who was on board, and used to be very intimate with me, if he would let me speak to her; but he said that being a prisoner I could speak to no one, much less to her. He abused me, and seemed to delight in my misfortune.'

Taylor and ten others were marched six miles in irons – some wore more than one set, each weighing between 20 and 30 pounds. Two sick prisoners had to be carried on poles. Their guards encouraged the prisoners with their bayonets and those who lagged behind were flogged. At San Fernando, Taylor saw men and women tortured and flogged to death. He saw an Argentine officer taken away to be flogged and return with the whole of his body raw. Unable to speak, the Argentine wrote with a stick in the sand '100'. The next day, when he returned, he wrote '200'. The third day he was shot. Others were simply bayoneted to death 'in the most cruel way'. Taylor saw more than 700 people slaughtered at San Fernando. Still more died of starvation and exposure. Their prison was in the open air. It was a rough piece of ground where they were secured in lines by '*el cepo de lazo*' or rope stocks. These were fixed between two stakes and tightened until they were as taut as harp strings. In itself this was extremely painful. The prisoners were left like that, lying on the ground all day, exposed to the burning sun, tropical storms and the bites of swarms of insects. Sentries beat and kicked them as they pleased. A request for water would invite a flogging. Their only food was the offal of animals killed for the troops. They were given no salt and prisoners would sell their clothes for a handful of bread or a spike of maize. And the women were treated just as badly as the men – kept naked, starved, flogged and tortured, though some were given little A-shaped straw huts to give them some shade, but no shelter from the rain.

Francisco's favourite torture was the *cepo uruguayana*. Devised in Bolivia at the time of Simón Bolívar, this means of torture was originally known as the *cepo boliviano* – or Bolivian stocks. But it was such a painful and effective way of extracting a confession that López introduced it to Paraguay and, after Estigarribia's surrender at Uruguayana, he renamed it *cepo uruguayana*.

'This is how I suffered it,' said Taylor. 'I sat on the ground with my knees up. My legs were first tied tightly together, and then my hands behind me, with the palms outwards. A musket was then fastened under my knees; six more of them, tied together in a bundle, were then put on my shoulders, and they were looped together with hide ropes . . . two soldiers hauling on the end of it forced my face down to my knees and secured it so.

'The effect was as follows: first the feet went to sleep, then a tingling commenced in the toes, gradually extending to the knees, and the same in the hands and arms, and increased until the agony was unbearable. My tongue swelled up, and I thought that my jaws would have been displaced; I lost all feeling in one side of my face for a fortnight afterwards. The suffering was dreadful; I should certainly have confessed if I had had anything to confess.' But when he was questioned afterwards he was physically unable to speak.

Taylor had been left in the *cepo* for two hours. 'I considered myself fortunate in escaping then; for many were put in the *uruguayana* twice, and others six times, with eight muskets on the nape of the neck,' he said. He was told that he had been kept in the *cepo* for only a short time, due to the clemency of His Excellency Marshal López.

It was only much later – after he was released – that Taylor discovered that, in common with the other prisoners, he had been charged with treason. The evidence against him was that his son's Italian teacher had invited him to become a Freemason. Under torture, the teacher testified that Taylor had signed a paper saying that he wanted to join. When the authorities decided that there was no truth in this, the teacher was shot.

Although he was entirely innocent – and there was

now no case against him – Taylor was not released. But despite the terrible privations he suffered he considered that he got off lightly. He had seen Eliza's former lady-in-waiting and confidante Juliana Martínez tortured in the *cepo* six times, then flogged and beaten with sticks until not an inch of her skin was free from wounds.

By the time they began the hundred-mile march from San Fernando to Villeta on 28 August – a month since Taylor had been arrested – he was suffering from rheumatism, ague and dysentery. However, he had managed to fashion a tiny pipe out of a piece of clay and could comfort himself with a little tobacco. Before the march began the prisoners' fetters were removed, but they had to carry them. In bare feet, they walked over fallen leaves that hid sharp spikes and waded up to their waists through bogs at bayonet point. Their route looped along the edges of lagoons and impenetrable forest from one piece of high ground to another. Sometimes they had to walk four miles to cover one. At night they were put in the *cepo de lazo*. Although they were allowed to light fires to keep warm, they were given nothing to eat. Twenty-seven people died on the march.

According to Taylor, of the 260 prisoners on the march, fourteen were foreigners and at least four were women. These were the beautiful Dolòres Recaldè, the two aged sisters of Señor Ejusquiza, López's agent in Buenos Aires, and Juliana Martínez, once a pretty young woman, whose body was now covered with wounds, her face blackened and distorted. On the march, she asked Taylor whether one large black mark over her eye would disfigure her for life. It would. Two months later, she was shot. She was just 24. Her only crime was to be married to the man who had been forced to surrender Humaitá when López had left the garrison to starve.

On the journey to Villeta, Francisco's sisters Inocencia and Rafaela were spared the trouble of walking. Not that they were any better off. Each was imprisoned in a covered bullock cart, or *carreta*, just seven feet long and four feet wide, like the carts used at the time to carry wild animals about for exhibition. At the back was a door secured by a padlock; at the front, a slit through which food was passed. They were shut up in these for five months. Later, at Villeta, Masterman saw them being trundled past to the *fiscàles*, where they were interrogated, and heard children crying inside, but he was not sure if they were theirs.

When Masterman, Bliss and Baltazar arrived at Villeta, they were pulled from their mounts, beaten and dragged in front of a tribunal under Padre Maiz. They were told that they had not been brought there to defend themselves – their guilt was already an ascertained fact. They were there to make a full confession. When they refused to say that they had conspired against López and that Washburn was the ringleader, they suffered the *cepo uruguayana*.

'These savages, like those in *The Last of the Mohicans*, ought to have expressed regret that their means of inflicting pain were so primitive,' wrote Masterman. 'One of the men tied my arms tightly behind me, the other passed a musket under my knees, and then putting his foot between my shoulders forced my head down until my throat rested on the lower musket; a second was put over the back of my neck, and they were firmly lashed together.' Two soldiers then hauled on the ropes and sometimes pounded the muskets with a mallet to tighten them. This painfully compressed the abdomen. When Bliss was put in the *cepo*, he said he could hear his vertebrae cracking. Throughout the torture, the good Padre repeatedly told the victim in a monotonous voice that he must confess and 'receive the mercy of the kind and generous Marshal López'. Masterman suffered this torture twice, saying nothing until blood from his cut lips almost choked him and he fainted from the excruciating pain. Threatened with the *cepo* a third time, he confessed. The priest told him that he was a fool – Bliss had confessed straight away. In the background, Masterman heard Baltazar praying as his fingers were smashed with a mallet and pitied him. Unlike Masterman and Bliss, who had discussed Eliza's accusations with Washburn, Baltazar did not know enough about the supposed conspiracy to make any sort of confession and could not even save himself by admitting that he was guilty. After suffering appalling torture, Baltazar starved himself to death.

Masterman found making his confession easy enough. He gathered from his interrogators 'several valuable hints as to the course I had best adopt'. He found that the more he abused Washburn the better they liked it and referred to him as 'the great beast' throughout. 'I got on swimmingly,' he said, though he was grateful that Washburn was safely on board the *Wasp*. The others he named were already dead. He justified defaming the deceased by reasoning that, if he and Bliss died, there would be no one to clear their names later. Masterman said that his interrogators threatened him with torture another twenty times 'and twice were on the point of doing so when I luckily remembered something Mr Washburn had said against López'. As a finishing flourish he even apologised to his judges for having put them to the trouble of torturing him.

Bliss did not do so well initially. He had to rewrite his confession five times and his torture went on for days on end. He eventually decided to frighten López by inventing a conspiracy involving practically every country in the world, while Dr Stewart cheekily confessed under torture that there was a plot 'to kill off the soldiers of the Republic by poisoning the wine in the public storehouse' – even though all the wine in the country was in Eliza's well-guarded cellars.

During their interrogation they slept outside in a compound, where Taylor saw them, though he did not dare talk to them. Masterman recalled waking one morning to find he was wet through and lying in a pool of water. It had rained heavily that night and the wind was bitterly cold.

'On one side of me was tied Dr Carreras, still sleeping, and the corpse of Lieutenant-Colonel Campos on the other,' said Masterman. 'He had died, untended and unheeded, during the night, and lay there staring at blankly at the rising sun.'

Campos was an Argentine prisoner of war. After the rest of the prisoners were awoken with a rain of blows, his body was thrown in the river. 'What, only one this morning?' remarked the guard as he dragged the corpse away.

On the whole, though, during his interrogation, Masterman found the soldiers relatively kind. It was Padre Maiz and the other priests who urged more torture. One, named Padre Romàn, reminded Masterman of Torquemada.

'Romàn could outrage innocent girls and mothers, as he did Señora Martínez and Doña Dolòres Recaldè, and then send them to be shot without a sign of remorse or pity,' he said.

After the interrogation was over, Masterman and Bliss were moved to another enclosure on a hillside which contained some 40 prisoners. As far as they could see, in every direction, there were similar enclosures. Important people, such as Francisco's brothers Don Benigno and Don Venancio, had accommodation that, Masterman said, was 'somewhat luxurious, for each prisoner had a little straw kennel to lie down in'. They were not tall enough to sit up in, but offered some protection from the rain and a little shade. The others had no shelter from either sun or rain. The prisoners of war among them were also fortunate as they were not fettered, although they were 'in the last stage of misery, some quite naked, covered with wounds and the majority too feeble to walk'. Then there were common criminals distinguished by only having a single iron ring on the right ankle – 'These looked scarcely human, were without a rag of clothing and generally lay in a huddled heap on the ground.'

In the hillside compound Bliss and Masterman met Taylor and caught up with Dr Carreras again. Padre Maiz had tortured him in the *cepo uruguayana* for three days and smashed his fingers with a mallet. Masterman also saw the two ex-Foreign Ministers Berges and Benitez. Both old men were naked and 'evidently in their second childhood'. One day Masterman saw Benigno López being taken away to be tortured. Benigno had already made a full confession and Masterman wondered whether he might have to undergo his own terrible ordeal again.

Others in custody at the time were Bishop Palacios, the remains of López's cabinet with the exception of Vice-President Sánchez, Leite Pereira and two other Portuguese nationals, two Germans, six Frenchmen, nine Spaniards, fifteen Italians, 25 Argentinians, 33 Brazilians and countless Paraguayans.

Alonzo Taylor noted that, although the prisoners were 'of all nationalities and of all grades and positions, with the heat, wear and tear, the rain and wind, they were soon all alike, nearly naked'. Bliss said that some people he knew had been tortured so badly that it took a long time before he could recognise them.

They were fed scraps left by the soldiers, usually animal entrails, thrown to them twice a day. They had to cook these themselves. Masterman said he saw the former Prime Minister of Uruguay 'eagerly gnawing the gristle from a few well-picked bones, contemptuously thrown him by a passer-by'. Water was fetid and scarce. Prisoners jealously guarded any receptacle that could carry it – one Brazilian had an old wellington boot. But the most prized possession was a spoon.

Every day prisoners were tortured, flogged to death and shot, sometimes in the middle of the enclosures. Again there were women there too, some 'from the best families in the country'. When they were flogged, their cries were pitiful, according to Taylor. Masterman saw a sixteen-year-old girl there who never moved, though tears often ran silently down her cheeks. Many were simply put out of their misery. Others were brutally executed, after being tortured into confession. Between June and December 1868, Dr Cecilio Báez reckoned, 'the number of executions of distinguished people for imaginary crimes reached 1,000, not counting the 7,000 or 8,000 soldiers shot for minor offences, and the hundreds of families sacrificed by the lancers, for no purpose except to despoil them of their jewels and silver. Among the tyrant's victims, one counts hundreds of distinguished women and young ladies, whose only crime was in being the mothers, wives, daughters or sisters of supposed conspirators.'

Bliss and Masterman put their survival down to the fact that they could write. After confessing they were furnished with pen and paper and asked to write down everything they knew about the conspiracy. Both realised that they should pad out their accounts with lengthy passages abusing the 'great beast' Washburn – 'the evil genius of Paraguay' – and even longer ones praising the wisdom, kindness and virtue of López, in the hope that Washburn had been able to persuade the American squadron to return for them. They even came up with a fanciful plot, whereby Washburn was being paid by Napoleon III and Pedro II to carve up the whole of South America between the houses of Bonaparte and Braganza. Masterman recalled that he relished his task as he could put in the mouth of Washburn opinions and remarks that he dare not say himself – that López was a cruel, avaricious tyrant and an incompetent general pitted against a superior foe – 'and thus open the eyes of people to the true state of affairs,' he said. The result – with the addition of further details of the conspiracy – was published as a pamphlet of a dozen pages or so which was widely circulated. Only one fault was found with his writing. He was told that it was tautologous to say: 'Mr Washburn conspired against His Excellency the President and the Government of Paraguay.'

'His Excellency *is* the Government,' Masterman's torturer pointed out.

Bliss was a professional writer. His work ran to 323 pages and López was so pleased with it that he had it published under the snappy title *La Historia Secreta de la Mision del Ciudadano Norte Americano Charles A. Washburn cerca Gobierno de la Republica del Paraguay – Por el Ciudadano Americano, Traductor titular (in partibus) de la misma mission*. Hundreds of copies were sent abroad to show the world how he, López, had defeated the 'greatest diplomat and the boldest, most unscrupulous intriguer, who had ever sought to make kings and emperors the mere titular dignitaries of the chessboard'. According to *La Historia Secreta*, Washburn was also a drunk, a glutton, an inveterate gambler, a kleptomaniac and a rake who was expelled from school for stealing the silver, failed in his ambition to become a Grant or a Napoleon when he flunked the entrance examination to West Point and was sacked from his job in Washington for giving himself up to 'the pleasures and orgies of the capital with the dissolute youth he met there'. He went on to become a lawyer with no clients and a doctor whose patients ordered their coffins before consulting him. After that he took over San Francisco and subjected the city to a reign of terror. Fleeing from its outraged citizens, who wanted to hang him, he wrote a pornographic novel, which was clearly autobiographical, then compiled a joke book full of old jokes that he had stolen and new ones that were so unfunny he had to go around to readers' homes in person to explain them. Bliss even devoted six pages to vicious criticism of poetry that Washburn had never written. But Washburn's biggest crime, according to *La Historia Secreta*, was that he had seduced Bliss from his devoted loyalty to the 'greatest warrior of the age' – Mariscal Francisco Solano López.

Bliss put his prodigious literary imagination down to the fact that his 'ideas were not clogged by over-indulgence at the table' – like the other prisoners, he survived on morsels of unsalted offal – though his output may have been aided by the fact that he was forced to work twelve or fourteen hours a day with an armed guard standing over him. He was frequently awoken at night to correct proofs. Then when he found that he was working faster than he hoped, he purposely introduced errors to slow things down.

While Masterman put his real thoughts about López in the mouth of Washburn, Bliss came up with the device of pretending that Washburn had been writing a book himself, defaming both López and Paraguay. He then began to quote huge chunks of this from memory. In these imaginary quotations, Bliss related what was actually going on in Paraguay and described López's real character and actions. According to Bliss, Washburn had said that Francisco was a coward with a criminal dis-regard for the life of his subjects and, compared to his atrocities, 'the rule of the autocrats of all the Russias is mercy itself, and the worst rigours of the Holy Inquisition are tender caresses'. But the irony was lost on López, who had numerous extracts printed up as eight-page pamphlets and distributed to the army – which must have done wonders for morale.

It is not known whether Eliza read either Masterman's or Bliss's literary works or, if she did, what she made of them. They circulated widely and it would have been hard for her not to have come across them. She was certainly sophisticated enough and literary enough to have decoded them, and their use of irony would surely have appealed to her Englishness. But maybe, as she was largely responsible for inventing the conspiracy in the first place, she had begun to believe her own propaganda.

'I have since learnt that she took every opportunity to talk about the conspiracy,' wrote Masterman, 'abusing Mr Washburn and his friends to López, incessantly harping upon his generosity as a rule, and their base ingratitude. "Oh, Your Excellency, how you have sacrificed yourself for the sake of your country," she would say to the fat, drunken sensualist after dinner, "and how these wicked men have conspired against you. *Es muy triste, Señor.* Oh very sad indeed." Not from any desire to destroy us, but simply for her own safety's sake. She could be sure that a man who had imprisoned his brothers, flogged his sisters, shot their husbands and threatened his mother, would scarcely respect any other tie.'

Not everyone was fooled. Padre Maiz said to Bliss *sotto voce* that, while pretending to quote from Washburn, he was actually writing a scathing criticism of López. So Bliss, knowing how to bend with the wind, added a passage denouncing all the priests in the country as a vile horde of intriguers and spies who knew no more Latin than was necessary to mutilate the words of the Holy Office – with the exception, of course, of the good Padre himself. Maiz placated, Bliss went on to compare Paraguay to Dante's inferno and López to the tyrant

Nero and the vulture that ate Prometheus's liver. He called him a madman and a flagrant criminal, and quoted Washburn quoting Shakespeare: ' "A horse, a horse, my kingdom for a horse" – in such a case López would have been satisfied with a jackass.' Every word of this was read by López and passed by him for publication both in Paraguay and abroad.

To be fair, Francisco probably did not understand Bliss's frequent use of Latin quotations, citing classical authors neither López nor his cohorts would have heard of, not least as many of them were made up. Bliss also used this exercise to play upon López's superstitious nature, sprinkling the prose with signs and ill-omens and claiming that López was cursed by the letter B, then V, then W.

'Never, perhaps, in the whole history of the world, have so many lies been crammed into so small a space,' wrote Masterman jealously.

Ironically, when Washburn left Paraguay he was condemned both for criticising López and for leaving Bliss and Masterman behind. But when his book came out, Bliss himself was condemned for his criticism of Washburn. Washburn, however, praised Bliss's book as an intellectual and literary feat and described its author as both heroic and noble; Washburn was, after all, all too aware under what circumstances it had been written.

Bliss ended his 323-page diatribe with these paragraphs:

'We have sketched with free strokes the history of the greatest violation of the duties of a neutral diplomat that modern times can offer. We denounce to the Divine anger, to the opprobrium of the world, and to the condign punishment of his country, Charles Ames

Washburn as guilty of high treason, and particularly of an enormous conspiracy against the government to which he was accredited, and against the life of the supreme Magistrate of this Republic of Paraguay.

'Our present task is concluded; but at laying aside the pen we swear solemnly, if God gives us the opportunity, to follow Washburn through all the earth until he shall receive the just punishment of his unheard-of and execrable crime.'

Francisco was delighted and Bliss and Masterman were freed from their fetters. But God was not about to give them the opportunity to leave Paraguay in pursuit of the evil Washburn just yet.

Towards the end of 1868 – after four years of senseless slaughter – Caxias finally twigged that, rather than have his men fight their way against fanatical resistance through the disease-infested swamps along the east side of the River Paraguay, they could simply build a corduroy road up the deserted Chaco side and outflank the enemy with the minimum loss of life. So in November 1868 he took his entire army of 32,000 men across the river and marched them across the Chaco. Then he crossed back over the river above the Paraguayan positions at San Antonio, four miles north of Villeta, and attacked López by surprise from the rear.

To keep them out of the hands of the advancing Brazilians, the prisoners were taken on another long forced march.

'Men, women and children, in three divisions,' recalled Masterman, 'were hemmed in by soldiers on foot and horseback, fully armed and with sticks in their hands, with which they thrashed those outside and those that fell from exhaustion; whilst the officers, with drawn swords, rode amongst them, dealing out blows right and left with wanton cruelty.'

The less fortunate, usually those who could in no way be connected to the 'conspiracy', were told by a rueful López that due to an unexpected movement of the Allied troops, they were to be shot to prevent them from falling into the enemy's hands. Masterman recalled that a group of prisoners were beaten and slaughtered as Eliza rode by in a carriage.

'She bowed with a gracious smile,' he said. 'We took off our caps to her, all well knowing that a word from her could send us to the scaffold, or worse, on the morrow.'

Masterman, Bliss, Taylor and the rest of the surviving prisoners eventually arrived at Pikysyry where they staked out in a huge encampment on a dried-out bog. At first they were lucky. The cold southerly winds merely covered them with dust. Later it began to rain and they found themselves living in a swamp. The torture, suffering and random executions continued as before. One afternoon, Masterman saw the English sculptor Monygham, formerly an assistant to the Italian master Marochetti, who had come to Paraguay to carve some figures for López's new palace, in the *uruguayana*. But, for most of the British and Americans, there were some small creature comforts.

'One evening an officer came round with a number of little boxes, containing gifts from Mrs Lynch, to be divided amongst those mentioned in a list he held in his hand,' Masterman recalled. 'I received some cigars, sugar, *yerba* and a bottle of rum; and after living upon scanty meals of boiled meat, often without salt, for two months, it may be imagined with what satisfaction I discussed them.'

From the list, Masterman discovered that Major Manlove was still alive, though he was not to survive for much longer.

With the Brazilians now attacking from the north, López had to have new trenches dug to keep his house, which had previously been safely in the rear, out of rifle range. But there was no time to dig a trench all the way around the house and the east side was left open.

'This, however, did not signify with a general like Caxias, who was certain to find out which was the strong side and attack it,' wrote Colonel Thompson.

Although Thompson's batteries at Angostura were now in operation, the Brazilian ironclads had already passed them and the whole of the river was now under their control. However, neutral shipping was allowed to make contact with the Paraguayans at Angostura. HMS *Beacon* turned up to take away any remaining British subjects, but Captain Parsons was informed that none wanted to leave and was given the plum-pudding treatment by Eliza. Eventually he was allowed to talk with an English mechanic who, owing to the deaths of his superiors, had risen to become head of the arsenal and was drawing a large salary. Even then the conversation had to take place within earshot of López. In the end, López relented and allowed Dr Fox and a dozen English women and children to leave, along with a large number of copies of Bliss's book – so that Britain, too, would know of Washburn's villainy. Fifty-two other foreign nationals were allowed to leave on an Italian gunboat and a French ship came to take away the Chancellor of the

French Consulate, M. Libertat, who had confessed under torture to being paid £8,000 to join the conspiracy. He was one of only three Frenchmen, out of over 100, to survive the war. According to Cecilio Báez, Eliza made use of this neutral shipping to smuggle more goodies out of the country. And Colonel Thompson, who was Commander at Angostura at the time, noted: 'Some of these steamers took away a number of heavy cases, each of which required some six to eight men to lift; they probably contained some of the ladies' jewellery, which had been collected in 1867, as well as a large number of doubloons.'

On 3 December 1868, the USS *Wasp* returned. That same day Masterman and Bliss were freed from their shackles. Masterman received gifts of tea, sugar, biscuits and cigars, while Commodore Kirkland and Captain Ramsey were wined and dined by Eliza. Over dinner López told them that, much as he would like to release Bliss and Masterman into their custody, they had been found guilty of conspiracy and what became of them was up to the investigating tribunal. But then he agreed to let them go, provided that they were tried in the United States.

An extradition hearing was hastily convened under Padres Maiz and Romàn, and the army's chief torturer Major Aveiro, formerly a secretary in the Internal Revenue Service. Bliss and Masterman were warned to repeat what they had said in their confessions and were reminded that their lives depended on their discretion. Kirkland and Ramsey sat in on the hearings, while Bliss and Masterman were cross-questioned. The two naval officers noted down the evidence of Masterman and

Bliss's guilt, so that they could stand trial in the United States. Between sessions the two American naval officers were plied with *caña*, cigars and gifts of expensive lace, while Bliss and Masterman were lightly tortured to remind them that they were still very much in Francisco's hands.

Masterman and Bliss were forced, once again, to declare that they were guilty of conspiring against López. Their detailed confessions took days to reprise. Masterman did not much care about lying in front of Kirkland and Ramsey as he assumed that Bliss alone would be released as he was an American, but he began to fear that they were being discredited in front of the American officers so that they could be shot without any diplomatic repercussions.

To his surprise, at the end of the hearings, Masterman was told by Padre Maiz that the President had seen fit to commute his death sentence to banishment for life, provided he spent the rest of his days praising the clemency of Francisco and denouncing the wickedness of Washburn. Masterman promised to tell the truth, which he duly did in *Seven Eventful Years in Paraguay* – though it was not the truth as López or Maiz would have wanted it told.

Bliss was then told that he had not only been pardoned but forgiven, López had been so convinced by Bliss's literary masterpiece. The two men were to be released on the condition that they help prosecute Washburn in the United States for 'malfeasance in office'. López provided Bliss with 40 copies of his own book, so he could distribute them to influential people in the USA, and $60 in gold coin for his trouble. Bliss was tactful enough to ask López what he should do with the $5,000 in silver, and $5,550 in currency that he had admitted under torture that he had been paid for his part in the conspiracy and had already sent abroad. López generously said that he could keep the fictitious money or, if his conscience troubled him, hand it in at the Paraguayan Legation in Paris. The two men shook hands with their torturers and shared a glass of rum with them. Then, after three gruelling months at the mercy of López, they were released into the custody of the US Navy.

As they clambered up the gangplank on to the *USS Wasp*, they thought they were free. Instead they were sent for'ard, kept under guard and forced to sleep on the bare deck like criminals. Although Commodore Kirkland really thought they were innocent, according to Masterman, 'he had been so ingeniously flattered and cajoled by López and Mrs Lynch that he looked on the plot as reality'.

Although Kirkland and Ramsey seemed to accept Masterman and Bliss's confessions at face value, the ship's surgeon lavished his attention on them – Bliss was still suffering from the effects of the *cepo uruguayana* – and a petty officer smuggled some clean clothes to them. They had been wearing the same clothes for three months. At Montevideo, they were transferred to the flagship *Guerriere*, where they were given the run of the ship and ate in the officers' mess – though they were still, technically, under arrest. At Rio, they were sent on a merchant steamer, the *Mississippi*, to the United States, on their honour to report directly to the Secretary of State. When they did, he told them that they were free to go; there was no case against them. Bliss then published a full retraction of *La Historia Secreta*, while Masterman went home to write *Seven Eventful Years in Paraguay*, which was published in London in 1869. In it he revealed to the outside world the devastation that had been caused by Eliza and López.

'The Paraguayans exist no longer,' he wrote, 'there is a gap in the family of nations; but the story of their sufferings and of their heroism should not perish with them.'

When the *Wasp* had arrived at Angostura, it had brought with it Washburn's replacement, General Martin T. McMahon. On 12 December 1868, he presented himself at Francisco's headquarters in Pikysyry. The last thing López wanted was trouble with a new American Ambassador and he invited him to dinner. Nor did McMahon wish to find himself in Washburn's position and he quickly made it clear his sympathies were with Paraguay as the underdog in the war. He saw no reason to interview Bliss and Masterman and reported back to the US Secretary of State that, under the benign leadership of Francisco Solano López, political prisoners were not being treated with 'unnecessary harshness'.

McMahon cannot have been unaware of the mass execution of political prisoners that took place on 21 December. Many of them were flogged before being shot, some receiving up to 2,000 lashes, according to Captain Adolfo Saguier, a torturer who himself was put to torture when some of his victims refused to confess. Benigno López was nearly cut to pieces before being shot in front of his sisters Inocencia and Rafaela. That same day Doña Inocencia witnessed the execution of her husband. Dr Carreras, the former President of Uruguay, it was said, 'shrieked most piteously' while being beaten with hide ropes and sticks before his execution. Bishop Palacios, Dean Bogado, Juliana Martínez, Dolòres Recaldè, Doña Mercedes Ejusquiza – her sister Maria had died in prison – and many others faced the firing squad that day. According to Padre Maiz, a few minutes after the executions, Captain Miranda, an officer in charge of one of the firing squads, encountered Eliza crossing the encampment on foot. Her eyes were red and she had a handkerchief balled in her hand.

'You are weeping?' he asked in astonishment. 'For them?'

Eliza, it is said, looked at him scornfully. 'Only a fool would weep for them,' she said.

Perhaps McMahon reported none of this as 'unnecessary harshness' because he had already fallen under Eliza's spell. In public, he referred to her as 'Her Excellency'. And later, when asked to described Madame Lynch to the US Congress, McMahon painted a glowing portrait.

'She is a lady of Irish parentage, of English birth, and of French education,' he said. 'She has lived with the President for some fifteen years and is recognised and regarded by López as the mistress of his household and the mother of his children and is very much respected and loved in Paraguay, as far as my observation went. López has no other family that I am aware of; he has one son, older, who was born before he knew Mrs Lynch; but I heard of no other. Mrs Lynch always presided at his table and took care of all the internal affairs of his house, educating the children and everything of the kind. She is a woman who has been grossly maligned, I think, by the press of Buenos Aires which charged her with all sorts of immoralities, such as being cruel, instigating the President to unheard-of deeds of atrocity and with everything that could be written about a woman.' On the contrary, he said, she was 'one of the most bewitching and gallant ladies it has ever been my privilege to meet'.

The day that López was murdering his political prisoners, he should have been saving his bullets. For, on 21 December 1868, a series of battles began that were to be his Waterloo. The Paraguayans fought with characteristic valour – 'as if for liberty rather than their own perpetual enslavement' in Washburn's view.

'There were children of tender years who crawled back, dragging their shattered limbs, or with ghastly bullet-wounds in their little half-naked bodies,' wrote McMahon. 'They neither wept nor groaned, nor asked for surgeons or attendance; and, when they felt the pressure of the merciful hand of death heavy upon them, they would lie down and die as silently as they had suffered. Yet these children, many of them, had mothers not far off.'

When the fighting began, López acted with 'characteristic prudence', as Dr Stewart put it, cowering behind the walls of his headquarters at Pikysyry. Constantly beside him was his 'Lady Macbeth' – ever ready to 'incite him to his barbarities and to keep him from deserting his post'. But again, on occasions she had trouble in doing even that. He would withdraw so suddenly that even Eliza would not know where he had gone. She would search the battlefield and, when she found someone who had seen him make off, she would set off after him on horseback. Afterward, though, Eliza was 'at great pains to impress on all that he had exposed himself with reckless valour'. She even claimed on one occasion that one bullet had passed through his whiskers, while another ricocheted between his legs.

While the Paraguayan foot soldiers were mindlessly brave, the Brazilians were characteristically circumspect. Their cavalry muffed a chance to overrun the Paraguayan headquarters and capture López. According to one of the more fanciful accounts of the war, when Eliza saw that Francisco was in danger, she leapt upon a horse and led a regiment of half-naked Guaraní women bare-backed into battle to rescue him.

'The Brazilians, seeing a horde of wild women coming towards them like a tidal wave, turned tail and fled,' wrote Henry Lyon Young. At that moment, Eliza's horse stumbled. Apparently, its lungs had burst with effort, she had ridden it so hard. Eliza was trapped under the dead animal. Von Wisner and six men had to lift it off her. Bruised and bleeding, she was carried off on a crude litter to face the wrath of López, who cursed her for risking her life.

When Sir Richard Burton was in Paraguay in 1869, he heard similar tales. It was said that at Lomas Valentinas, López had two horses shot from under him, while Eliza sustained three wounds. 'Of this I believe not a word,' said Burton.

Something, however, must have put the wind up López, because on 23 December 1868 he wrote his will. It read: 'I, the undersigned, Marshal-President of the Republic of Paraguay, by this present document, declare formally and solemnly, that, thankful of the services of Madame Elisa A. Lynch, I make in her favour a pure and perfect gift of all my goods, rights and personal actions, and it is my will that this disposition be faithfully and legally complied with.'

The document was witnessed by the two British doctors, Stewart and Skinner, and named McMahon as executor, although he had only arrived at López's head-quarters eleven days earlier. McMahon also became custodian of the López children, who he took out of harm's way to Piribebuy – which succeeded Luque as Paraguay's capital – while Eliza stayed behind at Pikysyry to bolster Francisco's courage.

Two days later, on Christmas Day 1868, the Allies called on López to surrender, making it clear, once again, that their war was with the dictator of Paraguay, not with its people. In López's enormously long-winded reply, he said that his country had imposed on him the duty to defend the Fatherland and 'I take glory in fulfilling it to the last; as for the rest, history will be the judge and I owe an account of my actions only to God'.

By this time his troops were outnumbered by more than six to one. The situation was hopeless and López could no longer afford to waste men or bullets on executing his political prisoners. So they were simply left staked out in fetters in places where they were exposed to Brazilian shellfire.

'I felt no fear,' said Taylor, who found himself laid out in a *cepo de lazo* under enemy bombardment. 'The shocking misery I had suffered for five months had blunted, indeed, nearly obliterated, all feelings, moral and physical.'

Then, after four days, he got lucky. Eliza rode through his prison enclosure with López. She pointed out Taylor, von Treuenfeld and a number of other foreigners. López feigned not to know what they were doing there and had them released – from the *cepo de lazo*, though, not from the enclosure. Out of some 500 staked out there, ten were lucky enough to be freed. This did not guarantee their survival. Some were killed in the final charge two days later. Taylor was wounded in the shoulder by a rifle ball. He escaped into the woods and, later that day, fell into the hands of the Brazilians, who were far from merciful. Prisoners who did not have the strength to move were killed. Taylor himself was too weak to walk, but Caxias took pity on him.

'I was a miserable object, reduced to a skeleton and enfeebled to the last degree,' he said. After four days' recuperation, Taylor set off on horseback for Asunción, but suffered terribly on the road 'for I had scarcely any flesh on my bones, and had not strength enough to keep myself in the saddle'.

When he boarded the gunboat HMS *Cracker* at Asunción to be taken down-river to Buenos Aires, he weighed just 98 pounds, compared to 178 pounds five months earlier, when he left Luque. By the time he was rescued his wife and four children were out in the cordilleras, but they survived and were reunited the following August. Alonzo Taylor was not alone in believing that he had been saved from certain death by the intervention of Eliza. The *Buenos Ayres Standard* of 26 August 1869 carried reports of her kindness towards the British survivors and McMahon sent a cutting from a Buenos Aires newspaper into the Congressional record which said: 'We publish today an interesting narrative of one of the English Paraguayan sufferers just come down. He speaks in the highest terms of the kindness shown to himself and his wife and also to all of the other English in López's employment by Madame Lynch, and he, in common with all the sufferers, denounces in the most indignant terms, the calumnies and slanders that have, from time to time, appeared in some of the organs of the press against this heroic woman who has ever exerted herself to mitigate the suffering which the war entailed upon the Paraguayan people.'

But none had a good word to say about López. After seven days of fighting among the wooded swamps and low hills of the Lomas Valentinas, he suddenly fled alone to Cerro Leon, his old training camp some 30 miles inland, leaving Eliza to her fate. According to Colonel Thompson, she 'went among the bullets looking for him'. When she found that he had gone, she mustered all those who could find horse – some 60 in all including the Generals Resquin and Caballero – and made off after him.

As a professional soldier, Colonel Thompson was particularly appalled by López's flight. 'He repeatedly swore to the troops that he would stay and conquer, or die with them,' said Thompson. 'On this going away, almost without smelling power, the men, though so well trained as to think everything he did as perfectly right, yet felt disgusted with him, and I have heard many of them who were taken prisoners descant upon his cowardice.'

The foot soldiers were simply abandoned without orders. Few were taken prisoner as they continued fighting whatever the odds, men throwing themselves single-handedly at battalions. Even those who were surrounded or terminally wounded fought on ferociously. There was no point in doing anything else. Those who surrendered knew that their families would be killed; those who escaped the enemy faced torture. But Thompson had no wife and children in Paraguay to worry about. After López fled, he found that he been left surrounded at Angostura, without any provisions. And when ammunition ran low he surrendered with 800 fighting men, 500 women and 400 wounded, and went home to England to write *The War in Paraguay*.

Even though he had a family, Dr Stewart risked staying behind at Pikysyry to attend the wounded and was captured. He was taken to Rio de Janeiro where he told the Emperor of his low opinion of López. When this was reported in the newspapers, he feared for the safety of his wife and children who were still in Paraguay. Eliza later claimed that Stewart had deserted – that he had 'taken advantage of the attack' to defect to the Allies. His wife and children were arrested. One child died in captivity and only a sudden Brazilian advance prevented the rest of his family from being starved to death.

Even though Eliza was happy to slander Dr Stewart, though the lives of his wife and children were at stake, she would have nothing bad said about Francisco. After the flight from the Lomas Valentinas, Eliza told the French Consul M. Cuberville: 'We have had a great disaster, we owe it to Monsieur Caminos.'

Caminos, who was now Minister of War, was shot.

López had 'withdrawn' so swiftly from Pikysyry that his clothes, his baggage, his female slaves and his papers were all captured. Among them were a copy of his will and a diary written by López's loyal lieutenant General Resquin, which contains the names of hundreds of people who had been executed for their part in the supposed conspiracy. It covered only the period 17 June to 14 December 1868, during which 605 people had been executed or 'died in prison' – that is, tortured to death. These included 220 foreigners and 224 Paraguayan nationals. In other cases, the nationality was not known. Another 85 were executed on a single day, 22 August. Among them were the hero of the Battle of Richuelo John Watts, the Argentine Ramon Capedevila and his brother Aureliano, Confederate Major James Manlove and an English merchant named William Stark. When Stark was arrested, Thompson said, all his money was taken – including money he had in safekeeping for others – right down to the loose shillings in his wife's pockets. Her fate is unknown, though her name does not appear among those of the survivors.

So who was ultimately responsible for these atrocities? Washburn had no doubt – Eliza.

'To this bad, selfish, pitiless woman may be ascribed many of the numberless acts of cruelty of her paramour,' he wrote. 'That she was the direct cause of the arrest, torture, and execution of thousands of the best people in Paraguay there is no doubt, and it is equally certain that it was for her benefit and that of her children that so many hundreds were arrested and robbed of their property, and afterwards tortured as conspirators or traitors, and then executed, that they should never, by any contingency of war, survive to reclaim their own.'

Others blamed Palacios for the numerous cruelties of the regime – López himself blamed Palacios, until he was disposed of and, mysteriously the atrocities continued. In her book *Exposición y Protesta* Eliza herself said that the atrocities were carried out by individuals under the command of Francisco, but without his knowledge. The details were then leaked to the Allies to use as anti-López propaganda.

Colonel Thompson said that some of the blame must be shared by the Brazilians for failing to capture López once again. Even though Caxias had 8,000 cavalry and fresh horses, he let López slip through his fingers at Lomas Valentinas. And when Francisco fled from Pikysyry, Caxias did not pursue him. Even though Cerro Leon lay in the middle of a wide, flat valley that was impossible to defend – even if López had had the men to defend it – Caxias did not attack. According to Thompson, a professional soldier, Caxias could have taken López at that point without the loss of another man. And he wondered why he did not do so: 'Was it from imbecility, or from a wish to make money out of army contracts? Was it to have an excuse for maintaining a Brazilian army in Paraguay, or was there an understanding between Caxias and López? Or was it done with the view of allowing López to reassemble the remainder of the Paraguayans, in order to exterminate them in "civilised warfare"?'

Masterman agreed that the last may, indeed, have been the case. Back in Croydon correcting the proofs of his book, Masterman said that he had 'seen a gentleman, recently returned from the Plate, who has had unusually good opportunities of forming a correct judgement of the way the war was conducted'. This was probably Sir Richard Burton, who had then returned to England. 'He is of the opinion that the war was intended, from the first, to be one of utter extermination; that Caxias did blunder most miserably, but also that he intentionally protracted the war in the hope that the unfortunate Paraguayans would die from want and disease; and that Brazil intends to absorb all she has left of the Republic,' Masterman wrote in an appendix.

Burton had met Caxias at his headquarters in López's farmhouse on the Tebicuary and called him the 'Wellington of South America', though he shared Thompson's opinion that he was slow to act decisively and always attacked at the strongest point. And in August 1869, when Masterman's book was published, Burton also declared that the Paraguayan race was 'doomed'.

Instead of finishing off López at Cerro Leon, Caxias turned on Asunción, which fell without a resistance. He had a *Te Deum* sung in the unfinished cathedral and returned to Brazil, proclaiming on 21 January 1869 that the war was over. This was welcome news: the war had been costing Dom Pedro $60 million a year – the Uruguayans and Argentinians having long since stopped sending even token contributions. Caxias was honoured, enriched and ennobled. López set about digging in once more, while, in London, Thompson summed up the situation.

'The termination of the Paraguayan war now entirely depends on the state of López's pantry,' he wrote, 'and will end when his stock of wine and other good things has been consumed as he will then think he has done enough for glory.'

Of course, the wine and other good things were Eliza's department.

13

DOWNFALL OF A TYRANT

Five years before, Eliza had been first lady of the most powerful nation in South America and her realm showed every sign of expanding. But due to the strategic ineptitude of her lover, Paraguay had lost control of the Paraná river and its outlet to the sea. With the loss of Humaitá, López had also lost control of the Paraguay river, so the entire country now lay at the feet of the enemy. Finally, with the flight from Lomas Valentinas and the loss of Angostura, the remnants of the Paraguayan Army had lost all contact with the river and, with it, any hope of help from the outside world.

The barracks at Cerro Leon, which had once held 60,000 well-trained fighting men, was now one huge hospital. A high proportion of the wounded were women and children. Even the uninjured were half-naked and as thin as walking skeletons, but they knew better than to complain. The merest hint of discontent was a crime punishable by death. Most received that reward in any case. As food supplies fell dangerously low, López drove those too weak or too badly wounded to aid the war effort out of the camp to starve to death in the countryside.

Meanwhile, back at his old training camp, López began rebuilding his army.

Even before Asunción fell, López had taken the precaution of moving the capital from nearby Luque to Piribebuy, a town of whitewashed houses built around a central square and a church that dated back to 1767, about 40 miles east of Asunción. The move was a somewhat theoretical exercise as most of the members of López's government were either dead or in chains. Piribebuy's peacetime population of 3,000 to 4,000 was trebled by the newcomers, though their number was kept in check by cholera. Food was scarce and people slept in corridors. But they did manage to keep clean. At the foot of the slope on which the town was built runs a clear and rapid stream where the entire population of Piribebuy bathed every day – 'the women generally after nightfall', observed McMahon, who had established the new US Legation at Piribebuy. This is one of the numerous places around Paraguay where Eliza is said to have bathed in a stream or taken a shower under a waterfall. A story is also told of a daring train raid on occupied Asunción from the station at Patiño while Madame Lynch spent the day bathing in Lake Ypacaraí. To this day, the Paraguayans like the idea of the beautiful Eliza taking her clothes off.

Dr Stewart had visited Eliza at Piribebuy before he was captured. He had joined Eliza and von Wisner and McMahon in the evenings to play whist or sit on the verandah, smoking and drinking what Dr Stewart said was excellent claret.

'Even in this backwater,' said Stewart, 'Madame Lynch's house exuded an air of Europe.'

Another of Eliza's guests was the son of Admiral

Davis, who headed the squadron of the US Navy operating on the river. According to Navy surgeon Dr Marius Duvall: 'Young Davis ... when he came back spoke of having a splendid time, driving in a coach and four with Mrs Lynch, and was particularly delighted with the little arrangements of Mrs Lynch, when she had some of the prettiest girls in Paraguay to wait on the table, veiled very faintly indeed.'

Davis himself visited McMahon at Piribebuy and found that the new Legation was next door to Eliza's house. It was said that they were lovers. She seemed to be free with her favours to anyone who could secure her future. According to McMahon, things seemed to be patched up between Eliza and Doña Juana at the time. At Francisco's behest, Eliza took the children to dine with their grandmother on her birthday. McMahon was also invited, but declined. However, McMahon's picture of Eliza and the former *La Presidenta* playing happy families at last must be taken with a pinch of salt. He also told a Congressional committee that Inocencia and Rafaela had not suffered at their brother's hands, while many others saw them imprisoned and flogged.

In April 1869, while romance blossomed between McMahon and Eliza, Sir Richard Burton was making his way up the Paraguay river. He had heard much about Eliza in Buenos Aires and was keen to see around her house at Paso Pucú. At Villeta, he noted that the Paraguayan dead remained unburied and he saw the corpses being robbed by deserters from the Allied armies who had set up a maroon colony in the Gran Chaco.

Arriving in Asunción, he was greatly impressed by Francisco's 'Buckingham Palace'. He also visited one of

Eliza's impressive country estates, where he was struck by her outdoor plunge-bath in a grassy hollow – now a national monument. Like so many Paraguayans, Sir Richard also seems to have been fascinated by the idea of Eliza taking her clothes off.

Burton never aquired the photograph of Eliza that he had been repeatedly promised. But he recorded a detailed description:

'An English officer who she had impressed most favourably described her as somewhat resembling Her Imperial Majesty of France,' he wrote, 'tall, "belle femme", handsome, with grey-blue eyes – once blue, and her hair *châtain-clair* [light chestnut] somewhat sprinkled with grey. These signs of age are easily to be accounted for; her nerve must have been terribly tried since the campaign began, by telegrams which were delivered even at dinner time, while every gun, fired in a new direction, caused a disturbance. She and her children have been hurried from place to place, and at times she must have been a prey to the most wearying and wearing anxiety. Her figure threatens to be bulky, and to accompany a duplicity of chin: it is, however, a silly rumour which reports that, like another La Vallière [the mistress of Louis XIV], she lost her influence over her "fickle lord" since she inclined to stoutness . . . Only on one occasion did she betray to my informant some anxiety as to whether the British Minister would visit Paraguay.'

Burton was also concerned that the large number of 'unutilised women' he saw should be put to use repopulating the country. But there was a problem. For centuries, he wrote, it had been noted that in Paraguay the birth rates were unequal with many more girls than boys being born.

'This peculiarity would doubtless be the effect of a hot damp climate of the lowlands affecting the procreative power of the male,' wrote Burton, 'and combined with the debauchery of the people, would, to a certain extent, tend to limit multiplication.'

Since the beginning of the war few marriages had been permitted in Paraguay and Burton concluded: 'Unless she establishes polygamy her history is at an end.'

However, Burton was not heartened when he discovered that a vigorous start was being made. On his tour of the still unfinished cathedral, he was 'startled by the impudence of a French '*Frère ignorantin*', who, disturbed in fierce love-making to a pretty Paraguayan, stared fiercely at me from his stray corner as if I, forsooth, had been the offender'.

Although the war had officially been over for several months, by the time of Burton's visit to Paraguay, fighting had already broken out again. At some point Dom Pedro realised that holding Asunción or even occupying the entire country was not enough. As long as López was still at large, the war was not over. So he sent his son-in-law, the Comte d'Eu, Francisco's one-time rival for the hand of Princess Isabella, to Paraguay to finish the job. By this time López had gathered up an army of stragglers which he moved from Cerro Leon to the Ascurra Pass in the cordilleras, which he fortified to bar the road to Piribebuy.

With Francisco out of town at Ascurra, Eliza was still free to pursue her affair with McMahon, though the circumstances were not always conducive to romance. McMahon regularly awoke to find the bodies of women who had starved to death at the gates of his legation. However, he reported to Washington that people were even worse off in Asunción, though it is hard to see how. Eliza's affair with McMahon may have had motives other than the entirely amorous. It was alleged that there were some peculiar pecuniary arrangements between the two of them. As Burton noted when he saw the house next door to Francisco's palace in Asunción that Eliza had bought to turn into a hotel: 'In Paraguay money-making is a passion even more passionate than love-making.'

After five months in Paraguay, McMahon received a letter from the State Department recalling him. Washburn seems to have been behind this; he was still very much involved with the situation in Paraguay. Indeed they may have been in correspondence as Washburn wrote to McMahon asking him to let him know 'something of Mrs Lynch and her brats'. But Washburn came to fear that McMahon was closer to Eliza and Francisco than was appropriate for the best conduct of American foreign policy and was repeating in his despatches their allegations that Washburn was the mastermind behind a conspiracy to overthrow the Paraguayan Government. However, there had been in the meantime a change of government in the United States and Washburn's brother Elihu B. Washburne – with an 'e' – had been appointed Secretary of State in Ulysses S. Grant's first administration in 1869. The press deplored the appointment, suggesting that it threw 'grave doubts upon Grant's fitness to hold office'. Washburne survived just eleven days in the post, but the day before he left office he recalled McMahon.

Despite being ordered home, McMahon hung on in

Piribebuy for another four weeks. When he went it was noted that he had a great deal more luggage with him than when he had arrived. Washburn speculated that he was smuggling out still more of Eliza's ill-gotten property. Cecilio Báez claimed that McMahon took a number of boxes containing gold coin and jewellery belonging to the womenfolk of Paraguay out of the country for Eliza. According to Báez, the delay in his departure was caused by the amount of time it took to count out $900,000 in gold and silver coin. Apparently the counting went on all night and day in an office near the town's political headquarters under the auspices of the veteran Don Manuel Solalinda. The boxes were taken out of town one morning in full view of the people of Piribebuy. But no matter how pecuniary the affair, it seems to have left McMahon in a poetic mood. On his departure he wrote the ode *Resurgirás Paraguay*.

McMahon also took with him a copy of Francisco's will. López was sad to see him going. It was a blow to have a sympathetic American ambassador withdrawn after so short a time, but López consoled himself with the idea that McMahon was such a good friend that he might still be able persuade the United States to join the war on Paraguay's side. This gave Francisco new heart and further prolonged the war, according to Eliza. However, McMahon did not go straight back to Washington to plead Francisco's cause. Even though he was scheduled to appear before a Congressional committee, he went to Paris instead – though first he found himself taunted in Buenos Aires by an effigy of himself in a woman's dress. The *porteños* found it amusing that he had acted as nursemaid to Eliza Lynch's children while she fought on the battle fields. He delivered 500 ounces of gold to Emiliano López, Francisco's son by Juana Pesoa, who worked at the legation in Paris. This was the young man that Eliza later adopted. It was thought that McMahon then visited London where, according to Báez, he deposited 4,400 ounces of gold and 5,600 silver dollars with the Bank of England, in the account of Dr Stewart on the understanding, Eliza would later claim, that it would be returned to her on demand. When McMahon eventually returned to the United States, he wrote a piece about the plucky Paraguayans and their war effort in *Harper's Magazine* and told Congress that Francisco was in an impregnable position and had all the food he needed to hold out. But, by then, López had already abandoned Ascurra and was on the run in the interior, and neither Congress nor President Grant could see any reason to intervene on his behalf.

The torturer turned victim Adolfo Saguier also reported that treasure stolen from foreigners, along with more from the Treasury, was smuggled out of the country from Piribebuy. Apparently, McMahon was not the only diplomat to extend his services to Eliza. When Masterman related Saguier's story, he reported that the French and Italian consuls were still living in Paraguay on the most intimate terms with López, 'receiving presents from him and Mrs Lynch, making speeches in his favour at the public entertainments, and dining tête-à-tête with him and his mistress, whilst their countrymen, whom they had been sent to protect, were being put to death, day by day, after suffering the most appalling tortures and misery'. The money left the country on French and Italian gunboats in boxes that were 'marked as belonging to Mrs Lynch'.

McMahon and Washburn ended up slugging it out before the House Foreign Affairs Committee. While Washburn accused McMahon of smuggling valuables out of the country for Eliza – even alleging that McMahon, too, had come out of Paraguay a much wealthier man than he went in – McMahon countered by accusing Washburn of meddling in the domestic affairs of the country. After hundreds of hours of hearings and thousands of pages of testimony, the Congressional committee decided that both of them had acted in a manner unbecoming to a representative of the United States and put an end to both their diplomatic careers.

McMahon had been right when he said that López had been well dug in at Ascurra. Thompson estimated that his troops could have repulsed ten times their number in a frontal attack. But the Comte d'Eu was not a general in the Caxias' mould. He did not find López's strongest point and attack it. Instead he outflanked Ascurra, massacring the populations of Pirayú and Paraguari on the way, and attacked Piribebuy on 12 August 1869. The town was defended by a semi-circular trench and a ring of small bombs called 'pussies' – in the lubricious sense – because they could destroy a man. When the Brazilians entered the town itself, they found it defended by women and children armed with clubs and led, it was said, by Eliza herself. The battle lasted five days and, towards the end, the heroines of Piribebuy resorted to throwing stones, bottles, broken glass and clods of earth. The final slaughter took place in the church in the centre of the square. Human remains have been found under the altar. The savagery of the attack was unequalled during the war. The Brazilian cavalry rode back and forth over their helpless victims, who included babies in their mothers' arms. Six hundred wounded were burnt to death when the invaders set fire to the hospital and the garrison commander, who had surrendered honourably, had his throat slit. After the slaughter, the Brazilians toasted their victory in Eliza's champagne.

'Unfortunately, the quantity of champagne was quite small,' wrote Alfredo d'Escragnolle Taunay, a captain in the Brazilian cavalry and later a celebrated writer. However, he found a large number of silver coins in her house and an expensively bound copy of *Don Quixote*. Unfortunately, not all the Brazilians were as cultured as Senhor Taunay. The remains of the national library and the national archives were burnt and, according to Padre Maiz, 'a large amount of gold and silver was divided among the Allies with Satanic greed'. Paraguayan depictions of the Battle of Piribebuy also suggest that the surviving women were raped.

López celebrated with a *Te Deum* when he heard that the Brazilians had attacked Piribebuy instead of Ascurra, where he was. It was only afterwards that he realised that he was now surrounded. Over the next two nights, López withdrew all his men from Ascurra to Caraguatay, a village to the north which, at the time, was no more than a collection of reed huts. According to Cunninghame Graham, 600 carts were assembled for the final plunge into the wilderness. He quoted Paraguay historian Dr Carlos Zubizarreta, who said that the carts contained 'most of the money of the public Treasury, much of the jewellery that Madame Lynch had extorted from the Paraguayan women, along with wines and provisions enough to last for months, and above all, all the salt López could lay his hands on'.

The contingent sent out on the first night, led by López himself, got through. But the second night's party, which comprised the main part of the army, were caught by the Brazilians. Much of the remaining artillery and the bulk of the army's provisions were lost. And only six men escaped.

Not only had López lost his third seat of government, but he also lost the right to rule. On 15 August 1869, a provisional government was formed in Asunción, comprising a triumvirate of Paraguayan exiles. At the same time the Brazilian government declared López to be an outlaw. So by extension Eliza had gone from being the putative Empress of South America to being a bandit queen.

In the first four years of the war, the slow-moving Caxias had allowed López to flee periodically, then dig in. But the Comte d'Eu never gave him the chance to regroup and pursued him relentlessly across north-east Paraguay. He forced López to withdraw almost immediately from Caraguatay to San Estanislao, over unexplored mountains and through swamps and virgin forest, inhabited by jaguars, pumas, tapir and Carrigua Indians, armed with blowpipes. For Eliza, it was a nightmare of mosquitoes, malaria and massacres.

'During this march,' said General Resquin, 'many women and children died, the soldiers often losing their way, since the road was heavy going, and they made scarcely any halt to eat or sleep.'

It is also said that, somewhere along the way, the remains of the Paraguayan treasure was hidden, rather than let it fall into the hands of the Brazilians. One tale is that emaciated men, loaded like pack animals, climbed to the top of cliff in Mbaracayo range and threw the gold over the cliffs. It was claimed that López ordered the bearers to throw themselves over to their deaths after it, so that its exact whereabouts would remain a secret. Treasure hunters have been searching for it ever since.

As he went, López drove the entire civilian population before him on the grounds that the Brazilians would slaughter them. They were largely women and children as any male over the age of nine was in the army. Even so, he did not have enough troops to keep such a large number of women and children in order. So when they came across more women and children, his soldiers simply slaughtered them – to prevent the Brazilians from doing so. Those taken had no shelter and survived on wild oranges and palm nuts. Tens of thousands died of starvation, while stragglers were butchered before they fell into enemy hands. The Brazilians pursuing them frequently came across heaps of mutilated bodies left unburied. Women and children, particularly, were expendable, because the troops employed to guard them were of more use fighting the enemy. Besides, López said that, were he to fall, no Paraguayan should survive him. This included the remaining members of his family.

'When we were ordered to march after the battle of Piribebuy, a soldier offered to carry the hides we used as beds,' said Inocencia. 'It was lucky he did this, otherwise we would have all perished of hunger, for along the march we used to scrape the hair off and roast the hide. This was our only food. On arriving at the place designated by López, such was our awful condition that the girls, almost perfectly naked, had to wander through the woods, in the terrific heat, in search of a frog, or a snake, or any kind of insect to eat. The Carrigua Indians at times would bring us a piece of meat of some unknown animal, or cassava or maize, for which we gave them a gold ring or some other valuable trinket. But our moral suffering was even worse. How often have we seen a mother weeping over her unfortunate child expiring from famine.'

López saw little of this suffering. He never accompanied his army on the march. Eliza, Francisco and the children travelled by carriage some two days ahead – 'well out of danger of the scouting parties of the Allies', in the words of Cunninghame Graham. Along the way Eliza's imported landau collapsed and she was forced to resort to an old Spanish carriage with high wheels and leather springs. Worse, she had to abandon her beloved piano at a place that is known to this day as Piano, Paraguay.

Things were going so badly that López began to suspect another conspiracy. A man and a woman had been captured outside Caraguatay, but the man had escaped. The woman was brought to Francisco's headquarters for interrogation when they reached San Estanislao. Under torture she confessed that the man had been a Brazilian spy and that he had learnt from a soldier named Aquino that part of López's escort was planning to assassinate him. Captain Aquino was beaten and put in the *cepo* until he confessed – telling López that it was not he who he wished to destroy, but the country. Then Francisco showed a kindlier side. He ordered that Aquino should be given something to eat and drink. Aquino then denounced others who, under torture, denounced still more.

'So at one blow were executed 86 individuals of the troop and sixteen officials,' said Resquin. Among them were the commandant of the escort, Colonel Mongilo, and his second in command, Major Rivero – not because they were conspirators, but because they should have known about the plot. The men were flogged to within an inch of their lives in front of López, then shot. But that was not enough to satisfy him.

Writing in the newspaper *La Estrella* on 10 September 1869 an Italian priest named Father Geronimo Becchi said: 'More than 8,000 people were martyred by López, mostly killed by the lance . . . López killed manifestly to make himself master of the goods both of his fallen countrymen and of foreigners, taking good care to destroy the traces of his villainy, thus it was that after their executions he killed the executioners.'

Soon, the rest of world's press, which had supported López up to this point, turned against him. Reports of the supposed conspiracy and López's reprisals soon appeared in the *Anglo-Brazilian Times* and *The Times* of London. The only detail that varied was the number of people who died. A new newspaper published in Asunción called *Regeneracion Paraguay* reported that two Paraguayan women, named Vicenca and Marcellina, who had escaped to the Allied lines, said that López had shot 1,000 men 'after which the tyrant went to contemplate the corpses one by one'. The story goes that, hearing continuous fusillades of shots, a sentry asked his sergeant whether the Brazilians were attacking.

'No,' said the sergeant, 'they are only shooting the prisoners.'

Regeneracion Paraguay also reported that the retreating

column was on its way to Bolivia with twelve cart-loads of money. And behind it, on the road, López had left guards with orders to lance any men or women who turned back.

While the Comte d'Eu made a fresh landing 60 miles upriver from Asunción at Rosario to attack López from the west, the Allied vanguard took San Joaquín, blocking the pass in the Caaguazú Cordilla and preventing López moving east or south. He had no choice but to turn northwards towards Ygatimy and the unpopulated quarter of northern Paraguay. Instead of trying to outrun the Brazilians, the column stopped on the way to Ygatimy for six days for a further investigation of the latest conspiracy. This time 60 more were shot, including Aquino. By then, even the ultra-loyal Resquin was in fear of his life.

'López was a monster, and so entirely disregarded the lives of those next to him,' Resquin said later, 'that for no reason whatever he would order his most faithful followers to be killed.'

But Francisco did not see himself as a monster of course. Quite the opposite. It is said that, along the way, he had an altar built and Padre Maiz convened the 'Sacred College of Paraguay' which elected to make López a saint. Those who did not vote for this blasphemous act were shot. Twenty-three more died. Then a bizarre ceremony was performed at the roadside shrine.

'Rows of black-hooded priests, perspiring in the tropical night intoned the *Magnificat*,' wrote Henry Lyon Young. 'Francisco stood before the altar looking like a bull and was anointed, glorified, beatified and sanctified.

Six hundred voices burst into song and chanted Gloria in Excelsis.'

Santo Francisco Solano II of Paraguay was then swathed in costly robes and a gold biretta was placed on his head, while Padre Maiz announced that Francisco's birthday – 24 July – was to be the saint's day of the newest of heaven's elect. But even being a saint did not prevent the ungodly from conspiring against you.

López had had the wife of Colonel Hilario Marco – the former police chief of Asunción and widely believed to be the most feared man in Paraguay outside the López family – arrested. Under torture, she denounced her own husband, along with Francisco's surviving brother Venancio, his mother and his sisters. They were planning to put poison in his food, she said. Doña Juana, the former *Presidenta*, was arrested once again and Inocencia and Rafaela, who had been at liberty for some time, were flogged and returned to their carts.

Summoning Resquin and his other senior officers, López asked them whether he should put his mother on trial for treason. All of them, except Major Aveiro, the renowned master of the *cepo*, counselled that it would be better if he did not. López went wild. He agreed with Major Aveiro. She should be tried like any other common criminal. Of course, they would need witnesses against her, so Colonel Marco was flogged until he confirmed his wife's confession and also denounced Doña Juana.

Dr Frederick Skinner, the English physician who took over as Surgeon-General of the Paraguayan Army when Dr Stewart was captured, was present at the summary trial. Doña Juana, Inocencia, Rafaela and Venancio were all found guilty. Although Doña Juana was now over 70 years old, she was sentenced to regular floggings for her part in the conspiracy, though she 'piteously pleaded her advanced age and disease of the heart'. It did her no good. The punishment was carried out in public, by a common soldier. Inocencia and Rafaela were beaten every day, while Venancio was flogged until he was barely living, then stabbed to death.

Skinner, who was with Francisco up to three minutes before his death, described López as an 'unparalleled brute' and worse. In a letter to Washburn, he wrote: 'Who but he ever flogged his own mother and sisters, and killed his brothers – one, after a mock trial, by bullet; the other, by starvation and flogging with a double lasso, a lance-thrust finishing the scene of torture when the victim could no longer move. Who else exterminated a whole people by starvation, while he, his mistress and bastards, passed a life of comfort, feasting, nay drinking choice wine *ad libitum*, surrounded by every convenience attainable in a retreat from a pursuing army?'

Skinner also said that at the time of his death López 'had stores sufficient to have saved numbers, amongst them several cart-loads of salt, which his victims and followers had not tasted for months. I felt the want of it more than any other privation.'

While Francisco and Eliza continued to live well, the Brazilians relentlessly forced them on across swamps, through jungles and over mountain ranges. Doña Juana had joined her daughters in a prison cage on the back of a cart. And dragged along behind them was Pancha Garmendia, once the 'jewel of Asunción' who had rejected Francisco's loathsome advances 23 years earlier. According to Washburn, she had been 'kept alive apparently with no other motive than that she might bear floggings that were almost daily visited on her once fair and round, but now emaciated and shrunken shoulders'. She was lanced to death in the closing days of the war.

Juana Pesoa, López's former mistress and mother of Emiliano, who Eliza was to adopt, also seems to have perished on this final death march. Washburn says: 'She was exposed to the most terrible hardships, and, it is supposed, perished of want and exposure.'

Countless thousands of nameless men, women and children died of fatigue, disease and starvation, and those who could not walk or got left behind were shot or bayoneted to save ammunition.

The main column was down to about 1,200 men, along with a battalion of women and six artillery pieces, when they crossed the Mbaracayo range in the Cordillera del Amambay and began hacking their way through the virgin forest of *Ilex paraguayiensis* – the trees that *maté* leaves come from – to make a path for Eliza's coach. They established their last capital at a natural amphitheatre called Cerro Corá, on the banks of the Aquidaban in the extreme north-eastern corner of Paraguay, on the night of 6 February 1870. Cerro Corá can only be approached by two gorges, the Chiriguelo and the Picada de Yateho. This meant the enemy would have to attack through one of these narrow passes, while the other would be an escape route in case of defeat. López's plan was to set up a rump state out in the jungle and continue his struggle. He had already made treaties with the local Indian tribes and had contrived to get them published abroad by allowing copies to fall into the hands of the Brazilians. If he fought on long enough, López believed that the world would come to see that he was invincible. According to Cunninghame Graham, even towards the end of 1869, López believed that the United States, France, or Britain – or all three – would intervene to stop the war.

In the meantime, life went on much as always for Eliza and Francisco. When not on the march, López rose generally at about nine o'clock, drank chocolate, smoked a cigar or two and dallied with his toilet until it was time to sit down to a substantial breakfast with Eliza and his five sons. He would spend the rest of the day fulfilling his military duties or dispensing summary justice. Then, when evening came, Eliza would set a table that would have shamed most fighting generals, among trees strung with garlands of bright lianas.

While Eliza, Francisco and the children ate well, his mother and sisters were kept at the edge of starvation. He was scrupulous on this point. They were not to die, otherwise he would be deprived of the pleasure of torturing them. Their jailers were ordered to give them 50 lashes a day until the day they died, but they were to be killed immediately if the Brazilians broke through.

The army was also on the point of starvation and Francisco's conspicuous consumption did little for morale. Before, when Madame Lynch had served up sumptuous meals to her overweight lover, it had been done behind closed doors. But at Cerro Corá, under the lianas, the starving soldiers could see the pair, all dressed up for dinner, dining from the best china and silverware all the delicacies that the enlisted men were denied and guzzling wine from crystal. Just the smell of food hanging on the hot summer-night air must have driven the starving troops crazy. Reconnoitring parties and pickets began to melt away. So there was no warning when, early on the morning of 1 March, the Brazilians under General José Antonio Correa da Cámarra arrived unannounced and in force. The soldiers guarding the pass fled at the sight of them. Thinking the enemy was miles away, López was asleep. By the time he awoke, it was too late to organise any serious resistance. So he mounted the horse he kept permanently saddled and galloped off. Eliza ran to the carriage she always kept prepared for such an eventuality and got the younger children on board. And, with a small escort under seventeen-year-old Panchito, who was by now a full colonel, she made off into the woods, fleeing the remnants of her empire. When the Brazilians arrived at López's headquarters, they found little opposition. A few surviving members of Francisco's inner circle were killed. General Resquin and Major Aveiro surrendered, while General Caballero got away with a handful of men.

Dr Skinner was also captured, but he was set free. He was so thin and weak that 'the Comte d'Eu ascertained that I was one of the monster's victims, not one of his accomplices'. He had suffered financially too. The pay he had received for nine years' service was not enough for him to pay his passage home to England and he had to stay on in Paraguay after the war.

'Now that the war is over', he wrote in his letter to Washburn, 'all the dreadful atrocities of the unparalleled brute López cannot fail to be brought to light . . . I was very much grieved and disgusted at hearing them doubted in some papers, and attempts made to gloss over, or rather to deny, the fact of his being the very worst devil that ever polluted this earth.'

What happened to López after he fled we cannot know for certain as there were no independent witnesses present. So, in this case, we ought to allow history to be written by the victors. Their story is that, to make good his escape, López had to cross a little tributary of the Aquidaban called the Aquidaban Nigui. The ground near the bank was muddy and the horse got stuck. López dismounted and made off across the narrow brook on foot.

The Paraguayan version is less ignominious: López was wounded in the battle and was helped down to the river by two colonels.

In either case, when he was half-way across the river, the Brazilians caught up with him. General Cámarra gave the order that he should be taken alive. A corporal named Lacerda, known as *Chico Diablo* – 'Little Devil' – went to disarm him. López drew a gun and tried to shoot Cámarra but, according to an eye-witness, *Chico* 'thrust at the tyrant with a lance and he fell head first into the muddy stream'. He got to his feet, then sank to his knees and begged to be spared. But he was hit by a shot from an unknown hand – a Paraguayan one perhaps. According to legend, he cried: '*Muero con mi patria*' – 'I die with my country'. Then he expired.

With his death, the spell was broken. Until then, no one had raised a hand against him. Now, when his body was retrieved from the stream it had to be guarded from the surviving Paraguayan women, who wanted to tear it to pieces. Meanwhile, those who had been his most loyal torturers and murderers became the loudest to denounce him.

Eliza was captured – it was said she was fleeing

through the jungle in a ball gown. When Panchito stepped in to protect her, he was ordered to put up his sword. He refused, replying that it was the duty of a Paraguayan officer to die rather than surrender. A Brazilian ran him through with a lance. When she was brought back to the camp, Eliza, too, had to be protected from the surviving women who, it was said, would have 'dug out her eyes with bodkins, stripped her of the elegant silks and jewels she still wore and thrust her mutilated body into the Aquidaban to become food for the alligators'.

López's mother and sisters were also captured, but the women of Paraguay showed no enmity towards them. They were considered fellow victims and, like the other women, the López ladies once again cursed Eliza. Nevertheless, when Doña Juana saw Francisco's body, she wept.

'Why do you weep, Mother?' asked Rafaela. 'He was no son, no brother. He was a monster.'

It seems that General Cámarra gave Eliza permission to bury Francisco. She had to dig his grave with her bare hands. Panchito was buried nearby. The Paraguayans have a different version. They say that Mariscal López's body was being mutilated for sport by the Brazilians and that Eliza, leading a phalanx of loyal Paraguayan women, stole it at night, carried it away into the jungle and buried it secretly.

The news of López's death reached the outside world via a letter which General Cámarra wrote to the Emperor from his camp on the left bank of the Aquidaban on 1 March 1870.

'I write to you from López's encampment in the Sierra,'

it said. 'The tyrant is routed, and, having refused to surrender, was killed before my own eyes. I intimated to him to surrender when he was completely defeated and seriously wounded, and having before refused, he was killed.'

'Having lived like a tyrant he died like a soldier,' commented *The Times* of London. But this was to damn with faint praise. Summing up his contribution to what it called 'one of the strangest and most terrible chapters in the history of mankind', *The Times* went on to say: 'He was ahead of his age in soaring ambition and behind it in military science. He lacked generals and the smallest spark of military talent . . . As a patriot he was nothing, for he refused to leave the country when Gould offered him the most honourable tools. As a soldier he was still less, for he never figured on the battlefield until hunted down at Aquidaban.' The newspaper also condemned his 'terrible cruelties, which have spread a pall over his native land' and concluded: 'The only act of this extraordinary man since the war began that commands admiration is his death.'

By contrast, the mysterious Mrs Lynch received a remarkably good press. By this time, a large number of British survivors had made their way to Buenos Aires and were full of praise for the compassion she had shown them when they were in captivity.

'All are agreed that during the war Madame Lynch has done her utmost to mitigate the miseries of the captives, and to make the so-called '*détenus*' [prisoners] comfortable,' wrote Sir Richard Burton. Which only goes to show that some people can fall in a sewer and come out smelling of roses.

❦ 14 ❧

ELIZA IN EXILE

The women were taken to Concepción, the nearest town on the river. From there steamers took them to Asunción. The city was virtually a ruin, partly due to storm damage which occurred after its evacuation and partly due to the Brazilian occupation. Doña Juana, Inocencia and Rafaela went ashore there. For some time they were held under surveillance, then they were allowed to occupy one of their old houses. Eliza was held on board the Brazilian gunboat *Princeza* – for her own safety.

Estimates of how many people died in the war vary considerably. The *Encyclopedia Americana* says that the male population was virtually exterminated. Of the Paraguayan population of 1,200,000 at the beginning of the war, it says, 200,000 women and only 28,000 males survived – largely returned exiles and boys. Washburn reckons that, of 450,000 women at the beginning of the war, not 60,000 were left alive and, of 350,000 men, only 20,000 survived – if you included boys under ten – and just 10,000 if you did not. Most of these died, not from gunshot wounds or fighting, but of disease and starvation. Two English engineers caught up in the conflict – Percy Burrell and Henry Valpy – reckoned that 120,000 women and children died of hunger and exposure between the withdrawal from Pikysyry on 27 December 1868 and their escape on 21 August 1869, after which the mortality rate increased. The Allies lost 300,000 men. So at the very least Eliza's war consumed over one million people, making it the bloodiest war in the Americas – the four years of the American Civil War cost the United States 618,000 lives.

Paraguay lost 50,000 square miles of territory to Argentina and Brazil, including its two richest provinces in the south, and continued paying reparations to Brazil into the 1930s. In 1870, Brazil estimated that the war cost them $600 million. Indeed, the Brazilian Minister of War had told the *Anglo-Brazilian Times* of 23 June 1869: 'If the war lasts ten months longer, Brazil will be ruined.' When López fell on 1 March 1870, there were still two months to go.

Paraguay would probably have been dismembered completely if the Allies had not fallen out directly after their victory. The Brazilians were the major occupying force and encouraged fresh insurrections in Uruguay and Argentina to maintain the upper hand in Paraguay. But Brazil itself was also unsettled by the participation of so many slaves in the war. Its first anti-slavery law, the 'Free Womb Act', which freed children born to slaves, was passed in 1871 against the wishes of Pedro II and fatally undermined his authority. Argentina's influence in the region was further diminished when it was forced to return a large tract of the Chaco to Paraguay in 1878, after arbitration by US President Rutherford B. Hayes. The province now bears his name. But rivalry among the former Allies continued to destabilise the country. In the

84 years between the end of the war and 1954, when Stroessner seized power, Paraguay had 41 heads of state. In one year alone, three were sworn in – a record even the Italians would envy.

After all Paraguay had suffered, its people felt someone had to pay. López was dead. But Eliza was still alive and in Allied hands. The provisional government in Asunción demanded that she be handed over. The Brazilians refused. The women of Asunción got up a petition outlining the wrongs they had suffered at her hands. She had seen them imprisoned, tortured and starved, while she robbed them of their jewellery in the pretence that it was being used for the defence of their country. In fact, it had been taken for the benefit of Madame Lynch and the offspring of the tyrant who had murdered their husbands, brothers, fathers and sons.

Even the end of the war had not alleviated their sufferings. When they returned to Asunción emaciated and naked, walking down the street without shame, they found themselves the sport of the Brazilian and Argentine troops who were occupying the city. The victors did little to help. It has been said that, when it was heard that Mariscal López was dead, a ball was held in celebration – the first for many years not organised by Eliza. Under the circumstances, this seems unlikely. As it was, the women of Ascunción now pleaded that Madame Lynch 'should not be allowed to leave with the property of those she had robbed to spend in another country'. As a result, on 4 May 1870, the provisional government passed a law confiscating all Eliza's property – and all the property the López family acquired since Carlos came to power in 1841. Unfortunately, it was too loosely worded for its purpose and a second act had to be passed on 10 July 1871.

By then Eliza was long gone. The Brazilians had released her and sent her down the river on board the steamer *Jauru*. At Montevideo, she and her four surviving sons boarded the *City of Limerick* bound for Europe. She also took with her Rosita Carreras, another of Francisco's children who she raised as her own – though some sources maintain that Rosita was little more than an unpaid servant. And she took Isidora Díaz, the sister of one of Francisco's favourite generals, who had perished in one of his purges. As Eliza headed out across the Atlantic, she must have thought back to the adventurous voyage she had made in the other direction on board the *Tacuari* seventeen years earlier. Many of the adolescent dreams she had had on that trip had now been sunk. Her empire had collapsed. Hundreds of thousands of her subjects were dead. Others were dying. Her adopted country was in ruins and she was going into exile. She was just 35.

She may have lost an empire and a lover, but she was not exactly penniless. Although some of the other women had grabbed her carriage, gowns and some of her silver plate at Cerro Corá, she had managed to hang on to a large casket. On 21 May 1870, on board the *Princeza*, the Brazilian authorities made an inventory of her possessions. The box contained: six gold bars; $14,000 in – now worthless – Paraguayan currency; another 391 ounces of gold; promissory notes signed by McMahon and the Italian Consul who had also been smuggling her valuables out of the country; 55 assorted pieces of jewellery, including 40 gold rings; 23 fastenings in precious metals including six gold cuff links and five gold waistcoat buttons; twenty watch guards and chains; sixteen bracelets, including two made out of human hair; eleven gold watches, nine of them men's; ten pairs of earrings; six silver *bombillas* trimmed in gold; five silver *maté* spoons; four gold *peinetas de oro* head combs, one studded with diamonds; two rosaries and one crucifix made out of gold and red coral; one gold crown; and one Commander of the Order of Christ pendant and medal.

She also had some keepsakes of Francisco's: two gold snuff boxes; the gold book given to him by the grateful people of Paraguay and another in mother of pearl given to him by the citizens of Buenos Aires when he negotiated the end of the Argentine civil war; a gold cigar holder; a number of rosaries strung on gold chains; his marshal's baton and whip with the initials *F.S.L.* picked out in diamonds. She had also managed to salvage nineteen sets of children's toys, twelve in gold. And a box belonging to Rosita Carreras was found to contain 51 pieces of jewellery and seven pairs of toys in gold and topaz.

Eliza may have intended to return to Paris and settle there as her sons spoke French, the language the López-Lynches had used *en famille*. But Paris was no longer a safe place to be. The Franco-Prussian War had just begun and, by July, Eliza was ensconced in a fashionable house not far from Hyde Park in London. From there it was but a short coach ride to visit her money. She had on deposit in the Bank of England over 4,000 ounces of gold, worth more than $64,000 at the time.

When Eliza was younger she had followed in the footsteps of the Empress Eugénie. Now it was Eugénie who followed. In July 1870, Eugénie had encouraged

Napoleon III to declare war on Prussia. It was said that she was so excited at the prospect of war it made her look ten years younger. Her enthusiam was short-lived. When Napoleon III was defeated at the Battle of Sedan in September 1870, the Second Empire collapsed and Eugénie had fled to England. While Francisco had managed to postpone his ultimate defeat for nearly six years, Napoleon III had lost everything in two-and-a-half months. Eliza had lost Francisco at Cerro Corá, while Eugénie shared her exile with Napoleon for two-and-a-half years before he died, though she lived on for another 50 years as a widow. She would also learn what it was like to lose a son in battle. Her only son, Louis, was killed in the Zulu War in 1879.

Eliza put her remaining sons into school either in Richmond or at St Joseph's College in Croydon. Sources differ. But her youngest, five-year-old Leopoldo Antonio, perished on 21 July 1870 from convulsions brought on by congenital malaria, which was apparently exacerbated by London's damp climate. He is buried in the cemetery of St Mary's Church, on the Harrow Road in Kensal Green. The death certificate says that he was the son of the President of Paraguay. Present at the death was Emiliano López, the son of Juana Pesoa. He signed the certificate as witness. Perhaps Eliza was too distraught with grief to attend. Nevertheless, nine days later, on 30 July 1870, she was composed enough to instruct a solicitor to fight for the £100,000 that was in Dr Stewart's hands and which she claimed was rightfully hers. This included $70,000 in gold coin and the profits on the sale of a large quantity of *yerbe maté*.

Stewart had already been sued in the Scottish courts by

Eliza's agent Antoine Gelot over a bill of exchange for £4,000 he had signed. Stewart claimed that, towards the end of 1866, Eliza had summoned him to her house in Paso Pucú and, 'after intimating that López designed some terrible act of violence, opened the question of money'. Stewart was already in disfavour with Francisco for excusing sick men from duty. Eliza had claimed that she had plenty of money, but it was of no use to her inside the country. She wanted to make a remittance to Europe, but could not find a way to do it easily because of the blockade; she asked Dr Stewart for a bill for £4,000 to be paid by his brother Robert, a banker in Scotland. At first he hesitated but, in May 1867, she told him: 'I fear the President is going to do something, for which I will never forgive him.' Although he pretended not to be afraid, Stewart drew up and signed the bills she required. If he had refused, he said, he feared Eliza 'would have used her influence with López to have had him tortured or executed for some pretended offence'. Eliza remitted the money to Europe, but in Paraguay she did not pay up.

López also gave Stewart £12,000 in bullion to ship out of the country on an Italian gunboat and quantities of *yerba maté* that his brother George was to sell in Buenos Aires. He did not tell López that he intended keeping the money against what he was owed – 'that would have been equivalent to shooting myself,' he said. Stewart maintained that his salary of £800 a year – making him the highest paid foreigner in López's service – remained unpaid and that estates belonging to his Paraguayan wife had been confiscated, along with valuables lodged in the US Legation in Asunción. As far as Stewart was aware López did not know about the bill he had signed for

Eliza, which was a private affair. However, Eliza certainly knew of the financial arrangements that he had made with López.

In September 1868, after being taken prisoner by the Brazilian Army, Stewart returned to Scotland. He was sued by Gelot in the Court of Sessions in Edinburgh for the monies, which he had refused to pay on the grounds that the bill had been extorted from him with 'force and fear, without value received'. In his defence, Stewart told the jury what was going on in Paraguay: how López conceived the wildest jealousies of his best friends and most faithful servants – even, indeed, of his own family; how his suspicions meant imprisonment, torture, and death; and how Madame Lynch, his ruling favourite, exerted a unique power over the President.

'I have seen many executions,' Stewart told the court. 'I have seen from twenty to seventy and eighty a day, laden with irons, led out of the place where the prisoners were; I have seen a body of infantry accompany them; I have heard the discharge of musketry, and a little while afterwards I have seen the infantrymen return with the irons, saying they had despatched the prisoners, and now the irons were ready for more. But generally the executioner's work was forestalled by the mere effects of imprisonment.' Dr Stewart said that very few were ever released from prison and, with scarcely an exception, all who were not immediately executed died in jail. 'Hundreds of respectable people of the country' and at least a dozen British subjects shared the same fate, according to Stewart.

Washburn, Masterman, Laurent Cochelet, Burrell and Valpy all testified that Stewart was in real fear of his life.

They related the horrors they had witnessed in Paraguay and all of them testified that Eliza was the real power behind the throne.

'She was a very designing, very cunning and very avaricious woman,' said Valpy. 'She worked on the feelings and ambition of López, and did an immense deal of harm to the country.' He also told the court how Eliza used fear of López to make 'sharp' bargains. 'I have known her to buy several estates with a few bags of salt.'

Valpy testified that anyone who fell foul of her for the slightest of reasons suffered: 'I have been told of a Frenchman being cast into prison for saying Madame Lynch wore false hair. He was only let out of prison to die of his sufferings.'

After she had returned to Britain in 1870, Eliza was able to take up the case on her own behalf. But Stewart claimed that, as she was a married woman, Eliza had no right to sue. Eliza went so far as to get a letter from Quatrefages, dated 7 December 1870, granting her power of attorney. Then Stewart claimed that the Scottish courts had no jurisdiction and the matter could only be adjudicated under the laws of Paraguay. His solicitor produced documents from the provisional government of Paraguay, showing that Eliza and her lover had systematically robbed the country, that they had abrogated López's will and had given Stewart permission to hold on to anything he could get against his back salary.

Eventually the Edinburgh court found that Eliza had to find more proof that the money Dr Stewart had belonged to her. However, the court also found that, as Francisco's rightful heir, she should have the proceeds from the sale of the *yerba maté*. Stewart promptly filed for bankruptcy.

Eliza told the sorry tale in 1875 in her book *Exposición y Protesta*: 'In 1865, Marshal López sold Dr Stewart a large quantity of *yerba maté* from his own private holdings, worth about 112,000 gold pesos; George Duncan Stewart acted as agent. The latter gave a letter of acceptance for the sum in favour of his brother, the doctor, payable in Buenos Aires as soon as the Argentine government raised its embargo. Marshall López ordered Dr Stewart to endorse this letter in my favour and he did so. After the embargo was raised, George Duncan Stewart sold the *yerba* for 350,000 gold pesos, approximately, according to the papers.

'In 1868, I handed over to Dr Stewart 4,400 gold ounces [each worth about £3 15s at the time] and 5,659 *paticones* of silver, which were remitted in his name to Europe with some money belonging to other British subjects. In this remittance, Dr Stewart's private total was 800 gold pesos, according to his own letter and declaration.

'Moreover, in 1864, Robert Stewart, to whom the doctor made payment in Paraguay as one of the directors of the Royal Bank of Scotland, received from Marshal López over £400 sterling.

'As the result of all this, the fortune which I entrusted to Dr Stewart and which was exclusively mine amounted to 212,000 gold pesos, disregarding interest. To force Dr Stewart to return these deposits to me, I had to demand them of him before the Scottish courts, and when I won the case, he declared himself insolvent.'

But this was only the beginning of Eliza's legal battles. In March 1871, the government of Paraguay sued Eliza and General McMahon, who were seeking to obtain probate on Francisco's will – though McMahon claimed later that he had no standing in the case. The new government in Asunción wanted to prevent them getting their hands on 'divers sums of money and securities alleged to have been sent to England by the late President' on the grounds that the money belonged to the government of Paraguay and that a bill had been passed confiscating the dead tyrant's property. The following month Eliza countersued the Paraguayan government for abrogating Francisco's will. The Court of Probate and Divorce in London found in her favour, ruling that Francisco's will was valid under Paraguayan law at the time of his death.

But the victory was shortlived. On 19 February 1872, the front page of *The Times* – which, until 1966, printed personal advertisements – carried a notice from the Attorney of the Government of Paraguay in Great Britain, one Richard Lees, a solicitor in Galashiels, accusing Eliza of 'having robbed monies of the national treasury, of felony and of despoiling and extorting the fortune, money and jewellery of natives and foreigners and of being the adulterous accomplice in the assassination and tortures practised by the late ex-President Francisco Solano López'. These were not the sort of things matrons in Kensington were usually accused of in the Victorian era. Eliza was summoned to appear before the courts of Paraguay within four months and warned that, if she did not, she would be tried *in absentia*.

Eliza sued again, charging the government of Paraguay with defamation. Again the English courts found in her favour. The Paraguayan government tried once more, this time claiming in the London courts that 1,000 ounces of gold and over £3,500 sent to England by Francisco actually belonged to them. Yet again the courts found in favour of Eliza.

Even though the court case against Stewart had left her out of pocket, Eliza was by no means poor. Cunninghame Graham saw her several times in London in 1873, getting into her carriage at her house, which he remembered as being in Thurloe Square or Hyde Park Gate. In fact, this was socially rather a step up from 10 Southwick Street, on the north side of the park near Marble Arch, which was the address given on the death certificate of little Leopoldo.

'She was then about forty years of age, well made, beginning to put on a little flesh, with her abundant hair just flecked with grey,' said Cunninghame Graham. 'In her well-made Parisian clothes, she looked more French than English, and had no touch of the untidiness that so often marks the Irish woman. She was still handsome and distinguished-looking. Her face was oval and her appearance did not seem that of one who had looked death so often in the face, lived for so long in circumstances so strange and terrifying, buried her lover and her son with her own hands and lived to tell the tale.'

No one seeing her at the Brompton Oratory on a Sunday morning with her three surviving sons would have credited her story.

By 1874, Eliza had returned to Paris, now a very different city from the one she had left in 1853. Baron Haussmann had demolished the old slums and turned Paris into the 'city of light'. It was a richer city too, for her at least. M. Gelot, her agent, was holding more than half-a-million dollars worth of jewellery and currency for her and seems to have had other valuables belonging to Francisco, who would not be able to collect them.

Eliza had other business in Paris. Juan Bautista Gill – first as Paraguay's Finance Minister, then, after the assassination of one president and the deposition of another, as head of state – had invited her to return to Paraguay. After her victories in the British courts, Eliza was confident that she could prove she had come by the property she owned in Asunción honestly. In *Exposición y Protesta* she claimed that she had only made her acquisitions because Francisco's brother Benigno had put all his property on the market when the war was going badly and she was trying to avert a panic, though she admitted buying some downtown property near Francisco's palace to develop a shopping street there.

She also claimed that, when she was being held on the Brazilian gunboat in Asunción harbour, she had offered to return the title deeds to all the properties she had bought, if the vendors gave her her money back. But her kind offer was refused 'because they wanted to keep the property and the money'. This was typical, she said. She was always looked down on by people in society who 'shamelessly besmirched my good name, and that of my innocent children, the sons of the national hero, and tried to deprive me of all that was legally mine'.

Since then the 'heartless men in power and authority' in Paraguay had embargoed all her assets and nullified the deeds. As a 'defenceless woman at the mercy of the malicious multitudes', she was mortified at the way they repaid 'the myriad kindnesses I have always shown towards these unlucky people'.

To prove her case, Eliza needed the papers she had lodged with her attorney in Paraguay, a Frenchman named Edmon Berchon des Essart. Unfortunately des Essart had been assassinated – Eliza asserted – by a vindictive mob. The mob would have looted his house had the French Consul not intervened. He rescued the papers and sent them back to France where Eliza began the tortuous bureaucratic process of retrieving them.

In June 1875, Eliza and her son Enrique boarded the Royal Mail packet for Buenos Aires where, it seems, she had not been forgotten. According to writer Henry Lyon Young, she was taken to see a play based on her life story entitled *Madame Lynch*. While there, she tried to sue the Argentinian government for the possession of furniture looted from her various homes that, she claimed, was 'adorning the rooms of the National Government building'. Although Sir Richard Burton had seen furniture that was clearly hers in Buenos Aires, she was laughed out of court. By this time, Burton was on his way back to India.

In October 1875, she made the trip up the river once more, on the steamer *Cisne*. She must have felt almost as much trepidation making this trip as she had the first time. Criminal charges were still hanging over her head and an anonymous letter had appeared in *La Tribuna* claiming that she dare not go to Paraguay in case she was 'kidnapped and tortured to reveal where Paraguay's treasure lay buried'. Nevertheless she set out, eager, she said, 'to answer the charges made against me and to confront all my enemies at the very seat of their power, having no other support than that of my conscience and my deeds'.

On the way she saw the dismantled ruins of Humaitá and the other forts she had occupied with her lover. Although what she had seen the first time she came up the river had seemed primitive, it was now even less developed. Post-war Paraguay was wracked with poverty, hunger and corruption. According to a visitor, after the end of the war 'outcasts, tramps and adventurers corrupted with vices, the scum of humanity removed here to appropriate to themselves the estates of the perished Guaranís and to console the hundreds of thousands of bereaved widows and maidens'.

Eliza described her reception in Ascunción as rapturous. Word spread through the city that she had returned and people rushed to the quayside. When she disembarked she was surrounded by people who embraced her and kissed her and shook her hand.

'All of them wanted to touch me and talk to me,' she said. 'As we walked along the streets, people in their doorways recognised me and greeted me kindly. The merchants in San Francisco Square surrounded me with expressions of joy and affection and joined in my procession.'

Eliza stayed with Isadora Díaz, who had returned to Paraguay with Rosita Carreras and Emiliano López in 1872. She expected an invitation to the palace from Juan Gill who – after a short period of exile in Brazil – was now President. Instead, the 'daughters, wives, mothers and sisters' of Asunción drew up a manifesto, published in *La Reforma*, demanding 'in the name of the victims that the woman Eliza A. Lynch sacrificed' and the constitution that she either be expelled from the country or face criminal charges. Seeing the way the wind was blowing,

Gill reneged on the guarantees of immunity that he had given her. Consequently, according to Eliza, she 'decided to leave the country'. To help her on her way, it seems Gill provided an armed escort and a boat to take her back to Buenos Aires. Gill was assassinated soon after.

In Buenos Aires Eliza wrote *Exposición y Protesta*. It is said that she failed to pay the printer, spawning a fresh round of legal suits. She left her second son Enrique in Buenos Aires – to be joined later by his brother Carlos when the latter finished his education in Europe – to fight for her possessions in Paraguay, while she returned to London, where she faced yet more litigation.

Inflation caused by the Franco-Prussian War and the Paris Commune would have greatly reduced the value of any paper money Eliza had on deposit in her Parisian bank. However, the valuables she had sent over from Paraguay and the money she still had in England, would have meant that when she returned to Paris she could live in some style. She occupied a mansion at 1 Avenue Ulrich in the fashionable seventeenth *arrondissement*, though one writer puts her on the swanky Rue de Rivoli, where the Empress Eugénie would stay when she returned to Paris to shed a tear over the destruction of the Tuileries Palace.

It was said that Eliza made a pilgrimage to the Holy Land to repent her sins; surely a lengthy journey would have been required. It is also said that she visited Ireland, where she was treated as a Latin American version of Lady Hamilton. One glorious version of her story has her running into her old friend Franz Liszt, who expressed his regret that she had not taken his advice and gone on the concert platform. Regrettably there is no mention of this intriguing encounter in any of his biographies. A meaner tale has her returning to her old profession, as a Madam Lynch rather than Madame Lynch. Her family maintained that she spent the rest of her life trying to clear her own name and that of Francisco – apparently the family history even compares her to Joan of Arc.

Photographs of her in exile show that she grew rather stout and lost the luminous beauty of her youth. It is possible that she made another trip to Buenos Aires to sign all her Paraguayan possessions over to her sons. Eventually her funds ran low, perhaps as a result of her continuing taste for champagne and high fashion. By the time she died, she was living in a lodging house at Number 54 Boulevard Pereire. This was not the palatial living quarters that Eliza had been used to, but it enabled her to keep up appearances – after all, it was still in the seventeenth. The Parisian probate records show that she owned no substantial property when she died, but she was certainly not on the breadline. Her youngest son Federico Noel seems to have become a successful executive in a French phone company and she did not go to the pauper's grave that some sources suggest.

⁓§ 15 §⁓

EMPRESS AT LAST

Eliza died on 25 July 1886. But it was not until two days later that her body was discovered, when the police broke down the door of her apartment. The cause of death has been variously ascribed to stomach cancer or malnutrition. She was just 51. The death certificate describes her as the 'widow of Francisco Solano López' and as a woman of independent means. As she died in the seventeenth, she should have been buried in the cemetery of Montmartre. But her son Federico paid for a very small plot in Père Lachaise just two metres wide, the smallest available for an adult. She was buried in the ground, rather than in a tomb or 'cellar' as is usually the case there. It is not known whether Pedro II visited her grave when he was exiled to Paris in 1889.

'Ever since the Paraguayan War, I have been expecting a revolution, but it took me by surprise at this moment', he said. With his fall, slavery was finally abolished in Brazil.

They became near neighbours in death in 1891, when Pedro was laid out for a requiem mass at the Madeleine Church, built by Napoleon in honour of the Grande Armée, before his body was taken by train to Lisbon. His remains were returned to Brazil in 1920. He now lies in a chapel in Petropolis, the city named in his honour.

In May 1900, Eliza was dug up and moved up the hill to Division 92 to be reburied in the Martin family tomb with Estelle. Père Lachaise historian M. Charlet suggests that Eliza and Estelle were sisters or close friends. The Martins paid for the masonry. The López family inscription was added much later. On 26 March 1928, one Jeanne Martin was buried there too. It is thought she was Estelle's daughter. Next into the grave, on 25 February 1932, was a Pierre Xavier Coste de Champéron, whose wife, Lucienne Coste de Champéron, née Brisset, followed him on 10 July 1936. By that time, the reassessment of Francisco's reputation was under way in Paraguay and the replica of the national flag and great seal of Paraguay were added.

In the 1930s Francisco Solano went from being the 'worst devil who ever polluted this earth' to a hero in the eyes of Paraguayans because of a war – not the one that he lost but one that they won. Having fought her neighbours to the south so disastrously, Paraguay turned her attention to her neighbour to the north, Bolivia. Early in the twentieth century a long-running dispute began over the Chaco Boreal, the largely worthless area of scrub, forest and swamp that separated the two countries. Paraguay claimed the territory on the grounds that a handful of Paraguayan missionaries and settlers had inhabited the area, and strengthened its frontier garrisons. However, the War of the Pacific between Bolivia and Chile (1879–1884) lost Bolivia its Pacific coastal province of Atacama and left the country landlocked. Bolivia needed the Chaco Boreal to give it access to the sea down the Paraguay river. Then a rumour began that there might be oil in the Chaco. So far, this has proved to be unfounded, but oil has always been an excellent reason for armed conflict.

A series of border incidents in December 1928 precipitated full-scale war. In the ensuing conflict, Bolivia seemed to have every advantage. It had three times the population of Paraguay, which had yet to recover from the impact of Eliza and Francisco. It had the backing of Standard Oil and loans from several American banks, a well-trained and well-equipped army under the command of the German General Hans von Kundt. However, Bolivian morale was low and the Indians forcibly conscripted into its army were from the mountains. They proved susceptible to the endemic diseases of the lowlands of the Chaco and suffered many casualties from snakebites, while the Paraguayans were more knowledgeable and better suited to fighting in lowland swamps and jungle.

In August 1932, Paraguayan forces launched an offensive under General José Félix Estigarribia. He proved to be a more successful general than his namesake from Eliza's time, and later became President and lent his name to Mariscal Estigarribia, a major town of the Chaco, and a street in downtown Asunción. By 1935, the Paraguayans had driven deep into Bolivian territory. But more than 100,000 men were dead – making the Chaco War the bloodiest conflict in the Americas in the twentieth century – and both sides were exhausted. The peace conference in Buenos Aires stripped Paraguay of all its territorial gains and, although it gave Paraguay clear title to most of the disputed region, Bolivia was granted a corridor to the Paraguay river and the port of Puerto Casado.

The equivocal outcome of the war caused political instability in both Bolivia and Paraguay. In 1936, war hero Colonel Rafael Franco seized power in Asunción and made Paraguay Latin America's first Fascist state. In order to legitimise his authority, Franco looked for an absolute dictator from the past who he could promote as a national hero in his own likeness. So 1 March 1936, the sixty-sixth anniversary of López's death, became a day of national celebration. Francisco officially became the great hero of the nation, who had given his life on the battlefield when the fatherland had been invaded by a barbarous foe. Statues of him were raised across Paraguay, often showing him on horseback, sword in hand, galloping into battle, rather than – as would have been more appropriate – away from it. Streets were named after him – resulting in the incongruously named new shopping centre in Asunción, 'Mariscal López Shopping', which is rather like going to Berlin and finding the Adolf Hitler shopping mall.

Remains were disinterred from Cerro Corá. Although they were probably not his, they were taken to Asunción, to be enshrined with all due ceremony in the Panteón de los Héroes, as Francisco's replica of Napoleon's tomb at Les Invalides was now named. Eliza's son Carlos had returned to Paraguay, became wealthy and a leading figure in the Colorado party, which was founded in 1874 and ruled the country continuously for the next 30 years. Federico Noel also returned to South America. Francisco and Eliza's descendants re-established themselves there and their money helped finance a spate of books that re-evaluated Francisco's life and legacy – including the literary output of Juan E. O'Leary, whose name also adorns a street in downtown Asunción.

Within eighteen months Franco had fallen from power, but when Alfredo Stroessner seized power in 1954, he again turned to the 'national hero' Francisco Solano López to legitimise his rule. Cerro Corá became a national shrine. A huge monument was built on the battlefield, with a viewing platform; an avenue of statues of war heroes leads from the battlefield down to the cross that was erected on the bank of the Aquidaban Nigui where Mariscal López died. Stroessner also built an airstrip to allow him to pay flying visits to the site.

A cult surrounding Eliza seems already also to have sprung up. It is said that a Padre Bodgado performed rites in a grotto of Cerro Santo Tomas, where St Thomas was believed to have resided when he came to South America long before Columbus, and on top of the Dark Mountain, Cerro Hu, near her old summer home, the Casa Blanca – one of her many residences that still stands. And, to add a new dimension to the bogus national story, Stroessner wanted her body back.

Members of the López family who, by then, were well established in Paraguayan national life, had every interest in seeing Eliza restored to her position alongside the national hero Mariscal López. Novelists found her an intriguing figure and a couple of highly romanticised accounts of her life became bestsellers.

Eliza's reputation, so long a political football between the liberals and the López-loving Colorado party, who were in power continuously since 1949, was restored. In schools, young Paraguayans were taught that Madame Lynch was a national heroine because she led school children into battle against the enemies of their country. Indeed, this is part of her iconography. As you enter

Asunción from the airport, the first thing you see is a giant statue of the strong, independent and assertive woman who was largely responsible for the deaths of three-quarters of the population of the country, stealing much of its money and losing a valuable part of its territory. She bears a tattered flag in one hand and, at her feet, there is a dead Paraguayan – or, perhaps, symbolically, the dead Paraguay. In the other, she is holding the hand of a small child. Maybe I am missing something here, but I cannot see for the life of me what is so heroic about taking unarmed children out to be run down by cavalrymen wielding lances and sabres.

By 1970, a century after the end of the War of the Triple Alliance, the entire national fiasco had been satisfactorily rewritten, Eliza's reputation was redeemed and Paraguay was ready once again to celebrate her memory. The remains in the 'Museo Madame Lynch' were dusted off. Eliza's urn was carried from the National Defence Building in procession down the Avenida Mariscal López to the national cemetery at La Recoleta. There a huge mausoleum had been prepared, at enormous expense, not far from the tomb of Eliza's daughter Corina Adelaida. The urn of Paraguay's national heroine was placed in it with all due ceremony. There were more speeches. Bands played, and a plaque on the wall of the tomb was unveiled, saying that the mausoleum is

> a tribute by the people, government and armed forces of the nation to Eliza Alicia Lynch, who selflessly accompanied the greatest hero of the nation, Marshal Francisco Solano López, until his sacrificial death at Cerro Corá.

On the top of this shrine there is a life-size statue of Eliza. It is flanked by two crosses, which apparently symbolise the martyrdom of the Paraguayan people and her own martyrdom. In her hands, she holds a spade, though this is perhaps not meant to suggest that she is burying Paraguay, or its treasure. Nevertheless, in this huge memorial, Eliza has found, at last, a resting place fit for the Empress of South America − if, of course, the remains in the urn are hers. After all, the corpse which Teófilo Chammas dug up in Père Lachaise in 1961 had, he said, jet black hair that turned to gold when he opened the coffin. Eliza's hair was blood red.

SELECT BIBLIOGRAPHY

Anon, *A Narrative of Facts Relating to Dr Thomas Francia by an Individual Who Witnessed Many of Them*, W. Mason, London, 1826'

Barman, Roderick J., *Citizen Emperor – Pedro II and the Making of Brazil, 1825–91*, Stanford University Press, Stanford, California, 1999.

Barrett, William E., *Woman on Horseback*, Frederick A. Stokes Company, New York, 1938.

Bierman, John, *Napoleon III and his Carnival Empire*, St Martin's Press, New York, 1988.

Bishop, Nathaniel H., *A Thousand Miles' Walk Across South America*, Lee and Shepard, Boston, 1869.

Bliss, Porter Cornelius, *The Ethnography of the Gran Chaco*, Buenos Aires Typographical Society, Buenos Aires, 1863.

Box, Pelham Horton, *The Origins of the Paraguayan War*, University of Illinois, Urbana, 1927.

Brodsky, Alan, *Madame Lynch & Friend*, Harper & Row, New York, 1975.

Burton, Captain Richard F., *Letters from the Battle-Fields of Paraguay*, Tinsley Brothers, London, 1870.

Carlyle, Thomas, 'Dr Francia', *The Foreign Quarterly*

Review, Chapman and Hill, London, July 1843.

Charlevoix, Pierre François Xavier de, *The History of Paraguay*, Lockyer Davis, London, 1769.

Farwell, Byron, *Burton: A Biography of Sir Richard Francis Burton*, Penguin, London, 1963.

Graham, R.B. Cunninghame, *Portrait of a Dictator*, William Heinemann Ltd, London, 1933.

Hutchinson, Thomas J., *The Paraná with Incidents of the Paraguayan War*, Edward Standford, London, 1868.

Lynch, Elisa A., *Exposición y Protesta*, Fundación Cultural Republicana, Asunción, 1987.

Lynch, John, *Argentine Dictator: Juan Manuel de Rosas 1829–1852*, Clarendon Press, Oxford, 1981.

McMahon, General M.T., 'The War in Paraguay', *Harper's Magazine*, New York, February and April 1870.

Masterman, George Frederick, *Seven Eventful Years in Paraguay*, Sampson Low, Son, and Marston, London, 1869.

Maiz, Fidel, *Etapas de Mi Vida*, La Mundial, Asunción, 1919.

Miers, John, *The Apocynaceæ of South America*, Williams and Northgate, London, 1878.

Miers, John, *Travels in Chile and La Plata*, Baldwin, Cradock and Joy, London, 1826.

O'Leary, Juan E., *El Mariscal Solano López*, Félix Moliner, Madrid, 1925; *Un Denigrador Uruguayano del Mariscal López*, Asunción, 1921.

Ouseley, W. Gore, *Views in South America*, Thomas McLean, London, 1852.

Page, Thomas J., *La Plata, the Argentine Confederation, and Paraguay*, Trubner & Co, London, 1859.

Rengger, Johann Rudolph and Longchamp, Marçel François Xavier, *The Reign of Doctor J.G.R. de Francia in Paraguay*, T. Hurst, E. Chance & Co, London, 1827.

Robertson, J.P. and W.P., *Francia's Reign of Terror*, J. Murray, London, 1839.

Thompson, George, *The War in Paraguay*, Longmans, Green and Co, London, 1869.

Young, Henry Lyon, *Eliza Lynch: Regent of Paraguay*, Anthony Blond, London, 1966.

Warren, Harris Gaylord, *Paraguay: An Informal History*, University of Oklahoma Press, Norman, Oklahoma, 1949.

Washburn, Charles A., *The History of Paraguay*, Lee and Shepard, Boston, 1871.

Zinny, Antonio, *Cronologia de los Obispos del Paraguay*, Europea, Buenos Aires, 1887.

INDEX

Francisco 197–8; torture and ill-
treatment/murder of prisoners
123–4, 126–7, 129–30, 137, 196,
223–4, 229, 231; Uruguayana
capture and surrender 145–7;
withdrawal of Uruguay 180
Washburn, Charles: Burgos'
daughter's fate 87; Caacupé Virgin
154–5, 156; Carlos López 42;
'conspiracy' 200–20, 227–43; Eliza
– blamed for atrocities 251;
courage 159; fancy dress ball 116;
first meeting with Francisco 67;
McMahon's involvement with 259,
262; personal aggrandisement 153,
207–8; wife's visits to 113; forced
labour in Asunción 80; Francisco –
birthday celebrations 122–3; death
of Juana Pesoa 271; departure from
Asunción for Humaitá 141;
description/character of 47–8, 113,
160–1, 162–3; foreign ambassadors
trapped 180; ill-treatment of
Juliana Martínez 200; jailing of his
landlord 178; Pancha Garmendia's
ill-treatment 270–1; intervention
on behalf of Brazilian prisoners
124; Maiz' confession 103; Palacios
89; peace envoy role 177–9;

Skinner's letter to 270, 273;
Stewart's fear for his life 284;
valour of Paraguay troops 245;
Venancio López 46; women's
contribution to war effort 194
Washburne, Elihu B. 259
Watts, John 142–3, 251
Whytehead, William 79, 119, 164
women: Brazilian use as soldiers
194–5; drafted to plough the fields
and work the slaughterhouses 170,
194; jewellery taken for war effort
114, 136, 144, 151, 158, 188,
193–4; nursing role 152; Paraguay
Army 151, 193–4

Xarayes, Lake 11

Yegros, Col. Fulgencio 28, 31
yerba maté 23, 36, 43, 77, 85, 98, 132,
283, 286
Young, Henry Lyon 190, 246, 268–9,
289
Ysquibel, Doña Juana 30

Zavala, Bruno Mauricio de 21
Zinny, Antonio 109
Zola, Émile 65
Zubizarreta, Dr Carlos 263–4

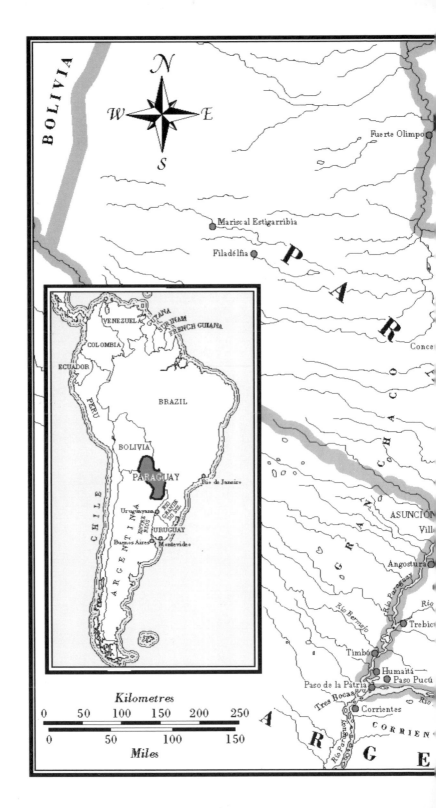